SPECIALIST BRITISH
Sports/Racing Cars
OF THE FIFTIES & SIXTIES

NOW SEE
Motor

SPECIALIST BRITISH
Sports/Racing Cars
OF THE FIFTIES & SIXTIES

A marque by marque analysis ~ from AC to Warrior ~ Bristol

ANTHONY PRITCHARD

Published in 1986 by Osprey Publishing Limited
12–14 Long Acre, London WC2E 9LP
Member company of the George Philip Group

British Library Cataloguing in Publication Data

Pritchard, Anthony
Specialist British Sports/Racing cars of the Fifties and Sixties.
1. Automobiles, Racing—History
I. Title
629.2′28′09045 TL236
ISBN 0-85045-643-6

Designed by David Tarbutt

Filmset by Tameside Filmsetting Ltd
Ashton-under-Lyne, Lancs
Printed in England by
BAS Limited, Over Wallop, Hampshire

CONTENTS

INTRODUCTION

The success of British sports/racing cars during the 1950s was an integral part of the growth of British motor racing power in postwar years. Two major British teams led from the front, Aston Martin and Jaguar, and while they do not form part of the subject matter of this book (for reasons explained shortly), their role in the book is important. They stimulated British interest in sports car racing, and their example encouraged small enthusiast constructors and entrants and, in the case of Jaguar, supplied many of the engines used by the smaller concerns.

Jaguar first entered Le Mans in 1951 with a full team of their new C-type competition cars powered by the 3.4-litre XK twin overhead camshaft engine. The XK engine, as modified for racing, was the one truly powerful, truly reliable British competition engine of the early 1950s and Jaguar, almost obsessed by the prestige of Le Mans victories, appeared to be the technical innovator, adopting Dunlop disc brakes as standard and rubber bag fuel tanks on the 1953 works C-type and dramatic aerodynamics and monocoque construction on the 1954 D-type.

While Jaguar won Le Mans five times between 1951 and 1957 and scored victories in the Reims 12 Hours race three times, Aston Martin were usually struggling for class success with their 3-litre cars. The David Brown team under the admirable direction of John Wyer followed a policy of gradual evolution, racing lightweight versions of the 2.6-litre production DB2 coupé until the end of 1951, introducing the DB3 sports/racing car at the 1951 Tourist Trophy and racing the DB3 with 3-litre engine in 1952 and the early part of 1953. For the 1953 Le Mans race Aston Martin produced the much improved DB3S, and three years later came the space-frame DBR1, which in its ultimate form had a power output of 255 bhp at 6000 rpm. Aston Martin also dabbled with the 4.5-litre V-12 Lagonda and the initially 3.7-litre DBR2, but these proved expensive and abortive diversions from their main aim of winning the Sports Car World Championship.

Aston Martin finally withdrew from International sports car racing at the end of 1959 with a string of successes that included wins in the three Goodwood Nine Hours races (1952, 1953 and 1955), wins in the Tourist Trophy at Dundrod in 1953 and Goodwood in 1958 and 1959, second places at Le Mans in 1955, 1956 and 1958 (the last of these successes by the private DB3S of Peter and Graham Whitehead), wins in the Nürburgring 1000 Km race in 1957–59 and culminated in a 1-2 victory at Le Mans and winning the Sports Car Championship in 1959 (by which time the Championship was limited to 3-litre cars).

When the works Astons and Jaguars met in British events, the Nine Hours races at Goodwood and the annual thrashes at Silverstone in May and July in each year, the Aston Martin team was almost inevitably the winner. Feltham took the British races much more seriously; while Coventry's eyes were firmly glued on Le Mans, Aston always ran a full team of very well-prepared cars and if they lacked the speed of the Jaguars, their roadholding was vastly superior and it was a matter of honour that one of the works Aston drivers led into the first corner.

It was against this background of two major British teams contesting the major International events that the specialist constructors worked in small workshops, sometimes only a lock-up garage, towing their cars behind old bangers or making do with a near derelict converted coach as a transporter; racing weekend after weekend at

Silverstone, Snetterton and Goodwood, concentrating very often on their main line of business during the week's working hours and preparing the cars in the evenings. This was how Lotus, Lola and others started, eventually fulfilling their creators' dreams of becoming fully fledged competition car constructors, whilst others, like HWM, Cooper and Tojeiro, ran garage businesses and at least had proper facilities for working on their cars.

Any specialist constructor wishing to compete in the larger-capacity classes was almost compelled to use a Jaguar engine or a large-capacity American production unit (as did Allard and one or two others). The Aston Martin engine was not readily available and, in any case, was insufficiently powerful. Although Jaguar sold both the C-type and the D-type as production cars, by the mid-1950s the C-type was obsolete and the D-type was patently unsuitable for short-circuit events. By 1955 the D-type engine and gearbox were available to friends of the factory and from 1957, by when Jaguar had withdrawn from racing, the Lister team was racing with very active works support.

In the 2-litre class, constructors, almost without exception, turned to the Bristol engine, the BMW-based 6-cylinder unit. The Bristol was used by Frazer Nash on what might be described as a proper contractual basis and the Frazer Nash Le Mans Replica was to prove the dominant car in the 2-litre class until challenged in 1953 by Bristol's own 450 coupés in long-distance events and by the Cooper-Bristol and Tojeiro-Bristol in short-circuit events.

It was a constant cause for complaint that there was no suitable engine for constructors to use in the 1500 cc class. In enlarged 1500 cc form the ubiquitous pushrod MG XPAG produced only 85 bhp or thereabouts (compared with the 110 bhp of the Porsche 550 'Spyder' engine) and in the early 1950s there was little choice apart from the Singer engine used by HRG. But the coming of the Coventry-Climax 1100 cc FWA single-cam engine for 1954, by 1956 available in limited numbers in 1460 cc form and in 1957 followed by a twin-cam 1500 cc unit, changed all that.

At Club and National level 1500 cc sports/racing cars were always popular; they were relatively cheap to maintain and race and the MG-powered cars and the HRGs could be driven on the road to race meetings. Until the coming of Coventry-Climax, MG-powered Coopers, the Lesters and Leonards and the HRGs flourished. With the availability of the Climax, the innovative engineering skills of Colin Chapman and the ingenuity of the Coopers this aspect of the sports car scene was transformed.

Colin Chapman was the only really advanced designer among specialist constructors in the mid-1950s, and where he led, so many others followed. Chapman constantly stretched the frontiers of engineering development; low weight, superb roadholding and brilliant aerodynamics (the work of Frank Costin) were the Lotus stock-in-trade. Tales of Lotus fragility were legion. Stalwarts such as David Piper and Bob Hicks, who toured the Continent, driving from minor meeting to minor meeting to compete with their Lotus Elevens, would find that chassis tubes had broken whilst the cars were on their trailers! In Roy Salvadori's autobiography (Patrick Stephens Ltd., 1985), Roy narrates how he suffered three bent de Dion tubes, two in practice and one in the race, on a Lotus Eleven at Goodwood in 1957.

So far as I am aware, however, no driver was ever killed at the wheel on an early Lotus sports/racing car. Undoubtedly the forté of the Lotus was the short-distance British event and the cars raced by Team Lotus at Le Mans and in other long-distance races were much strengthened and very carefully, if sometimes rather hastily, prepared.

During 1955–56 the only serious opposition to Lotus came from the Coopers, also of course Coventry-Climax-powered, but with an unconventional rear-engine layout, an arrangement carried on from the Surbiton company's 500 cc Formula 3 practice. By chance, rather than judgement, the rear or more accurately mid-engine layout was to dominate Formula 1 racing in 1959–60 and prove to be the layout of the future. It is interesting to speculate how motor racing would have developed if in 1946 Charles Cooper had not chosen to copy the rear-engine layout first seen on Colin Strang's Vincent HRD-engined Strang Special 500 cc car. All 500 cc Coopers were rear-engined like the Strang Special, but not the MG- and Bristol-powered sports/racing cars or the Formula 2 Cooper-Bristol of 1952–53 which 'reverted' to the traditional front-engined layout. For the Climax-powered sports cars, Cooper adopted the rear-engine mounting and were a serious rival to Lotus until Cooper gave up sports car to concentrate on the new 1500 cc Formula 2 in 1957 (Cooper won the first Formula 2 race at Silverstone in July, 1956, but the Formula did not officially come into force until 1957). Two years later Cooper returned to sports car racing with the first of their long line of Monaco sports/racing cars based on their Formula 1 chassis.

From 1955 onwards the 1100 cc and 1500 cc classes proved one of the most popular and best-supported categories at Club, National and International level. These sports/racing cars did much to oust the old 500 cc Formula 3 that was Cooper-dominated (and some would say very boring) and nurtured a number of British Formula 1 drivers, including Graham Hill, Alan Stacey, Chris Bristow and Cliff Allison.

The old Sports Car World Championship came to an end in 1961, and from 1962 there was a new category known as Prototype racing, largely dominated by Ferrari and, in the smaller-capacity classes, Porsche, with Ford struggling for success. Alongside these giants there were initially few British cars competing, but Lola, Chevron and Mirage emerged to contest long-distance sports car races. Sports car racing continued to flourish at a purely National level and through the growth of the CanAm series. Most of the larger-capacity cars were powered by American engines, a trend initiated by Bruce McLaren when he re-engined the Zerex Special with an Oldsmobile engine.

As this book is concerned with the products of specialist constructors and some of the more successful 'specials', the decision was taken to exclude the competition cars of Aston Martin and Jaguar. Apart from the fact that these were the products of large and well organized companies, Jaguar is superbly covered by Andrew Whyte in his *Jaguar Sports Racing and Works Competition Cars* (Haynes, two volumes) and Aston Martin by John Wyer and Christopher Nixon in *Racing with the David Brown Aston Martins* (Transport Bookman, two volumes, 1980). Jaguar-powered cars are mentioned only in passing because they have been so well covered in *Powered by Jaguar* by Doug Nye (Motor Racing Publications, 1980) and the competition Cobras are ignored because these Anglo-American hybrids were more American than Anglo. Inevitably, the selection in this book is my own and I apologize to anyone whose favourite marque is omitted.

ACKNOWLEDGEMENTS

The author and publisher are grateful to the following for permission to reproduce their photographs: Aston Publications (photographs by T. C. March), *Autosport*, BP, Edward Eves, Geoffrey Goddard, Guy Griffiths, Louis Klementaski, London Art Technical (the photographic service to *Motor Sport* magazine), Pete Lyons, David Phipps, Quadrant Picture Library and Nigel Snowdon. In addition, the author and publisher would like to express their appreciation for the consent by Quentin Spurring, editor of *Autosport* to reproduce the tests by John Bolster of the Lister-Bristol and Lola-Climax and by B. T. Batsford Limited to reproduce an extract from *Racing and Sports Car Chassis Design* by Michael Costin and David Phipps.

Anthony Pritchard
Bourne End, Buckinghamshire
October 1985

AC Le Mans Aces

Although the Ace was primarily a production sports car, and out of a total of 225 AC-powered Aces and 466 Bristol-powered Aces only a very small number raced in Europe and the United States, it had an important role in sports car racing of the 1950s. The Ace achieved exceptional success at Le Mans and in SCCA Production Sports Car races in the United States.

The story of how the Ace evolved as a production car from the 1953 sports/racing Tojeiro has been told many times. Cliff Davis's Tojeiro-Bristol was a very well-built and well-finished car and if the Lea-Francis-powered example that Vin Davison showed to the Hurlock brothers in 1953 was as well turned out, it is hardly surprising that they were impressed. After all, the 2-litre saloon that AC was manufacturing was just about the most antiquated car on the British market, with an engine the development of which could be traced back to 1919, rigid axles front and rear, an enormous boxy body and a decidedly leisurely performance. Perhaps the enthusiast should simply be thankful that the Hurlocks were offered a really good design, as it seems that they would have jumped at almost any prospect!

Within a matter of months the Tojeiro was on display at Earls Court as the Ace (reviving a name used by the company in the 1930s), and alongside was a stripped chassis revealing John Tojeiro's simple but effective design of two large-diameter steel tubes linked at the centre by a cross-tube of similar diameter and by triangular box-members at the end carrying the all-independent suspension of transverse leaf springs, wishbones located beneath the springs and Girling dampers. In production form a large tubular member was added to form the scuttle, a smaller radiator replaced the standard saloon radiator fitted to the show chassis and the 'saloon' 70 bhp engine was replaced by a more highly tuned engine with triple SU carburettors developing 85 bhp at 4500 rpm.

Transmission was through a single dry-plate clutch, Moss 4-speed gearbox and an open propeller shaft to a hypoid bevel final drive. Wire wheels with knock-off hubs and Girling hydraulic brakes with Al-fin 11-in. drums were fitted. This

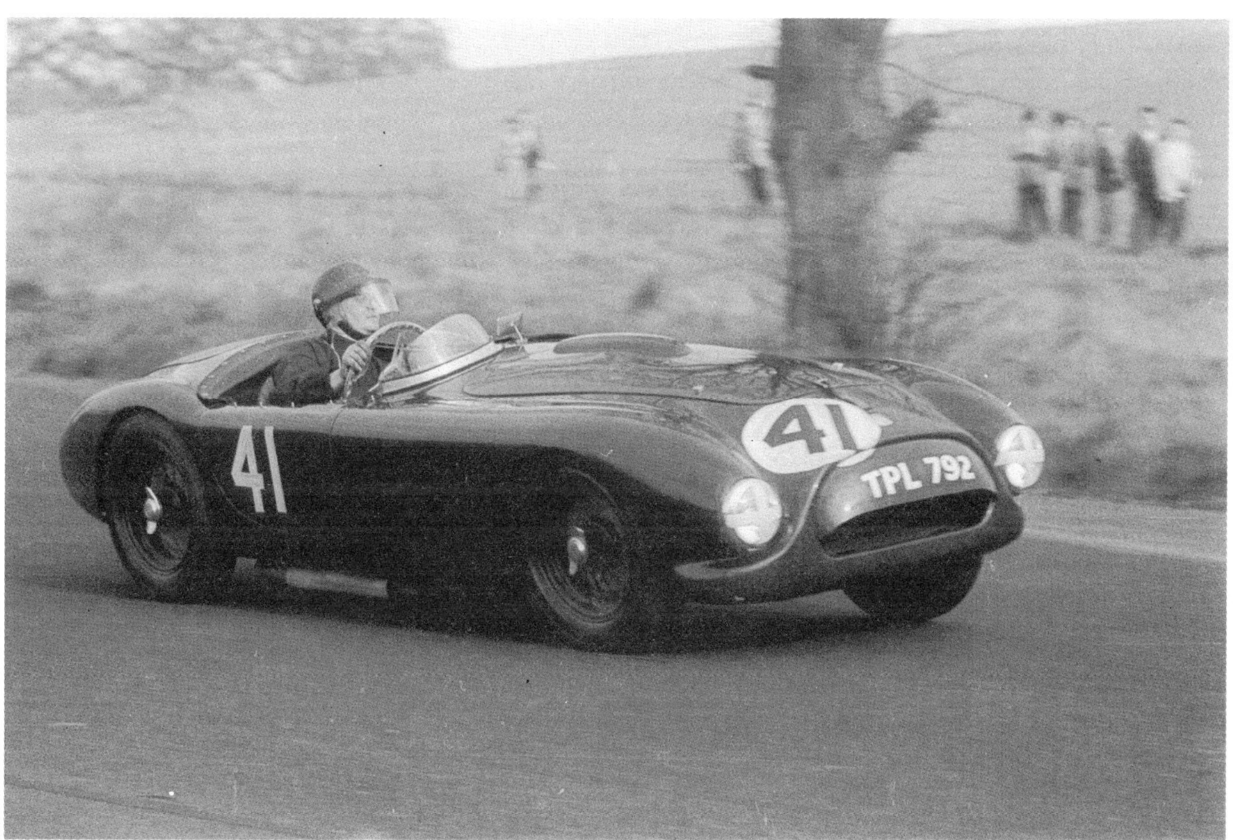

The Ace-Bristol with various modifications and in various degrees of tune was a popular car with Club drivers in the late fifties. This is Bob Jennings in the 1957 British Empire Trophy at Oulton Park (T. C. March)

simple, but highly effective chassis was clothed in an aluminium two-seater body, very similar to that fitted to Davis's Tojeiro and thus very similar to the Superleggera Touring 'Barchetta' design fitted to a number of Tipo 166 2-litre Ferraris.

For its day the Ace went exceedingly well, with a top speed of just over 100 mph, the ability to attain over 80 mph in third gear and to accelerate from rest to 60 mph in around 11 seconds. It also cornered superbly and its steering and brakes were excellent by the standards of the time.

The first competition appearance of the Ace came in the MCC *Daily Express* Rally in November 1953, with Cliff Davis/David Blakely (later murdered by Ruth Ellis) at the wheel of the prototype car, but it failed to win an award. By early 1954 production was beginning to get under way and the production cars differed by having raised front wings and headlamps and enlarged boot.

Throughout 1954 and 1955 that great AC enthusiast and dealer from Worthing, Ken Rudd, raced Aces in British events and he developed the engines of his cars to the point where they were producing over 100 bhp (the final production version of the AC engine developed 110 bhp at 5200 rpm). A typical Rudd drive remembered by the writer was at the first Boxing Day meeting at Brands Hatch in 1954, where Rudd battled in the Unlimited Sports Car race with Margulies' C-type Jaguar and Rogers' Cooper-Bristol until he ran out of petrol!

It was largely at Rudd's instigation that in 1956 AC adopted the option of the Bristol engine in the Ace and Aceca (the latter was the delightful coupé introduced at the 1954 Earls Court Show). Most Bristol-engined ACs were fitted with the 125 bhp 100D2 unit, but a number of earlier cars were re-engined with various Bristol types. From 1957 Girling disc brakes on the front wheels were available.

Rudd raced Ace-Bristols to second place in the 1956 and 1957 *Autosport* Series Production Championships. There was quite a kerfuffle about the results in 1956, as Rudd had not only scored the highest marks in the qualifying rounds (awarded on a class basis), but also won the three-hour final overall, only to be relegated to second place on the handicap results of the final alone. The rules were changed for 1957, and although Rudd won the three-hour final at Snetterton (now a scratch race) from Bekaert's C-type Jaguar, he was still only

second to Ian Walker (Lotus) on the basis of points won in the qualifying rounds!

At Le Mans in 1957 the AC factory entered an Ace for Rudd and Peter Bolton. Modifications were limited to a new bonnet with smaller air intake (with fog lamps mounted in the grille), full-width curved perspex windscreen and the exhaust discharging just ahead of the right-hand rear wheel. There was strong opposition in the 2-litre class, including a very quick Gordini, but most of this fell by the wayside and the Ace finished second in the class (tenth overall) to a Ferrari.

In the United States, Aces dominated Class E of the SCCA Production Championship, winning the class in 1957, 1958 and 1959, and were then transferred to a higher class with stronger opposition and won again in both 1960 and 1961. Aces won the 2-litre Grand Touring class in the 1958 Sebring 12 Hours race and took the first three places in the class in 1959.

Encouraged by the performance in the 1957 Le Mans race, AC built a special car for the 1958 24 Hours event. In reality this was a version of the contemporary Tojeiro sports/racing car with multi-tubular space-frame chassis, front and rear suspension by double wishbones and coil springs and at the rear a low pivot diagonal swing axle arrangement (instead of the Tojeiro's de Dion axle) with which AC had been experimenting for some while. The familiar Bristol engine and gearbox were retained, which led Denis Jenkinson to comment in *Motor Sport*, '. . . the Bristol engines in the ACs were embarrassing to see, for on the day before the race there was a gathering of prewar Le Mans cars and there were present two BMWs with virtually the same engines.'

This special Le Mans AC had disc brakes front and rear, with those at the rear mounted inboard on either side of the final drive unit. The body was designed by artist Cavendish Morton and was clearly inspired by the previous year's Ferrari, the Tipo 290MM. Low and sleek at the front with faired-in headlamps, there was a large scoop on the bonnet to clear the very deep Bristol engine, full wrap-round perspex windscreen, swept-up tail with streamlined headrest so that the rear wings formed small rounded fins and a high 'boot' to clear the spare wheel mounted on the fuel tank. There were one-piece front and rear body sections so that there was excellent access for the mechanics to work on the car during a race.

At Le Mans the works car was driven by Dickie Stoop and Peter Bolton, while a production car was entered by the Swiss AC distributor Hubert Patthey with Berger as co-driver. The Swiss-entered car was crashed by a mechanic while being driven back to the team's headquarters after practice and made the start after only a frantic, almost complete rebuild. In a race run in particularly bad conditions with heavy rain that resulted in a number of very bad accidents the works car ran well, slowed in the

LEFT *This slightly modified Ace-Bristol was driven at Le Mans in 1957 by Ken Rudd and Peter Bolton and finished second in its class (LAT)*

BELOW *The 1958 Le Mans AC designed by John Tojeiro seen at the Thames Ditton factory shortly before it left for France*

ABOVE *The AC-Bristol seen at Le Mans. It ran well to finish eighth overall, but developed a crack in the rear of the chassis towards the end of the race*

closing hours of the race by a broken chassis tube, to finish eighth overall and win the 2-litre class, with the Patthey/Berger car in ninth position.

It was a remarkable performance by a car that had been completed only a couple of weeks before the race and not tested before it reached the Sarthe circuit. It should also be noted, however, that there were no other finishers in the class apart from the Jopp/Crabbe Peerless, which had covered insufficient distance to qualify for an official placing. The Le Mans car reappeared in the Tourist Trophy at Goodwood in September driven by Mike Anthony/Ted Whiteaway, but was plagued by overheating problems and finished at the tail of the field. This car survives in the ownership of Barrie Bird.

AC success at Le Mans continued in 1959 when a Rudd-prepared, secondhand, virtually standard Ace-Bristol driven by Whiteaway/Turner finished seventh overall and won the 2-litre class (there were no other finishers in the class). As late as 1961 Bob Staples won the BARC Marque Championship with his Ace-Bristol, and in the 1962 Le Mans race the Martin/Magne Ace-Bristol with modified bonnet, having a small air intake and faired-in headlamps, retired with clutch failure. By this time production of the Bristol engine had ceased (although the last Ace-Bristol did not leave the Thames Ditton factory until 1963), the Ford 2.6-litre engine available in various states of Rudd-speed tune up to 170 bhp had appeared in the Ace at Earls Court in 1961 (only 38 were built) and the Cobra was in full production.

Allard

In prewar days Sydney Allard established a considerable reputation as a constructor of trials cars with Ford V-8 engines. He formed the Allard Motor Company in 1945, and early in 1946 set up a production facility in Park Hill near Clapham Common and showrooms and offices in Clapham High Street. A range of V-8 Ford-powered cars in two-seater, tourer, saloon and drophead forms was soon in production. In 1947 they were joined by the J1 competition two-seater intended primarily for trials work. Although in later years production slumped dismally, there was initially considerable demand for these good-looking and fairly quick sporting cars and Allard continued as a manufacturer until 1959. Sydney Allard was a great motoring enthusiast, competing in most branches of the sport: trials, rallies, racing, hillclimbs and sprints. He won the 1949 RAC Hill Climb Championship at the wheel of his own Steyr-powered single-seater and his greatest triumph was victory in the 1952 Monte Carlo Rally at the wheel of onc of his own cars. In addition Allard competed in endurance racing with cars of his own company's manufacture and there were in all three series of sports/racing cars.

Jim Tiller with his J2 Allard accelerates out of the Esses at Wiscombe Park Hill Climb in 1962. The swing-axle front suspension is working very hard (Michael Ware)

The J2

The prototype J2 first ran at Prescott hillclimb in July 1949 and was soon in production. It featured a chassis broadly similar to that of the existing range, box-section construction for the main side-members with substantial box-section cross-members. There were three tubular hoops to provide extra stiffening and support the body. At the front there was the same independent suspension by split Ford axle and transverse leaf spring, while at the rear there was a de Dion axle suspended on coil springs, a layout derived from that used on the Steyr single-seater. On the 1950 production J2, coil spring front suspension was adopted. The body was a neat two-seater with cycle front wings, rear wings integral with the bodywork and separate headlamps. In standard form the J2 was fitted with the Ford V-8 3622 cc side-valve engine and Ford 3-speed gearbox (which meant that the performance was pretty pathetic), while export cars had the Mercury 3917 cc engine, which improved the performance a fraction.

During 1949 Sydney Allard ran the J2 in a number of British events and he campaigned a car actively in 1950. Anglo-American Tom Cole had ordered a J2 in which he installed a Cadillac V-8 5420 cc engine; this transformed the performance and, although this engine was not available in the ordinary way in the United Kingdom, it was installed in quite a number of J2s that were exported, and Allard himself raced a car with the Cadillac engine.

In April 1950, partnered by Tom Lush, Sydney Allard drove the J2-Cadillac in the arduous Tour of Sicily road race, but after a couple of minor prangs was eliminated when the car caught fire. At Le Mans Sydney co-drove Tom Cole's J2-Cadillac. They had worked their way up to second place by the early hours of Sunday morning when a gear-selector jammed. The selectors were fixed in the top gear position and Cole and Allard worked their way back through the field to finish third behind the Talbots of the Rosiers and Meyrat/Mairesse. Subsequently cars ran in the Production Sports Car race at Silverstone, where Sydney Allard finished third, and in the Tourist Trophy at Dundrod, where no success was gained. One of the best performances of the year was Erwin Goldschmidt's win in the sports car United States Grand Prix at Watkins Glen. Sydney Allard, partnered by Lush, drove a 3917 cc-powered J2 with Ardun head in the 1961 Tour of Sicily, but retired because of a broken piston. In the Mille Miglia, Allard retired after damaging the J2's steering in a minor accident, and the J2s were out of the picture in the Production Sports Car race at Silverstone and both entries retired at Le Mans.

Throughout its life the J2 was hampered by the lack of a suitable engine for British events, and even the exported cars that were shipped without engines still had the rather unsatisfactory Ford 3-speed gearbox. Some Ford engines were fitted with the Ardun overhead valve, light aluminium cylinder head conversion devised by Zora Arkus-Duntov (later responsible for the Chevrolet Corvette), but apart from the fact that supplies of these kits were limited, they proved unreliable. There were problems with the blown head gaskets, broken pushrods and oil starvation and these were sorted only long after Allard had ceased to be a force in motor racing. In all production of the J2 amounted to 90 cars.

The J2X

At the 1951 Tourist Trophy on the Dundrod circuit the Allard team introduced the improved J2X model. This car, fitted with a Chrysler engine, was driven by Sydney Allard, but was eliminated with a broken drive-shaft after he had hit a bank. The main changes to the design were that the J2X had the engine mounted seven inches further forward in the frame to give more cockpit space, and this resulted in changes to the front suspension; the front axle halves were located by leading radius rods attached to extensions on the front of the chassis frame, whereas the J2 had trailing radius rods similar to those of production Fords.

In December 1951, *Autosport* published John Bolster's road test of the 5.4-litre Chrysler-powered J2X. What was most significant was the sheer lack of performance of the J2X at a time when the production Jaguar XK120 was good for 120 mph and the competition C-type (introduced that year) had a top speed of around 140 mph. Bolster achieved a maximum speed of 100 mph, 65 mph in second and 37 mph in first (the Ford 3-speed gearbox was still fitted), but acceleration was not too bad, 0–60 mph in 10 sec and this on a wet road.

Bolster commented, 'On taking my seat, I was amazed that a 5½-litre car could feel almost as small as an Austin Seven ... On moving off, it was at once apparent that the big motor developed a phenomenal torque at low speeds, and I soon realized that for normal road work the gear lever was all but superfluous. A touch of the accelerator was sufficient to send the machine surging forward with the curiously typical "V8 beat" rumbling from the four exhaust pipes. The Chrysler engine was entirely silent mechanically, and at a high cruising speed one heard nothing but the hum of the tyres and the wind. It was all most exhilarating and quite unlike any other car on the market . . . . The three-speed gearbox is no disadvantage on the road, but for racing one would prefer four speeds. . . .'

Generally Bolster was impressed with the J2X, praising the brakes highly, but obviously somewhat uneasy about the handling: 'My only criticism of the suspension concerns its behaviour when a corner is taken at racing speed. Under these conditions, the rear end breaks away rather suddenly, particularly on wet roads. This makes it difficult to slide a corner in one smooth sweep without a certain amount of "dicing" at the wheel.'

Bolster praised the construction of the car and with regard to the body said, 'The body is entirely functional and achieves exactly the right degree of sleek raciness, allied with almost animal ferocity . . . there is not an ounce of superfluous weight, yet there is nothing flimsy about the construction. It would be impossible to better the view from the driving seat, and all the controls are well placed, though the accelerator seems a thought far away.' The price quoted was $4500 delivered in New York.

During 1952 Allard developed an improved version known as the J2X 'Le Mans' with rather ugly full-width aerodynamic bodywork and selling at a higher price than the standard version. Two of these cars were entered at Le Mans, both with Chrysler engines, 4-speed gearboxes based on the Ford commercial vehicle gearbox and somewhat tidied-up appearance. The car driven by Jack Fairman/Sydney Allard worked its way through to fifth place before retiring because of failed big-end bearings and the second entry for Arkus Duntov/Curtis was eliminated by rear axle failure.

Total production of the J2X amounted to 83 cars, many fitted with Ford and Mercury engines, but the export cars were usually powered by Cadillac or Chrysler engines. The J2s and the J2Xs were popular mounts in Club and National racing in both Britain and the United States and at this level achieved a reasonable measure of success, despite their limited performance.

The Cadillac-engined Allard J2X, Sydney Allard at the helm, in the 1952 Production Sports Car race at Silverstone. For a while Allard held fourth place, but retired because of mechanical problems (Guy Griffiths)

ABOVE *Sydney Allard struggling with the JR—which is displaying considerable understeer—in the Production Sports Car race at Silverstone, May 1953 (Guy Griffiths)*

BELOW *Tommy Sopwith's Armstrong-Siddeley-powered Allard J2R known as the Sphinx was a formidable contender in 1954 Club races*

RIGHT *Sopwith with the Sphinx leads Crook (Cooper-Bristol) and Scott-Brown (Lister-Bristol) at Snetterton in October 1954 (LAT)*

The JR

For 1953 Allard produced an improved competition car with shorter 8 ft 0 in. wheelbase (the same as the Palm Beach production model), full-width aerodynamic bodywork with one-piece front wings and bonnet that hinged forwards and the 5.4-litre Cadillac engine, now developing a claimed power output of around 200 bhp, as standard. In all publicity material, the model was referred to as the J2R. At the 1955 London Motor Show Allard announced an improved J3R with torsion bar front suspension, but this was never built. At a time when the C-type Jaguar was available in production for a mere £1495 plus purchase tax (and had a vastly superior performance), there was very little demand for the J2R and only seven were built between 1953 and 1956.

In 1953 Allard contested Le Mans for the last time, after running in a couple of 'shake-down' races. At Ibsley in April Sydney Allard finished second to Ian Stewart's Ecurie Ecosse C-type Jaguar and tied for second place in a handicap. It was already evident that all was not well in the handling department and the J2R appeared to suffer from pronounced understeer. In the Production Sports Car race at Silverstone Sydney Allard went off backwards at Becketts and demolished the rear end of the J2R. For Le Mans the Allards were fitted by Pye with radio-telecommunication with the pits, and, perhaps remarkably for the time, the system seemed to function well. The driver pairings were Allard/Fotheringham-Parker and Arkus Duntov/Merrick. Remarkably enough Sydney Allard led on the first lap by some margin from Ascari's Ferrari, but was soon out of the race because of a brake pipe severed by a broken differential housing mounting bracket. The second car was plagued by overheating and this eventually resulted in the engine seizing.

An interesting variant of the J2R was seen in British Club racing in 1954. Tommy Sopwith, son of the famous T. O. M. Sopwith, had acquired a J2R chassis which was fitted with its own distinctive body style and an Armstrong-Siddley Sapphire 3.4-litre engine and gearbox. This device, known as the Sphinx, was financed to some extent by Armstrong-Siddeley, which was part of Hawker-Siddeley (of which T. O. M. Sopwith was chairman), and painted the famous Sopwith dark blue and entered under the name 'Equipe Endeavour'. During the year the car showed promise and with its Sapphire engine tuned to produce around 200 bhp (compared with the standard 125 bhp) it proved quite formidable in minor events. For 1955 Sopwith switched to Cooper-Jaguar and Cooper-Climax cars and in the 1960s the Sphinx was raced with a Jaguar engine.

Arnott-Climax

Arnotts Garages (Harlesden) Ltd. ran a small racing workshop alongside Canons Park 'tube' station in Whitechurch Lane, Edgware, and developed a sound reputation as a constructor of 500 cc Formula 3 cars. The 500s achieved no outstanding successes, but they were a favoured alternative to the ubiquitous Cooper and offered owners certain advantages. Run by Daphne Arnott, Arnott Cars was a small, friendly organization and at most Formula 3 meetings attended with their service van and mechanics to help owners with spares and technical advice. Although most 500 cc Arnotts were fitted with bodies built from 18-gauge aluminium sheet, Arnott pioneered the use of fibreglass bodies on 500 cc cars, they were probably the first to fit a roll-over bar (on their 1953 Mk 1 cars) and they were among the first to use seat belts.

As the popularity of 500 cc racing started to wane in the mid-1950s Arnott planned a sports car powered by the popular Coventry-Climax FWA engine. The new car was designed by Daphne Arnott and George Thornton and was based on a simple twin-tubular chassis with independent suspension at the front by unequal-length wishbones and coil springs and at the rear by wishbones, coil springs and torsion bars. Lockheed hydraulic brakes with Al-fin drums were used. The most interesting feature of the Arnott was neat open two-seater bodywork in fibreglass, a very advanced feature for the time. The bodywork was characterized by a large 'A' in the air intake; it sloped inwards behind the rear wheels and featured a very sloping tail line. It seems that only three of these cars were built, two with Climax engines retained by the works and the third supplied in kit form to a Mr Abbott, who fitted a Lea-Francis engine and gearbox and used it in Club racing for a year. One of the Climax-powered cars was sold to Jack Perkins, who competed with it regularly, and the third car was retained by Daphne Arnott.

In 1955 Arnott managed to secure an entry for their car at Le Mans and it was to be driven by Jim Russell and Peter Taylor, but in practice Taylor crashed at the Dunlop Bridge and the Arnott was posted as a non-starter.

Two years later Arnott developed a completely new and much more advanced sports/racing car. George Thornton designed an elaborate multi-tubular space-frame constructed from 18-gauge tube and said to weigh only 53 lb. The suspension was unusual in that it was based on very long double wishbones (fabricated from 1 in. 16-gauge steel) pivoted at the centre-line of the car on a common central shaft and acting on coil spring/damper units mounted on the chassis frame on the opposite side. Describing this layout in *Sports Car*, David Phipps commented, 'In this way a deflection of any wheel causes a weight transference across the car which is designed to increase the roadholding ability of the remaining wheels. This arrangement allows the track to vary, and wheel angles during cornering became rather unusual, but the system has the practical advantage of simplicity and, above all, preliminary tests have proved that it works.' Knock-on wire wheels were

Arnott in action—Abbott's Lea-Francis-powered car at Brands Hatch in May 1955 (LAT)

fitted and there were finned drum brakes, inboard at the rear. The Coventry-Climax FWA engine in Stage 2 tune was used with an MG TC gearbox. The body of the new car was constructed in aluminium with a very low bonnet, full wrap-round perspex windscreen, full metal tonneau, half-enclosed rear wheels and a very prominent streamlined headrest (from the rear this Arnott had more than a passing resemblance to the Grand Prix Connaught). The complete car was said to weigh a mere 7 cwt.

During the early part of 1957 Jim Russell tested the car extensively at Snetterton and apart from the necessity to lower the bottom wishbone pivots, fit stiffer rear springs and slightly modify the steering, Arnott found that few changes were necessary. An entry had been obtained once more at Le Mans, but Le Mans regulations insisted upon a full-width cockpit with two proper seats. Rather than modify the existing open body, Arnott built a new coupé body with rather less dramatic lines, high front wings with headlamps under perspex covers, gull-wing doors and a windscreen that had almost certainly started life as the back window for a Hillman Minx.

Arnott took to Le Mans both the coupé to be driven again by Russell and Taylor and the earlier Lea-Francis-powered open car. This year there were no major problems in practice and the team even found the time to try the older car out on the circuit and allegedly attained a speed of 125 mph on the Mulsanne straight. In the race the coupé ran steadily, but retired in the sixth hour because of a dropped valve. After this Arnott lost interest in racing, but the garage company survived for many years afterwards.

Astra (Costin-Nathan)

Roger Nathan raced Lotus Elites and a Brabham BT8 sports/racing car, as well as developing a business in Brixton selling tuning kits for Hillman Imps and in 1965 Frank Costin and Roger Nathan collaborated in the design and development of a new sports/racing car. With Costin's long experience as an aerodynamacist working on Lotus, Vanwall and Lister cars and his involvement in the design of the Marcos, it was not surprising that the new car should be both very aerodynamic and feature wood in its construction.

The basis of the Costin-Nathan was a monocoque centre-section built of resin-bonded plywood with front and rear end-frames constructed from 20-gauge round- and square-section tubing. At the front the suspension was by the usual double wishbones and coil springs, while at the rear there were links, radius arms and coil spring/damper units. The first cars used the Hillman Imp engine angled in the chassis 54 degrees to the right with a revised lubrication system to suit this arrangement and the Imp gearbox fitted with close-ratio gears mounted upside down. The gear-change was on the right-hand side of the cockpit and linked to the gearbox by flexible cable. The radiator and spare wheel were mounted in the nose. The fuel was carried in a 6-gallon tank on the left-hand side with the filler just ahead of the windscreen. Originally Lotus 13 in. wheels were fitted, but Minilite wheels were substituted later, and the brakes were 9.5 in. discs mounted outboard. On the prototype the body was constructed in aluminium, a low, sleek, open two-seater with a very small air intake and full-width perspex screen, but later cars had fibreglass panels.

During 1966 Roger Nathan moved to new premises at Fortis Green in North London and enjoyed an immensely successful season with the new car, painted distinctive blue and gold colours. The Costin-Nathan was first raced at Brands Hatch on Easter Monday, where Nathan won the 1150 cc class of the event for sports/racing cars and set a new class lap record. During the year the car ran six times, scoring five first places and a second and set five new class lap records. Probably Nathan's best performance was at Montlhéry in September, where he beat strong Abarth opposition.

In 1967 he produced a GT version of the Costin-Nathan and there were modifications to the chassis of both types; the suspension was strengthened and there was an improved brake balance arrangement. On the GT version there was a fibreglass cockpit top with glued-in windscreen strapped and bolted to the centre-section of the open car, with intakes let into the sides of the body to allow air into the cockpit. On the first of the GT cars, built for Le Mans, there was a 5-speed gearbox with a separate lever for reverse to the left of the centre tunnel. It had been necessary to bring the weight up to comply with Group 6 Prototype regulations and this was achieved through the installation of steel fuel tanks and similar modifications. In fact Nathan rather overdid building in extra weight and the car came out at 1220 lb, almost 100 lb heavier than the minimum weight, and the weight was pared down again on later GT Costin-Nathans. At Le Mans the car was driven by Nathan and Beckwith, but was eliminated in the fifth hour by an electrical fault.

The Costin-Nathans continued to do well in British events in both 1967 and 1968. In the latter year the cars, now being raced with BMW and Ford SCA engines as well as the Imp, won 21 races out of 27 starts, together with four second places, and set ten class lap records. Outright wins were gained in both the *Motoring News* GT Championship and the Tootal GT Championship. At Le Mans the Simca-powered Moynet, a Costin-Nathan with local modifications, was driven by Max/Ligonnet, but retired early in the race because of fuel pump failure.

In October 1968 the company announced that in future all cars would bear the name Astra and gave details of the RNR 1 model, a development of the existing design that complied with the latest Group 6 regulations. Initially the RNR 1 was powered by the 2-litre Coventry-Climax engine, but during the year the Cosworth-Ford 1600 cc FVA twin-cam unit was substituted and this was used with the Hewland FT200 combined 5-speed gearbox and final drive unit—standard wear on Formula 2 cars of the period. The fibreglass body had smoother, neater lines and under the shell there were many minor changes as the result of development work over a two-year period.

It was not until the Cosworth engine was installed that the Astra began to achieve real success and it was first raced in this form at the Crystal Palace on 2 August, 1969. Here Nathan won the 1600 cc *Motoring News* GT race and set a new lap record, a performance which he repeated in the *Motoring News* race at Mallory Park the following weekend. At Nogaro in France Nathan was third overall in the race for Group 4 and 6 cars,

TOP *The very streamlined and rather bulbous Costin GT tested by John Blunsden for* Motor Racing *in 1967*

BELOW *The open cars were much more practical in appearance. This Astra-Climax was entered for Roger Nathan/Clive Baker in the 1969 BOAC 500 race at Brands Hatch, but non-started after a practice crash*

won his class and set a new class record. It was back to Brands Hatch the following weekend and another win and class lap record. A week later at the August Bank Holiday Brands Hatch meeting Nathan finished second in the Lombank Trophy race for Group 4 and 6 cars to 2000 cc behind John Miles with the 2-litre works Lotus 62. In the Nürburgring 500 Km race he finished seventh overall and second in his class (admittedly the overall winner, Brian Redman with the new Chevron B16, was also the winner of the 1600 cc class) and Nathan rounded off the season with victories at Crystal Palace and Brands Hatch.

In *Autosport* for 16 October, 1969, Simon Taylor reported on his track test with the RNR 1 at Silverstone:

'As this was the first time I had driven an FVA-powered car, my initial impressions all revolved round the superb performance of this wonderful engine. Peak power of around 230 bhp is developed at 9200 rpm, and the power doesn't really start until 7000 rpm, but it will pull from much lower speeds. For the purposes of this test were were only using 8800 rpm, but even then the performance in a car weighing less than half a ton seemed fantastic for only 1600 cc. One of the FVA's characteristics, presumably due at least partly to the Lucas fuel injection, is a tremendously rapid throttle response, and under straight-line acceleration each gear is only held for a second or two, as the rev-counter flicks across the dial with incredible rapidity.

'. . . The gearbox gave me my biggest problem to start with, for although the right-hand change for the FT200 five-speed box (this is the one used on all Formula 2 cars) has an orthodox gate, with first to the left and back, and then the usual H-pattern for the remaining four ratios, at first the linkage seemed imprecise and I found it difficult not to miss the appropriate notch when going across the gate. In addition the revs need to be absolutely right to make the change, and a moment's hesitation while searching for the cog allows the revs to drop too much. Once I had mastered the technique, however, it was possible to make literally instantaneous changes, and snapping down three gears from fifth to second going into Becketts with the brakes hard on and the revs rising and falling as the throttle is blipped, brought a warm glow to the heart.

'. . . As set up to Roger's liking, the Astra has a strong understeering characteristic, and to get round a corner quickly the throttle has to be opened good and early to keep the power feeding through the back wheels to counteract it. With so much instant power on tap, this is not difficult, and the wide open spaces of the Becketts hairpin allowed me to sample this—lots of power early on, unwind the steering a little, and with the tail hanging out ever so slightly, the Astra rockets out of the corner . . . .'

For 1970 Nathan standardized on the 1800 cc Cosworth FVC engine, but the great days of the Astra were over; the cars were no match for the latest Chevrons and at the end of the year production and development ceased. By the end of 1969 some 40 cars of all types had been built.

Beart-Rodger

Francis Beart was the foremost tuner and developer of Norton racing motorcycles, with a career extending back into prewar days, and in the early postwar years became increasingly involved in the preparation of Norton engines for 500 cc car racing. For 1953 Beart built his own Formula 3 single-seater based on Cooper Mk VII components and with a Norton Manx twin-cam engine. In 1953 the Cooper was driven by Alan Brown. Stirling Moss drove for Beart in 1954 and in 1955 the driver was Les Leston.

It was partly as a result of the encouragement that he received from Moss that Beart decided to go ahead with the construction of an 1100 cc sports/racing car for 1955. Beart commissioned Bernie Rodger (responsible previously for building two sports two-seaters from Cooper Formula 2 cars and for the Warrior-Bristol) to design and build the car in the Beart workshop at Byfleet. The new car was based on a multi-tubular frame constructed from 16-gauge 1.5 in. and 18-gauge 1.25 in. tubing with wishbone and coil spring front suspension and at the rear a de Dion axle located by tubular radius arms and central A-bracket and suspended on a transverse leaf spring. Initially there were coil springs at the rear, but these were soon replaced. Inevitably the engine was the 1098 cc single-cam Coventry-Climax FWA front-mounted (which Beart later adapted to take four Amal carburettors), but the transmission was somewhat unusual. Francis elected to use a 5-plate Norton-based clutch and a Riley 4-speed close-ratio gearbox. The wire wheels used Borrani alloy rims (which Beart used on his racing motorcycles) and Al-fin brake drums, 9 in. at the front and 8 in. at the rear—the brakes were mounted inboard at the rear. The body was a neat two-seater built by Wakefield's of Byfleet with a large oval air intake, streamlined headrest and drop-down bottom-hinged doors. Because of his motorcycle racing background Beart was preoccupied with weight reduction and the dry weight of the Beart-Rodger was only around 1000 lb.

Stirling Moss had agreed to drive the Beart-Rodger when his other commitments permitted

DAILY EXPRESS
37
WPL 5

37
37

and, still unpainted and registered WPL 5, it made its debut at Goodwood on Easter Monday 1955. Moss was away to a quick start, but soon fell back and retired on lap 3 because of a broken throttle linkage caused by poor brazing. Moss reappeared with the Beart-Rodger, now painted the distinctive Ford Ludlow Green that Beart used for all his entries to make them easily recognizable, at the *Daily Express* meeting at Silverstone in May. Here the car was plagued by ignition troubles; it covered the last few laps with the driver's door hanging open and Moss finished last—something of a contrast with the previous weekend, when Moss had won the Mille Miglia with a Mercedes-Benz 300SLR.

By this time Beart had rather lost interest in the project (as had Moss!) and after it had been driven by Les Leston at Brands Hatch on August Bank Holiday Monday it was sold to Ian Forbes. Changing hands a number of times it continued to appear in Club events and hillclimbs. It later acquired an MGA gearbox and by 1961 a Ford 1172 side-valve engine with Aquaplane head and Ford gearbox with Buckler close-ratio gears had been substituted.

In mid-1955 Beart moved to new premises at Ladymead, Guildford, and work continued on a second sports car that had been ordered by J. W. Byrnes. This differed considerably from the first car, for although the chassis was of very similar design but with 2 in. longer wheelbase, larger 10 in. brake drums and, at the rear, knock-on hubs were fitted, and the body was a narrow two-seater with detachable wings. The power unit was a 1342 cc twin-cam 4-cylinder Osca and there was a 5-speed gearbox in unit with the final drive. The new Beart-Rodger made its debut in the Formula 2 race at the British Grand Prix meeting at Silverstone in July 1956, where it ran without wings and was driven by Ian Burgess. The car appeared in the Silverstone programme as an Osca. Burgess finished right down the tail of the field in 14th place. It was subsequently driven in a Formula 2 race by Burgess at Brands Hatch in September, finishing fifth, and in the Gold Cup race at Oulton Park later that month it finished eleventh. Compared with the Lotus and Cooper opposition it was uncompetitive and quietly disappeared from the racing scene.

LEFT *Two views of the unsuccessful Beart-Rodger-Climax driven by Stirling Moss in the Sports Car race at Silverstone in May 1955 (T. C. March)*

Brabham

Throughout the long history of Brabham cars, from the first MRD Formula Junior car of 1961 to the latest BMW-powered Formula 1 cars, the emphasis has always been on single-seaters. In the mid-1960s, however, Brabham produced a handful of sports/racing cars that are now almost completely forgotten.

In 1963 Brabham built their first two sports/racing cars typed the BT5—BT stood for (Jack) Brabham and (Ron) Tauranac, who, of course, designed all Brabham cars prior to the acquisition of the company by Bernard Ecclestone in 1972. The BT5 was a neat little car based on the Brabham Formula Junior single-seater, with multi-tubular space-frame chassis, front suspension by unequal-length tubular wishbones and coil spring/damper units and at the rear lower wishbones, radius arms and coil spring/damper units. The body was a smooth fibreglass two-seater with full-width perspex screen—very similar in appearance to the Lotus 23. There were 13 in. magnesium wheels and the disc brakes were outboard front and rear. The cars were entered by Ian Walker Racing, who also ran Brabham Formula Junior cars, and were fitted with Ford 1098 cc engines modified for Formula Junior or the 1594 cc twin-cam Lotus-Ford engine used with a modified Volkswagen gearbox. Walker's drivers were Frank Gardner and Paul Hawkins. The BT5 was not a great success and proved no match for the Lotus 23.

The following year Tauranac tried again with the much-improved BT8, broadly of similar concept to the BT5 with multi-tubular space-frame chassis, front suspension by unequal-length wishbones and coil spring/damper units and rear suspension by lower wishbones, radius arms and coil spring/damper units. Two 12-gallon alloy fuel tanks were installed, one on each side. The wheelbase was 3 in. longer, there were 15 in. wheels, the transmission was the Hewland Mk 1 5-speed gearbox and the BT8 was intended to be powered by the Coventry-Climax FPF 2-litre unit or the BRM V-8. The BT8 remained available until 1966 and it is said that 12 cars were built, although this figure cannot be verified.

Jack Brabham drove the BT8 with BRM engine on its debut in the Lavant Cup at Goodwood on Easter Monday, finishing third overall and winning the 2000 cc class. However, the Brabham Racing Organization was not happy with the BRM engine, allegedly because they thought that it was 'all revs and no power', and in future the cars were raced with Climax engines For the Targa Florio in May the Brabham team prepared a BT8 with 2-litre Climax engine to be driven by Wilks and Epstein. To quote Denis Jenkinson's report in *Motor Sport*, '. . . unfortunately during the official practice period something at the rear broke while Epstein was travelling at speed along the straight near the end of the lap and the car spun off the road, throwing the driver out with minor injuries and demolishing itself on a series of granite road-side markers; so badly that it was difficult to decide whether a rear wheel, spring or suspension failed first.'

During 1964 cars were supplied to Roger Nathan and SMART (Stirling Moss Automobile Racing Team, whose car was fitted with a 2.5-litre Climax engine), along with a number of other drivers. Nathan enjoyed a particularly successful year with his dark blue and gold 2-litre car, taking a class second at Silverstone in May, winning at Mallory Park at Whitsun, winning the Martini Trophy at Silverstone and at Snetterton the following day. In the Guards Trophy race at Brands Hatch in August Denis Hulme and Jack Brabham with works-entered cars took second and third places behind McLaren's Cooper-Oldsmobile (the former Zerex Special). The car crashed at the Targa Florio was rebuilt for Tommy Hitchcock, who raced it in North American Group 7 races with great success, usually cleaning up the 2000 cc class.

The Brabham BT8 continued its run of successes in 1965, and the racing record of the white and green car entered by Sid Taylor for Denis Hulme was formidable. Hulme's successes included a win in the 2000 cc class at Goodwood on Easter Monday, an outright win in the Tourist Trophy at Oulton Park after the failure of faster cars, fourth place and a class win at Silverstone in May, a win in the 2000 cc race at Mallory Park at Whitsun and fourth place and a class win in the Guards Trophy at Brands Hatch. In addition, Peter Revson finished

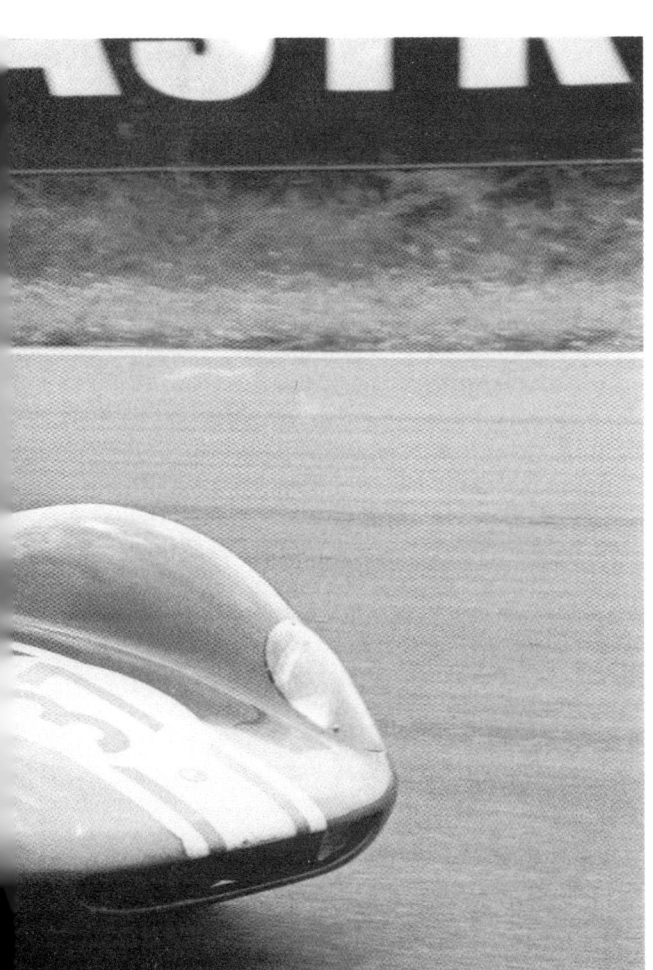

ABOVE *This BT8-Climax entered under the name 'Brabham/Sid Taylor Racing' and usually driven by Denis Hulme enjoyed immense success in 1965. Here, at the Clubmen's Championship at Silverstone in October, it was driven by Taylor himself (the author)*

LEFT *Tommy Hitchcock's Brabham BT8-Climax in the 1965 Tourist Trophy at Oulton Park (T. C. March)*

second to McLaren (McLaren-Oldsmobile) in the Martini Trophy at Silverstone. In 1965 Roger Nathan raced his BT8 with a 3.5-litre Oldsmobile V-8 engine, but it did not prove successful in this form. The cars continued to perform well in minor events and Clive Lacey raced the ex-Epstein, ex-Hitchcock car in 1967 with a coupé body. The coupé body had been designed for Epstein, who had originally intended rebuilding the Targa Florio car in this form and entering it at Le Mans with a 3.7-litre engine.

Despite the success of the BT8, Brabham, with one exception, built no more sports/racing cars and concentrated on Formula 1 and 2, which the team almost dominated in 1966–67. The one exception was the BT17 sports/racing car built in 1966, powered by the V-8 Repco 2994 cc (88.9 × 60.3 mm) engine with single overhead camshaft per bank of cylinders and with Hewland combined 5-speed gearbox and final drive. The engine and transmission were the same as fitted to the team's Formula 1 cars. The car was completed in a rush to

Jack Brabham with the Repco-powered BT17 in the 1966 Tourist Trophy at Oulton Park (T. C. March)

compete in the Tourist Trophy at Oulton Park in May 1966. It was driven by Jack Brabham, who finished at the tail of the first heat after delays in the pits to investigate an oil leak and retired in the second heat because of loss of oil pressure. The Brabham team was heavily committed with its single-seater racing programme and no serious attempt was made to develop the BT17, which was later sold to a private owner.

Bristol

When Bristol Cars Ltd. set up a racing section at the end of 1952 to build their own sports/racing cars, the marque was at the peak of its production and fame. The 401 saloon was in production, Bristol engines powered the Formula 2 Coopers which had enjoyed a successful season (especially when driven by young Mike Hawthorn) and the company was still a subsidiary of the Bristol Aeroplane Company, whose prototype Britannia turboprop airliner had made its first flight in August 1952. Bristol Cars were planning the 404 coupé (to be known familiarly as the 'Businessman's Express') and the much improved 405 that would continue the line of traditional, high-quality sporting saloons built in the Filton works. It made good sense to undertake a racing programme with sports/racing cars with a clear aviation affinity, especially as the basis of a suitable car was readily available.

During 1952 English Racing Automobiles Ltd. of Dunstable, headed by Leslie Johnson, had been racing the G-type Formula 2 car designed by David Hodkin and powered, almost inevitably, by a Bristol engine. The G-type was based on an exceptionally light and strong chassis formed by two oval-section thick-walled magnesium-alloy tubes. Front suspension was by unequal-length wishbones and coil springs; at the rear there was a de Dion rear axle located laterally by an A-bracket, the apex of which was ball-jointed to the chassis at the base of the final drive casing, and twin trailing arms and anti-roll torsion bar mounted on the frame. By changing the location points of the trailing arms the handling characteristics of the G-type could be varied to give understeer or oversteer as required.

As raced by ERA, the Bristol engine was converted to dry sump lubrication and the driver sat very low in the car alongside the prop-shaft so that the G-type had the appearance of being a two-seater. Other interesting features were the wheels, which had separate rims bolted to spiders cast integrally with the hubs, and the spiders were designed so as to deflect cooling air over the brake drums.

The ERA was raced in 1952 by Stirling Moss, but no success came the G-type's way, partly because the car was underdeveloped and ERA lacked the resources to develop it fully and partly because the Bristol engine was not really powerful enough to achieve much in the way of success. On the credit side the G-type had excellent roadholding and superb brakes. By the end of 1952 it was evident to ERA that they could not afford to continue development and the car together with drawings was sold to Bristol. Bristol's new racing section, headed by Vivian Selby, applied themselves to converting the G-type into a sports/racing car.

So far as the chassis was concerned, Bristol made few changes. The ERA chassis was built up into the prototype 450 and retained as a spare car, while three new cars were built with tubular steel chassis. At the rear the suspension was redesigned so as to incorporate twin parallel trailing arms on each side and the ability to adjust the handling characteristics was eliminated. Bristol used their own wet-sump BS series engine, developing around 150 bhp with new and very stiff crankshaft and 4-speed gearbox. The most startling feature of the 450 was the aerodynamic coupé body with steel and aluminium-alloy frame and aluminium-alloy panelling clearly aviation-inspired, very wide, with twin and very prominent tail fins extending from the roofline and over the sloping tail. This was the first time that tail fins had been used on a British sports/racing car. The curved side windows were in perspex to blend in with the curved body sides and the interior was a mass of hooded instruments, reminding many onlookers (especially those who knew little about aviation) of the cockpit of a fighter aircraft.

The Bristol 450 was based on the Formula 2 G-type ERA with offset driving position raced in 1952. Here designer David Hodkin is at the wheel (Guy Griffiths)

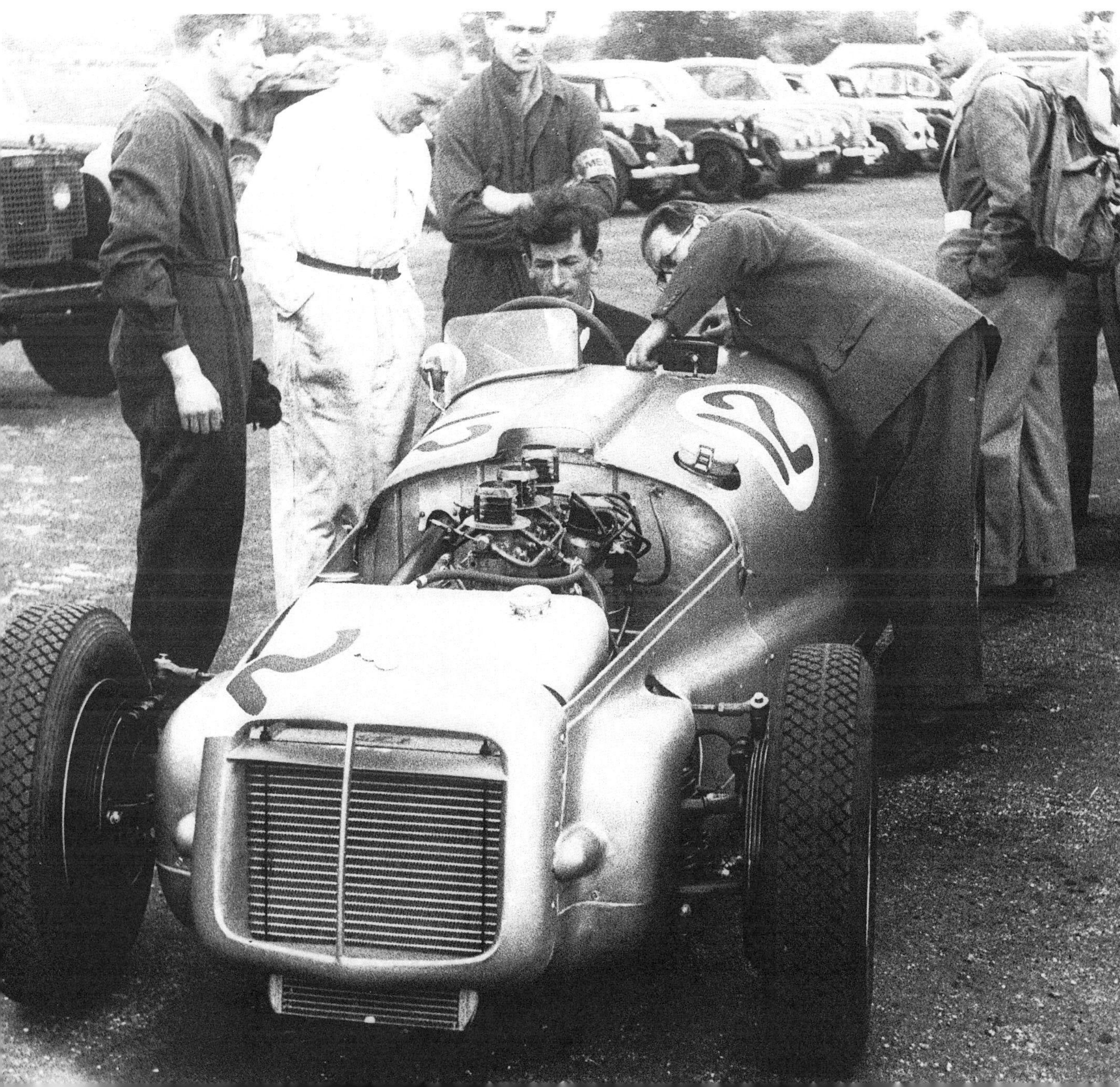

Another "BRISTOL" Success!

RHEIMS 12 hour race

FRANCE, SUNDAY · JULY 5th

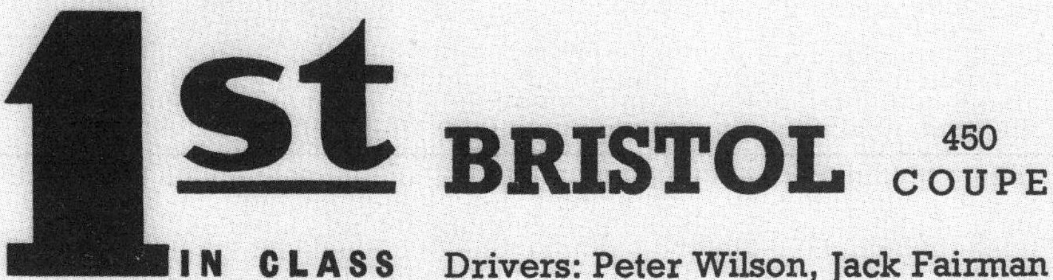

1st IN CLASS BRISTOL 450 COUPE

Drivers: Peter Wilson, Jack Fairman

BRISTOL 2 LITRE

The Bristol 450 Coupe is powered by basically the same 2-litre engine as that in the Bristol 403 Saloon.

5TH In General Classification

All results subject to official confirmation

THE CAR DIVISION OF THE BRISTOL AEROPLANE COMPANY LIMITED, BRISTOL, ENGLAND

London Showrooms: 80, Piccadilly, W.1

This Bristol advertisement following the team's success in the 1953 Reims 12 Hour race shows the very unattractive frontal appearance of the 450 in its original form

RIGHT *The class-winning open Bristol 450 of Wilson/Line at Le Mans, 1955 (T. C. March)*

The design showed very careful attention to detail. For example, the Le Mans regulations now permitted the use of a small hole in the rear wings so that the driver could see whether the tyres were wearing out. On the 450s the holes were covered with neat glass panels. But something had gone drastically wrong in the evolution of the 450 bodies and the basic smooth, aerodynamic lines were marred by a hump on the nose, by the protruding headlamps and foglamps, by the fuel filler and the bonnet-retaining straps.

During testing the 450's engines showed the reliability to last Le Mans, one of the cars attained 142 mph on the main runway at Filton and early oversteering problems were soon resolved. Bristol, managed by Selby and S. C. H. Davis, travelled to Le Mans full of confidence. Two cars were entered, to be driven by Lance Macklin/Graham Whitehead and Tom Wisdom/Jack Fairman. Both cars retired because the crankshaft balance weights became detached and punched their way through the sumps. It was a failure predicted by engineer Stuart Tresilian during a visit to Filton, but one that had not been revealed in Bristol's extensive pre-race testing.

Three weeks later the Bristol team was in action again in the Reims 12 Hours race with the driver pairings Macklin/Whitehead and Peter Wilson/Fairman. Already an effort had been made to 'clean up' the cars; the fog lamps had been removed, the oil cooler was now mounted inside the radiator air intake (instead of behind slats in the nose) and, most important, the crankshaft problem had been solved. Whitehead retired his car because of final drive failure, but Wilson/Fairman won the 2-litre class at 92.67 mph, finishing fifth overall. By October the appearance of the 450 had been further improved with the sleek noseline that was to characterize the 1954 cars and one of the improved 450s was taken to Montlhéry for Class E record-breaking attempts. Jack Fairman took the 200 miles record at 125.87 mph and with Lance Macklin sharing the driving they broke the 500 km (116.10 mph), 3 hours (116.42 mph), 500 miles (115.74 mph), 1000 km (115.49 mph) and six hours records (115.43 mph). To round off the two days of record-breaking, the 450 covered a flying lap at 126.11 mph.

Apart from the now beautifully smooth body lines and slightly raised roofline between the fins to reduce drag, the definitive 1954 Bristol 450s featured new twin-barrel Solex carburettors. The racing programme remained unchanged, Le Mans and Reims, but the team now entered three cars in each event. In the 24 Hours race the sleek coupés finished seventh (Wilson/Mayers), eighth (Wisdom/Fairman) and ninth (Keen/Line) to take the first three places in the 2000 cc class. Wilson/Mayers had covered 2179 miles at an average of 90.78 mph.

At Reims all did not go quite according to plan. During the early hours of the race, heavy rain fell

and the Bristols sucked into their air intakes water thrown up by cars in front, and were delayed by soaked ignition leads and plugs. They were not as fast as the Loyer/Rinen Gordini, which retired, and although all three Bristols finished the race in formation in the order Keen/Line, Wilson/Mayers and Wisdom/Fairman, they were pipped for victory in the class by the well-driven and carefully conserved 2-litre Ferrari of Picard/Pozzi, which was a lap ahead. They were also beaten by the Polensky/von Frankenberg Porsche 550 1500 cc car, which had led all the 2-litre cars for much of the race.

For 1955 the 450s were converted to open bodywork with a single prominent tail fin, metal tonneau over the passenger side and small wrap-round perspex windscreen. The unique styling of the 450 was completely lost, but the advantages were many. Drag was reduced, there were no longer problems with windscreen wiper failure (which had nearly caused Wilson to crash in 1954 at Le Mans), oil on the screen (the driver could look over the top of the perspex), misting-up of the inside of the cockpit or the very high noise level that was always present with closed sports/racing cars. Power output was now around 160 bhp, thanks in part to a new exhaust system that merged into a single tailpipe at the rear of the car (formerly three tailpipes emerged just ahead of the left-hand rear wheel).

The Le Mans race was a straightforward repetition of 1954, with Wilson/Mayers, Keen/Line and Wisdom/Fairman taking the first three places in the 2000 cc class. At one stage the Wilson/Mayers car held fifth place, leading the Porsche 550s, but was slowed by the Bristol pit as a precautionary measure. A problem on the leading car during the last 15 laps or so of the race was that the exhaust pipes came adrift at the manifold with the result that flames were shooting in the direction of one of the fuel tanks! Wilson/Mayers averaged 94.61 mph, had averaged over 100 mph during the first 12 hours of the race and were timed at 138.43 mph on the Mulsanne straight.

Sadly, the 1955 race was marred by the horrific accident involving Levegh's Mercedes-Benz, resulting in the withdrawal of the Mercedes team. A direct repercussion was the cancellation of the Reims 12 Hours race, and the 450s were never raced again. Motor racing is an expensive business and the Bristol directors concluded that their motor racing programme had fulfilled its purpose and, in any case, if the team were to continue racing, an engine with a lot more power would be needed to maintain supremacy in the 2000 cc class. Work that had started on a new car with multi-tubular space-frame was abandoned. The three steel-chassis cars built by Bristol were broken up, but the original ERA-based prototype survives, albeit without its original engine.

Buckler

As a supplier of components and chassis, mainly for Ford-based cars, Buckler Cars was the source of inspiration for a generation of 'Special' builders. Derek Buckler founded the firm at Caversham Road, Reading, in May 1947, and later expanded into additional premises at Crowthorne. Buckler manufactured a vast range of products—close-ratio gears for Ford gearboxes, light alloy cylinder heads, aluminium bodies and a vast range of chassis; by 1960 they offered 14 different space-frames.

Buckler's best days were in the early 1950s, when so many amateur competition cars were either built to the 750 Motor Club's 1172 Formula for side-valve Ford-based cars or simply used Ford components. The company tended to lose ground in the 1950s with the introduction of such sophisticated and readily available designs as the Lotus Mk 6.

All Buckler chassis could be used for competition work and the majority featured a multi-tubular space-frame (Buckler claimed to have built the first space-frame), swing-axle front suspension based on a divided Ford axle suspended on a transverse leaf spring (this layout used by so many constructors in post-war days was pioneered by L. M. Ballamy) and a Ford rigid rear axle suspended on a transverse leaf spring.

There were, however, two Buckler chassis aimed for competition work at a more sophisticated level, the DD1 and DD2 (DD stood for de Dion). Both cars featured a comparatively simple multi-tubular space-frame, but the swinging front axles were suspended on coil spring/damper units and, at the rear, a de Dion axle was suspended on coil springs. The DD1 was designed to take the Coventry-Climax FWA 1098 cc engine or the MG XPAG, while the DD2 featured a shorter wheelbase. Both these models, together with the Buckler 90, were usually fitted with low and very sleek aluminium bodywork having easily detachable nose sections and rear bodywork that hinged upwards.

The most successful Buckler was W. A. Liddell's car, which was raced throughout 1955 with a fair amount of success, albeit in minor events. Another

ABOVE *The Buckler was a popular 'home-build' at the lower end of the competition spectrum. This is a Mk X seen at Prescott in 1955 (T. C. March)*

BELOW *Cornish with the Halton-Buckler overtakes the Yeats' Special at the Eight Clubs meeting at Silverstone in June 1956. The Halton-Tojeiro also ran at this meeting*

BETTER BUILD A BUCKLER

BUY A BUCKLER MULTI-TUBE SPACE FRAME AND BUILD YOUR OWN BUCKLER

AMAZING STABILITY—EVERY MILE A PLEASURE

Complete range of frames to accept Ford 10; M.G.; MORRIS MINOR and COVENTRY CLIMAX UNITS including the famous 1172 Formula NINETY and D.D.I. CLIMAX for both of which we supply body panels as illustrated. Other models accept Mistral glass fibre bodies.

Buckler Close-Ratio Gears for Ford 10 Specials and New Prefects £10 - 15.
4:7 Crown Wheels and Pinions £8-8. High Comp. Cyl. Head Gaskets 10/-.
Goldtop H.C. Cyl. Heads from £4-12. I.F.S. Conv. for Populars ex. £26-10.

BUCKLERS 67 Caversham Rd., Reading—*Phone: Reading 54031*

This 1955 advertisement by Buckler cars reveals the vast range offered by Buckler and illustrates the 90 usually raced in 1172 cc form

much-raced variant was the Halton-Buckler, constructed by apprentice servicemen at RAF Halton for their commanding officer to drive. This successful Ford-powered car was raced throughout 1955 and in 1956 was sold to J. A. Cornish, who continued its career in Club events.

By the end of the 1950s most of the Buckler chassis and components were intended for use in road cars, but in 1961 Buckler introduced a new competition chassis intended for Ford power and based on a 'backbone' construction built up of steel tubing. Derek Buckler was seriously ill in the late 1950s, and Peter Hilton took over as managing director. Buckler died in March 1964 aged 53.

Chevron

Mancunian Derek Bennett was one of the most pleasant people in motor racing, a great enthusiast, an able driver and a very fine designer. In his early days he built Austin 750 Specials on a vaguely commerical basis (most of his customers were his friends) and in 1956 he constructed two rear-engined 500 cc JAP-powered Specials for midget speedway racing. The vogue for midget racing soon passed and Bennett moved on to building and racing a 750 Formula car (based on Austin 7 components) to comply with the regulations of the 750 Motor Club. For 1958 this car was re-engined with a Ford 1172 unit and for two years Bennett competed successfully in the 750 MC's 1172 Formula racing.

In 1960 he constructed a front-engined Formula Junior car with Ford engine and gearbox, but financial problems caused its early sale. Bennett's racing career continued in 1962 and 1963 with a Lotus Elite. He drove Gemini Formula Junior and Brabham Formula 3 cars in 1964 and started construction of two cars to comply with the Clubmen's Formula, where most of the opposition consisted of Lotus Sevens and Mallock-built U2s. Construction was delayed while Bennett raced a Brabham BT14, but the two new cars were eventually completed in 1965. One was to be raced by Bennett himself and the other was built for Brian Classic, now a well-known dealer in specialist cars. These were the first cars on which the name Chevron was used. Bennett had been desperately trying to think of a suitable name, and one day, when he was thumbing through the Highway Code, he saw a reference to Chevrons and the problem was solved.

The new cars, later typed the B1, were immensely successful in their class and won race after race. In 1966 he built four Clubmen's cars for customers and these were typed the B2. These early Bennett designs featured a multi-tubular space-frame with stressed prop-shaft tunnel and under-tray, independent suspension front and rear and Ford 1500 cc engine (with the exception of one production car that was powered by a BMC 998 cc engine). It was now that the future of Chevron was forged in the small works, part of a former cotton mill, at 105 Chorley Old Road, Bolton, and there followed a long and successful line of Competition Sports cars built by Derek Bennett Engineering Ltd.

B3

Bennett had been asked about the possibility of fitting a hard top to the Clubmen's car and he had discussed with a customer the possible conversion of a Lotus 23 into a GT car. With these thoughts in mind Bennett drew up the design of the B3 GT car and Digby Martland ordered the first Ford-powered car after being shown a model of the proposed design.

The basic structure of the Chevron B3 was formed by a multi-tubular space-frame constructed from 16- to 20-gauge, 1 in. to 1.5 in. square and round tubing, with the tubes running up the windscreen pillars to the roof area and stiffened by monocoque steel sills, two bulkheads and a stressed dural undertray running the full length of the car. At the front there were wide-angled double wishbones and coil spring/damper units, with the anti-roll bar operating on the upper wishbone, and using modified Triumph uprights. The rear suspension consisted of wide-based lower wish-bones, single top links, twin radius rods and coil spring/damper units. At the rear the anti-roll bar operated on the bottom wishbones, and the uprights were machined from magnesium castings. Steering was Triumph rack-and-pinion, the wheels were magnesium machined from castings and there were Girling disc brakes mounted outboard front and rear. The fuel was carried in a 12-gallon tank mounted transversely behind the cockpit but with additional 6- or 8-gallon tankage in the nose. While the water radiator was at the front of the car in the usual way, the 2-gallon oil tank was rear-mounted. The oil and water pipes passed through the sills of the chassis.

Digby Martland's car was powered by a Ford Cosworth twin-cam 1598 cc unit developing around 155 bhp at 7800 rpm and driving through a $7\frac{3}{4}$ in. twin-plate clutch and Hewland HD5 5-speed gearbox (later cars had the Hewland FT gearbox designed for Formula 2). The engine was canted about 17 degrees in the chassis, which improved water circulation, helped lower the centre of gravity and kept the rear decking as low as possible. The fibreglass coupé body had conventional doors with lightweight plexiglass windows (incorporat-ing half-moon swivelling cut-outs which aided ventilation and could be used for signalling); the nose and tail sections were detachable with quick-release fittings.

The Chevron B3 combined the then current single-seater chassis design approach with a practical GT competition body. Its space-frame was easier to build in quantity than a monocoque and far cheaper to repair in the event of accident damage. It was a very easy car to maintain, was exceedingly competitive, its handling was superb, and, like so many successful competition cars, it looked right.

During development testing at Oulton Park in 1966 both Peter Gethin and Bennett lapped faster than the GT record. It was a promise soon to be fulfilled, for on the B3's racing debut Martland scored a win at Oulton Park, and on his next outing at the Crystal Palace he was on the exhausts of David Piper's Ferrari 250LM throughout the race and finished a close second. As the racing season continued, Martland scored success after success.

The B3 was very much a prototype and only one other car to this specification was built in 1966.

B4

Alongside the Cosworth-powered cars, Bennett built the B4, which was powered by a BMW 1991 cc 4-cylinder engine developing 190 bhp at 7300 rpm and with similar transmission. It was reckoned that Bennett was taking a gamble using the BMW engine, which had proved largely unreliable in its competition career; initially the engines were detuned in the interests of reliability and later, after a visit by Bennett to Munich, most of the problems with these engines were ironed out.

Bennett drove the first B4 on its racing debut and later in the year John Lepp demonstrated the considerable speed and potential of the car in the Paris 1000 Km race at Montlhéry, where, with Peter Gethin as co-driver, they finished eighth overall and second in their class.

In the January 1967 issue of *Motor Racing*, John Blunsden reported on his track-tests of both the Ford and BMW-powered cars at Brands Hatch. The conditions were dreadful, with heavy rain and strong wind, and these factors must be taken into account when reading his comments on the B4:

'Starting the BMW-engined car is quite a tricky business, calling for a gradual opening throttle as the starter switch is operated . . . I was soon finding that I was having to concentrate so hard to stay on the road that it was difficult to evaluate the car's performance. Because of the conditions I used only 6600 rpm, but with a lot of power from 4500 rpm upwards this still gave a useful rev band for a 5-speed transmission.

'The centre shift works very well (there's a strong spring protecting first), and the only thing to remember with the BMW engine is to give the throttle a real boot during downward shifts to get a completely smooth engagement, due to the engine's slower than usual linkage. The clutch action was light, and the brake pedal quite firm, the car feeling very stable in the wet under braking. The engine is mounted very rigidly in the frame, having an extra pair of front mounts compared with the twin-cam, and these are to be modified to eliminate a certain amount of vibration which is transmitted to the cockpit, mainly at fairly low revs.

'The track conditions made the car something of a handful, and I found the front end ploughing straight on at most corners and losing me quite a lot of time, while inevitably a sudden lift-off would bring the back end round. I found myself taking some rather novel lines here and there, and a lot of concentrated effort and wheel twirling went into my best lap of 65.9 seconds.'

Later in the day, when weather conditions had improved somewhat, Blunsden drove Martland's Ford-powered car for a second time:

'Though the track was still wet, it felt a different car. The understeer was less than half what it had been, and now I could really use the power to neutralize what was left. Even the hairpin, which had been hopeless earlier on, was now giving some traction, and I began to understand why the Chevron GT has been so successful. It started to feel more like a single-seater, and I began using 7500 rpm for the first time, and finding that I could go through the wettest parts of Bottom and Kidney Bends under power without either end skating away from me. I felt I was driving it properly for the first time, and I was able to think about other things, such as the good mirror visibility through the vertical rear screen, and the fact that despite the fairings from roof to tail on each side, you can see what's happening close to your nearside rear wheel. Another good thing was the air flow into the cockpit, which prevented any misting up.

'The best lap time during the final short session was 61 seconds, which was a clear enough indication that the next time a Chevron GT competes at Brands Hatch in a Special GT race in the dry, the class lap record will take quite a bashing.'

ABOVE *In the 1970 BOAC 1000 Km race there were five B8s entered in the Sports Car category. This Worcestershire Racing Association entry driven by Bamford/Creasy/Tangye was eliminated by ignition trouble (Guy Griffiths)*

LEFT *The B8 with Cosworth FVA engine driven in the prototype class of the 1969 BOAC 500 race at Brands Hatch by John Bridges/John Lepp. They retired because of an engine misfire (Guy Griffiths)*

B5

This designation was given to a car supplied to David Bridges and powered by a 2-litre V-8 BRM engine and with Hewland 5-speed gearbox. The car did not prove a great success, mainly because of the unsuitability of the transmission. In 1969 it was acquired by Willie Green and, raced with BRM 2-litre centre-exhaust engine and 6-speed BRM gearbox, it enjoyed substantial success in British events.

B6

For 1967 this designation was given to the production cars, regardless of the engine fitted. In the main they were BMW-powered, but cars were constructed with Ford twin-cam, Cosworth FVA and 2-litre Coventry-Climax engines. Changes to the design were few, but the bodywork was now manufactured by Specialised Mouldings Ltd, and was to a much higher standard. Chassis frames were supplied by Arch Motors and engines direct from BMW. The air intake was larger to overcome the overheating problems suffered in longer events. During 1967 these cars enjoyed an immense run of success in British events. The writer recalls competing in a race at Oulton Park in September 1967 at which Brian Redman drove the works B6 and other Chevrons were entered—the speed of the Chevrons both along Oulton's short straights and through the bends was quite awe-inspiring to a novice who seemed to be spending the whole race trying to keep his Lawrencetune Morgan out of the way of one or other of the Chevrons that was travelling at what appeared to be twice his speed!

B8

The designation B7 was used for a prototype Formula 3 car, subsequently sold in the United States. The B8 was the 1968 GT car improved by having the undertray bonded to the chassis frame, larger radiators, oil pipes and tanks and an adjustable front anti-roll bar. Total production of B6 and B8 cars (excluding the prototypes) was 68 by the end of November 1968, and the cars were homologated as Competition sports cars (minimum production of 50) that year. The B8 was also remarkable value at £1800 ex-works.

By 1969 the cars were appearing regularly in international events and in the Daytona 24 Hours race in February a B8 driven by Kleinpeter/ Gunn/Beatty finished sixth overall in a rather depleted field and won the 2000 cc class. In British races the B8 was a familiar and successful sight; John Lepp with the works/Red Rose Racing car won the RAC British Sports Car Championship in 1969 and Chevron repeated this success in 1970 with a car driven by Trevor Twaites.

In November 1969 there was announced an open Group 6 Prototype body conversion for the Chevron B8 known as the Gropa MCM (the initials stood for Graphics Racing Organisation for Prototype Automobiles) and marketed by Andrew Mylius and designed by Nomad designer Bob Curl. The price of the conversion was initially only £500, it was approved by Derek Bennett and was said to take about two weeks to carry out. During 1970–71 quite a number of B6 and B8 cars were converted and their racing life extended. In 1985 the Chevron B8 is one of the most numerous and successful marques contesting the HSCC Historic Special GT Championship—and many of these are cars that have been converted back from Gropa configuration. By today's standards a Chevron B6 or B8 is a very reasonably priced historic competition car and the usual asking price seems to be in the £14,000 to £17,000 bracket—another advantage is that a good example is not too difficult to find.

B12

The designations B9 and B10 relate to Chevron single-seaters, and Bennett was superstitious about the number eleven. Accordingly the designation B12 was allotted to the special Group 6 Prototype car built for John Woolfe in 1968. Although the car was built in the Chevron works, it was not a car of which Bennett really approved. It was a B8 with lengthened engine bay and the wheelbase increased by 2.5 in. The power unit was the Australian-built Repco 90-degree V-8 with a capacity of 2996 cc (89 × 60 mm), single overhead camshaft per bank of cylinders, Lucas fuel injection and a power output of 330 bhp at 8800 rpm. This engine had of course been used in 1966–67 Formula 1 Brabhams. The B12 was also fitted with Brabham 15 in. Formula 1 wheels.

Although the B12 performed superbly in 10-lap British races, it was plagued by cylinder head gasket failure in longer races, and in 1968 Woolfe, co-driving with David Piper, retired at Watkins Glen and retired at Le Mans, with Digby Martland as co-driver, because of this problem.

B16

Bennett did not use the designation B13 out of consideration for other people's superstitions and the B14 and B15 were both single-seaters. The B16 was Bennett's vastly improved GT car, which was given its shake-down testing in August 1969 (with BMW engine), won on its first outing in an International event and was homologated as a Competition Sports car for 1970 (by this time the minimum production had been reduced to 25).

In every respect the B16 was an improvement on its predecessors. The chassis centre-section was now a full monocoque made up from a number of separate box-type structures with aluminium plating round the cockpit for extra stiffness; to this centre-section were attached tubular frames to carry the front suspension and mid-mounted engine and gearbox/final drive unit. The suspension layout was similar to that of the B8, but there were a number of detail changes. The engine was usually the Ford Cosworth FVC 1790 cc developing 245 bhp (but cars were raced with BMW and Mazda rotary engines) and the Hewland FT200 gearbox/final drive unit was specified. Whereas the body of the B8 had been attractive, the B16 was strikingly beautiful, with graceful curving lines and cut-off tail, and was clearly inspired by the Ferrari P3 and P4 prototypes of 1966–67. This body, the work of Specialised Mouldings, did as much to sell the car as its outstanding performance and modest price (around £5500 with Cosworth engine and Hewland trans-axle).

The new car made its debut in the hands of Brian

LEFT *An interesting entry in the 1970 Spa 1000 Km race was this B16 powered by a Mazda rotary engine, and driven by Deprez/Vernaeve. It was incredibly noisy, not particularly quick and finished at the tail of the field in 15th place (Nigel Snowdon)*

INSET *The installation of the Mazda engine in the Chevron chassis (Nigel Snowdon)*

The Skailes/Hine B16 entered by the works leads a Porsche 914/6 in the 1970 Le Mans race. Note the absence of headlamp covers and the stone-scarring round the headlamps (Guy Griffiths)

Redman in the Nürburgring 500 Km race on 8 September 1969. Because the new FVC engine was not ready, the car was fitted with the smaller FVA 1.6-litre unit. Despite handling problems during the first day's practice, on the Saturday Redman turned in a lap of 8 min 33.5 sec to take pole position, attaining 150 mph (9300 rpm in top) on the fastest part of the circuit. Redman agreed with Bennett that he would drive a cautious race, sitting behind the very fast Abarth opposition in the opening stages of the race, but instead he went straight into the lead, pulled out an advantage of several hundred yards over the fastest Abarth by the end of the first lap and, despite having to hold the car in third gear to prevent it jumping out, went on to win the race by a margin of nearly two minutes.

Postscript

The B16 was a car of the 1970s rather than the 1960s, and in 1970 Chevron won the nine-round European 2-litre Championship, mainly due to Redman's superlative driving, by the margin of one point from Lola. At the 1970 Nürburgring 500 Km race, Chevron introduced the B16S, an open Spyder version of the B16 which served as a prototype for the production B19 that followed in 1971. Chevron continued to score almost innumerable successes in British events (as well as finishing second in the 1971 European Championship), but with the passing of the years the emphasis shifted to single-seater design and production. With a strong team that included co-director John Bridges (originally a private entrant of Chevron cars) and Paul Owens as racing manager, Chevron flourished throughout the seventies. Sadly in 1978 Derek Bennett was killed in a hang-gliding accident; it soon became only too evident that the company could not survive without him and it was not long before liquidation loomed. Recently the name Chevron has been revived and the new company supplies parts for early Chevron GT cars as well as promoting new designs.

Connaught

L-Series

Continental Cars of Send in Surrey were Bugatti specialists, but when it became obvious in the 1940s that Bugatti would not be re-entering production, Rodney Clarke and Mike Oliver, who controlled the company, sought new ventures. After a great deal of thought they decided to go ahead with a sports car based on Lea-Francis components that would be suitable for competition work and cost far less, for example, than a Frazer Nash. It was decided to call the new car the Connaught.

The Lea-Francis Fourteen Sports 8 ft 3 in. wheelbase chassis with rigid axles front and rear was only slightly modified by using a higher steering ratio, adjustment to the shock absorber settings and choice of rear axle ratios. The 1767 cc Lea-Francis engine with twin camshafts mounted high on the block was modified by Peter Monkhouse and A. M. L. MacLachlan of Monaco Motors of Watford, working in liaison with Mike Oliver; there were new camshafts giving increased lift to the valves, a raised compression ratio of 8.2:1, new pistons, four-branch exhaust manifold with twin pipes, dry sump lubrication and twin SU carburettors. In this form the L1 'Sportsman's Roadster' developed 98 bhp, while the later L2 'Competition Two-seater' with wet sump lubrication and four Amal carburettors developed 102 bhp. Later development work increased these outputs to 107 bhp and 122 bhp, respectively. On alcohol fuel an output of 135 bhp was achieved.

The body, designed by Rodney Clarke and built by Leacroft of Egham, was constructed in aluminium, and costs were kept to a minimum by avoiding double curvature so far as possible. The whole of the front hinged forward to give access to the engine, but there was also an engine panel in the bonnet, and the rear of the body was detachable.

Initially three cars were built on chassis supplied through the Lea-Francis agents, Charles Follett, all to L2 specification, and these were registered MPH 329 for Kenneth McAlpine (then a customer of Continental Cars, who looked after his Maserati), MPH 995 for Mike Oliver and MPH 996 for Rodney Clarke. McAlpine drove the Connaught on its competition debut at Prescott in June 1949,

Ken McAlpine with one of the first L2 Connaughts at Silverstone in June 1949 (Guy Griffiths)

ABOVE LEFT *One of the later L3 cars with independent front suspension (the author)*

BELOW LEFT *A cockpit view of the L3 (the author)*

winning the class for unsupercharged sports cars up to 3000 cc, and the following weekend he raced at Silverstone, finishing fourth in his heat, but unplaced in the final. At Goodwood in August, Rodney Clarke won a handicap race with McAlpine second. Shortly afterwards, at Blandford, McAlpine and Clarke finished first and second in the sports car race.

Three more cars were built for John Lyons (son of Sir William Lyons of Jaguar) registered MPH 998, P. L. Jonas registered AHC 82 and Ken Downing registered OPC 3. Downing's car was fitted with the 1480 cc engine offered as an alternative by Continental Cars and two types of bodywork, full width for road use and stark cycle-wing for competition work.

McAlpine and Clarke continued to race their cars in 1950, but their efforts were increasingly devoted to the new A-series Formula 2 car, still with Lea-Francis-based engine, that made its debut at Castle Combe in October 1950. By this time Connaught Engineering had been formed to take over McAlpine's racing projects and the cars were now marketed by this firm. When Lea-Francis introduced independent front suspension by wishbones and torsion bars this was adopted on the Connaught. In this form it was known as the L3, but only two cars with standard full-width bodywork were built to this specification. To boost sales, Connaught introduced the L3/SR with narrow, two-seater bodywork, separate headlamps and cycle wings. This body was built by Abbott of Farnham on an ash frame. In all only three of these cars were built and there were two more with non-standard bodies. The last cars were sold in 1953 and in all only 14 had been constructed, despite strenuous marketing efforts.

They were not a great success commercially or in competition, but gained the company a great deal of useful design and racing experience before they plunged into International Formula 2.

ALSR

After four seasons of competing with 2-litre Formula 2 single-seaters, Connaught Engineering were hard at work over the winter of 1953–54 building the team's new 2500 cc Formula 1 contender. This was the B-series car to be powered by the 4-cylinder Alta engine and distinguished by its streamlined, aerodynamic bodywork. It was to prove a long development programme and, although the first car was demonstrated to the press in August 1954, it did not race until the Easter Goodwood meeting the following year.

Engineer Rodney Clarke had a very clear idea of just how long the development programme was likely to prove and both he and Kenneth McAlpine were keen to race a competitive car in the meanwhile (in fact McAlpine raced one of the obsolescent Formula 2 cars in a few events in the early part of 1954). The logical answer was a 1500 cc sports/racing car that incorporated many of the A-series Formula 2 components. That great enthusiast John Coombs, who had driven works Connaughts at some events in 1953, was keen to have a sports/racing car and so work was put in hand on two cars during the latter part of 1953.

The chassis of the ALSR was very similar to the Formula 2 cars, based on twin 3.75 in. steel tubes with a central tubular cross-member and a box-section front cross-member that also acted as the oil tank, with a capacity of 3½ gallons. At the front there was independent suspension by unequal-length wishbones with the lower and longer wishbones linked with torsion bars set across the frame. At the rear there was an important difference in that the de Dion tube ran behind the final drive and was located fore and aft by twin radius rods each side running back to extensions of the main frame members, which were inclined at an angle of 45 degrees. The tube was located laterally by a linkage on the left side of the car only, running from the end of the tube to the main frame member. The rear torsion bars ran longitudinally beside the main frame members, with the forward mountings just behind the half-way point.

Steering was Connaught's own rack-and-pinion system. The wheels were cast magnesium zirconium to Connaught design and cast integrally with the brake drums. Normal four-stud fixing was used and this was quite satisfactory for short races in which no wheel changes were needed.

Powering the ALSR was a 1484 cc (75 × 84 mm) version of the familiar Connaught engine based on the Lea-Francis with twin camshafts mounted high on the cylinder block. Apart from the basic layout the Connaught engine had little in common with its Lea-Francis ancestor and featured an aluminium cylinder block, dry-sump lubrication and four Amal 10 T.T. carburettors. With a compression ratio of 9:1 (compared with the 12.5:1 of the Formula 2 engine, which ran on alcohol fuel and sometimes with nitromethane additive) power output by 1955 was 115 bhp at 6000 rpm. With its oversquare cylinder dimensions and generally lower stressing Clarke reckoned that the sports/racing unit would prove more reliable.

As on the Formula 2 cars the 4-speed gearbox was of the Wilson preselector-type manufactured by Armstrong-Siddeley, whereby there was no clutch as such; the next gear was selected by a quadrant change mounted on the gearbox, which was separated from the engine by a short shaft, and engaged when the 'clutch' pedal was dipped. The Connaught-designed magnesium alloy final drive casing was mounted in a fabricated cage at the rear of the frame members. The body of McAlpine's car was a neat aluminium 2-seater with not particularly elegant lines, while Coombs' car was fitted with more stylish bodywork, reminiscent of the Aston Martin DB3S.

John Coombs' car (registered UPG 171) was ready to run in the BARC Members' meeting at Goodwood on 27 March, 1954, where it won first time out; Kenneth McAlpine first appeared with MCA 200 at the *Daily Express* Trophy meeting at Silverstone two months later and one of the new engines had been supplied to John Risely-Prichard for installation in his 'Disco Volante' Cooper. At Oulton Park Coombs finished second in his heat and was 10th overall (second car home in the 1500 cc class) in the handicap final.

At Oulton Park Colin Chapman had raced the new ultra-light, ultra-aerodynamic Lotus Mk VIII for the first time. It was too new to do well, but its MG engine developed a lot less horses than that of Coombs' Connaught and Coombs saw a way to have the best of both designs. The Connaught was superbly engineered in the traditional sense, beautifully made and immensely tough, whereas the Lotus was incredibly light and unlikely to last a European endurance race. By the British Grand Prix meeting at Silverstone on 17 July Coombs had transferred his Connaught engine to a Lotus chassis. The results of the 1500 cc sports car race were significant, Chapman (with the streamlined Lotus) winning from Peter Gammon (with an incredibly quick unstreamlined Lotus Mk VI), Hans Herrmann (works Porsche 550), Coombs with the new Lotus-Connaught and McAlpine with the works Connaught.

During the remainder of the season both Coombs and McAlpine scored a number of successes, but the works Connaught's best performance was in the Tourist Trophy on the incredibly difficult and dangerous Dundrod circuit, in which McAlpine partnered by Jack Fairman finished tenth overall and second in the 1500 cc class behind the Gordini of Cahill and Beauman. At the October Aintree meeting McAlpine managed to beat Chapman's Lotus into second place in the 1500 cc class of the sports car race. During the year the

BELOW *This photograph of the 1955 works ALSR Connaught shows off the car's superb lines*

RIGHT *A view of the cockpit of the works ALSR, showing clearly the 8000 rpm tachometer, the change for the preselector gearbox and many details of construction*

Coombs Connaught was sold to Peter Bell, fitted with a new 1484 cc engine, subsequently re-registered VPF272 and driven in a couple of events by Stirling Moss and Tony Marsh, albeit without success.

By 1955 Peter Bell's car was regularly driven by Les Leston. John Coombs was now racing a new Lotus Mk IX, without tail fins, using the Connaught engine. During the year another of these engines was fitted to Tommy Sopwith's Equipe Endeavour rear-engined Cooper.

The works car was rebuilt with the most superb-looking light alloy body; the frontal treatment was similar to that of the team's streamlined Formula 1 cars, with a small oblong opening feeding the radiator, above it an inverted triangular opening taking air into a duct to the carburettors and with small openings low down on either side taking air to the front brake drums. There was a single door on the driver's side. Twin tail fins dominated the rear of the car. The spare wheel was mounted in the tail above the main fuel tank. Altogether there were three fuel tanks, with additional tanks each side of the cockpit, giving a total capacity of 24 gallons and with each of the quick-action filler caps enclosed by a small panel. In real terms the works Connaught was not as aerodynamically efficient as the Lotus Mk IX, but it was the best looking car in its class.

Both Connaughts made their first appearance of the year in the British Empire Trophy at Oulton Park. Leston won the 1500 cc heat from McAlpine and was leading the final on handicap when eliminated by engine trouble. McAlpine went on to finish second in the final to Scott-Brown's Lister-Bristol. At the Easter Goodwood meeting Leston and McAlpine took first and second places in the 1500 cc sports car race. Another victory for Leston followed at Ibsley, but he was beaten into second place by Bueb's Cooper at Brands Hatch the following day. The following weekend at the *Daily Express* meeting at Silverstone, Leston and McAlpine were beaten into second and third places in the 1500 cc class of the Sports car race. McAlpine won the 1500 cc class of the Johnson's Trophy at Goodwood on Whit Monday from Parnell with Sopwith's Cooper-Connaught, and the same day Leston was again second to Bueb's 1100 cc Cooper-Climax at the Crystal Palace.

At Le Mans in June the works car was entered for McAlpine with former Aston Martin works driver Eric Thompson. The car was beautifully prepared; it clearly had the stamina for endurance

racing with speed to match and Connaught hopes of success were high. In the race the Connaught ran splendidly, holding third place in its class behind two works Porsche entries, and was timed at 135.47 mph on the Mulsanne straight (there was no speed published for the works MG-powered Lotus Mk IX, preventing comparison of the two entries). Unfortunately, during the eighth hour the Connaught's run came to an end because of piston failure.

The Connaughts were out of luck in the sports car race at the British Grand Prix at Aintree and McAlpine was trounced by Chapman with the Lotus-MG. Leston won at Charterhall, and then both cars were entered in the Goodwood Nine Hours race with McAlpine partnered by Thompson and Leston partnered by Scott-Brown. Leston/Scott-Brown enjoyed a completely trouble-free race to finish sixth overall and win the 1500 cc class, while the works car dropped to the tail of the field with brake problems. Incidentally, the works car ran on wire wheels with knock-off hubs in long-distance events to expedite wheel changes. Stirling Moss drove Bell's car in the *Daily Herald* Trophy at Oulton Park the following weekend; he missed practice, started from the back of the grid and drove a magnificent race to finish sixth overall and win the 1500 cc class. Another week passed and both cars were in action again at Aintree, where a newcomer to the Connaught works car, Tony Brooks, beat Leston for second place in the 1500 cc sports car race behind Chapman's Lotus.

Later in September the works car was entered in the Tourist Trophy with promising young newcomer Bill Smith (who had turned in some brilliant drives in 1955 with his private C-type Jaguar) and John Young at the wheel. It was an horrific race that resulted in the abandonment of the fearfully dangerous Dundrod circuit. Jim Mayers lost control of his Cooper-Climax, which struck a concrete post and disintegrated in flames; Smith crashed the Connaught into the blazing wreckage and four other cars crashed. Both Mayers and Smith died in the inferno. It was a tragic accident that cost the life of one of the most promising young sports car drivers, but it also destroyed one of the prettiest 1500 cc cars of all time.

Connaught were too preoccupied with Formula 1 to build any more sports/racing cars and it was only five weeks later that Tony Brooks scored Connaught's historic win in the Syracuse Grand Prix. Although the company traded and sold cars, Connaught was primarily Kenneth McAlpine's private obsession. It failed to attract commercial or industrial support, was always hopelessly under-financed despite the vast sums poured in by McAlpine and after a number of reasonable Grand Prix places in 1956 and the early part of 1957 finally withdrew from racing altogether after the 1957 Monaco Grand Prix. By 1956 Les Leston was racing a Cooper-Climax and the following year the Bell Connaught passed to amateur enthusiast Jock McBain. The ALSR Connaught had all the ingredients of a successful endurance car, but its potential was never fulfilled because of the team's preoccupation with Formula One.

RIGHT *Les Leston with the ex-Coombs, Peter Bell-entered Connaught in the Sports Car race at Silverstone in May 1955 (T. C. March)*

BELOW *McAlpine with the works Connaught in the same race. There is muck all over the nose and windscreen, possibly blown out by Hawthorn's Jaguar (T. C. March)*

Cooper

Cooper-MG

The first Cooper 500 had made its competition appearance at Prescott hillclimb on 28 July, 1946, and within two years production 500s were being turned out of the Hollyfield Road works in ever-increasing numbers and Cooper was the dominant force in 500 cc racing. John Cooper was keen to expand the small firm's activities by building a sports car, and as his father, Charles, was still a Vauxhall agent it made sense to use a Vauxhall engine, especially as the firm had a Vauxhall 10 engine in store. Much of the design work was carried out by Cooper's new draughtsman/designer Owen Maddock, and it proved to be a thoroughly professional little car.

Back in 1947 the Coopers had built a sports car based on the 500 cc chassis, with rear-mounted Triumph Tiger 100 motorcycle engine and very streamlined bodywork based on that built by Cooper's 'tame' panel-beater Charlie Robinson for Paul Pycroft's SS100 Jaguar, a successful car in Club events at the time. The Coopers had realized that there was not much of a future for a motorcycle-engined sports car and now had decided to pursue the more conventional path of building a front-engined car.

The chassis of the Cooper-Vauxhall, basically similar to the 500 cc cars, was based on welded box-section main members in $3\frac{1}{8}$ by $1\frac{5}{8}$ in. mild steel channel sections, boxed by welded 14-gauge mild steel sheet, fabricated suspension mountings front and rear, two central $1\frac{1}{4}$ in. tubular members which were extended outwards to support the body and a further $1\frac{1}{4}$ in. tubular cross-member. Front and rear suspension was independent by the familiar Fiat-derived Cooper system of transverse leaf springs and wishbones with telescopic dampers. The aluminium body, with more than a passing resemblance to the first of the postwar sports Ferraris, was supported on a superstructure of mild steel strip. The cycle wings turned with the steering and there were cutaway let-down doors hinged at the bottom. The 1203 cc Vauxhall engine, with twin SU carburettors, was tuned to develop something over 40 bhp and was used with the standard Vauxhall 3-speed and reverse gearbox. Other features were the usual cast alloy Cooper wheels with integral brake drums, Lockheed hydraulic brakes, 6-volt electrics and the head-lamps mounted behind a radiator grille similar to that of the 500 cc cars.

John Cooper believed the new car to have a maximum speed of around 85 mph, and with a weight as low as 9 cwt the acceleration was excellent. Although the Cooper-Vauxhall received rave reviews in the British press, John Cooper was convinced that the car needed more power and as a result negotiated with John Thornley of the MG Car Company for the supply of the XPAG 1250 cc engine, the standard unit powering most postwar British 1500 cc sports/racing cars. Early in 1950 the Cooper-Vauxhall was sold to Sir Bernard Docker, chairman of the BSA Group, and after it had been trimmed out by Hooper and fitted with a Daimler-style radiator grille was used by his son Lance Docker to drive round the family's estate at Poole.

In 1950 the first of the Cooper-MGs appeared, based on the longer, stretched 1000 cc chassis of the rear-engined single-seaters; it was very similar in appearance to the original Cooper-Vauxhall, but with fixed cycle wings. The main difference of course lay in the engine and transmission, which were MG. The engine was soon developed by John Lucas of Barwell Engineering, with a special head having oversize valves, raised compression ratio of 8.6:1, twin $1\frac{1}{2}$ in. SU carburettors and a power output of 75 bhp at 6200 rpm (compared with the standard 54 bhp).

The works prototype Cooper-MG, painted blue and wearing the Cooper trade plates 307 PD, made its racing debut at Goodwood on 17 June, 1950, at the BARC Members' meeting. Young Stirling Moss turned out to drive the Cooper on its race debut, but the engine was running rough and the best that Stirling could manage was fifth in a 5-lap scratch race. For the last race of the day, a 5-lap handicap, John Cooper took over the car—now running well—and Stirling's helmet to finish second. In August, John Cooper again raced the Cooper-MG at a BARC Members' meeting, winning a scratch event at 71.74 mph from Jim Mayers's Lester-MG (formidable opposition by 1950 standards) and after the meeting handed the car over to John Bolster of *Autosport*.

John Bolster drove the prototype Cooper-MG on the road for a weekend after trying it round Goodwood. He was very impressed with the performance and handling and wrote:

'I decided, in order not to show the performance in too favourable a light, to carry a heavy passenger and full equipment during the trials, and to take the mean of several runs in opposite directions. In spite of these handicaps, a standstill to 50 mph figure of some $7\frac{1}{2}$ seconds was secured, and the 0 to 60 time was under 11 seconds. With the driver only aboard, it was to excel these results, and of course some of the "one way" performances were better still.

'As the rev. counter flicked past the 6000 mark, the engine is still perfectly happy, and well below its ultimate capabilities. I respected the lion-hearted little unit too much, however, to find just how high it would go, but I did exceed 50 mph in second and 70 mph in third gear.

'It is in the upper ranges that the performance seems so uncanny, for one can cruise up quite steep main road hills at 70 mph on half throttle, and, in a few seconds, push the needle up to "80" with complete lack of effort. The low weight of the car (10 cwt as tested) obviously contributes to this result, but the body must be very well streamlined for acceleration to be maintained at such high speeds.

'Ninety mph comes up very quickly and one keeps exceeding it on the most unlikely pieces of road. Whether an actual timed 100 mph is available I neither know nor care, but it can certainly be achieved under suitable conditions if one is sufficiently heartless to ignore the rev. counter.

'. . . the Cooper feels safe, looks safe and *is* safe, even when swerving the curves at a most outrageous speed.'

Coopers Cars Limited were far too preoccupied with building 500 cc cars (which had been granted International status as Formula 3 for 1950) and the 1000 cc versions to tackle a serious production line of Cooper-MGs, but over the next couple of years parts were supplied for something approaching 20 cars to be built. The cars were supplied in component form so that owners could avoid purchase tax and also avoid clogging the already hard-pressed Cooper works. In the interests of simplicity I will describe the more important cars by reference to their registration numbers:

OPC 913

This was built up early in 1950 by John Coombs, who acquired a body and chassis from the works in which he installed a Rover 4-cylinder engine linered down to under 1100 cc and substantially modified to increase power output. It failed to achieve much in the way of success, passed to Peter Jackson and at some stage was fitted with attractive streamlined bodywork.

Cliff Davis at the wheel of his famous 'Barchetta'-bodied Cooper-MG (Guy Griffiths)

NKC 195

This was the registration given to the works car when registered. It passed to Francis Dundas, who used it mainly in rallies. It retained standard Cooper bodywork.

LLV 1

Raced in 1951–52 by Peter Reece, and its successes included third place on handicap in the 1951 British Empire Trophy in the Isle of Man. It was sold to Jack Sears, the Norfolk farmer who became best known for his drives with Lister-Bristol, Jaguar saloons and Cobra. For 1954 the car was acquired by Jack Hacking, who fitted it with a full-width body painted dark red and raced it in Club events. In Hacking's hands the car went very well and the writer remembers vividly him winning two races with it at the North Staffs MC meeting at Silverstone in October 1954.

JOY 500

This was the most famous Cooper-MG, which was acquired in 1951 by Lionel Leonard, who had previously raced a 1087 cc MG Magnette and was a well-known tuner of MG engines. The most striking feature of Leonard's car was the beautifully proportioned polished aluminium body closely following the lines of the Superleggera Touring 'Barchetta' body fitted to a number of 2-litre sports/racing Ferraris. During the year this car had its engine enlarged to 1467 cc, in which form it developed 85 bhp, but Leonard never seemed to be able to get the car to run well and towards the end of 1951 sold it to Cliff Davis. In Davis's hands—and after an engine rebuild—it proved one of the most successful 1500 cc cars in British events, vying for success throughout 1952 with the Lester-MGs raced by The Monkey Stable. Davis retained JOY 500 for 1953 and the following year sold it to Peter Jackson, who raced it with success in Club events. In 1952 John Bolster tested this Cooper-MG for *Autosport*, achieving maximum speeds in the gears of 1st, 33 mph; 2nd, 55 mph; 3rd, 83 mph; and top, 114.6 mph. The best time for the standing ¼-mile was 18.25 sec.

KOY 500

In 1952 Lionel Lenonard acquired a second Cooper-MG, which he raced with cycle-wing bodywork, but never achieved much in the way of success. Later in the year he sold this car to Bristol garage proprietor Horace Gould (better known for his exploits with a Cooper Bristol Formula 2 car and with the ex-Bira Maserati 250F). Gould fitted Cooper-Bristol Mk 1 suspension and two leading shoes brakes from the same model front and rear. Gould enjoyed a fair measure of success with this car before he sold it in 1954 to I. E. Davidson. Davidson's only claim to fame seems to be that he ran the bearings of the MG engine on the start line for a sprint at 6000 rpm!

Probably a dozen or so cars were completed with MG engines, but others had Ford Zephyr, Lea Francis and Riley engines. Where the Cooper-MG scored over its rivals was in its low weight and its superior roadholding. It also did much to encourage Harry Lester and other constructors in the 1500 cc class to improve their cars.

Cooper-Connaught 'Disco Volante'

One of the most successful 1500 cc cars of the 1950s—within its limited aims—was John Risley-Prichard's 'Disco Volante' Cooper, a pure 'one-off' that displayed a remarkable performance. Risley-Prichard, who was a director of Willis, Faber & Dumas, the leading London insurance brokers, raced one of the ex-Hawthorn TT Rileys in 1952. For 1953 he decided that he wanted something rather faster and decided to install a spare Riley 1500 engine at the front of a 7 ft 3 in. wheelbase Cooper 500 cc chassis. It was not so very different from what Coopers had done themselves when they built the Cooper-MG and Ken Flint had done the same thing to create his own Cooper-MG in 1952.

What was so different about Risley-Prichard's car was the magnificent 'Disco Volante' bodywork directly copied from photographs of the 1952 Alfa Romeo sports/racing car (in fact it was never raced in this form). It was such a close copy that it is worth including a photograph of the original so that readers can pick out the differences for themselves! The main difference, however, was the

ABOVE RIGHT *After selling the 'Barchetta'-bodied Cooper to Cliff Davis, Lionel Leonard acquired a second car with normal bodywork, registered KOY 500. It is seen at Silverstone in 1952 (T. C. March)*

BELOW RIGHT *In 1953 KOY 500 was raced by Horace Gould, seen here at Snetterton in August (LAT)*

SU
Fit & Forget
GRIFLEX
Flexible Fuel & Oil Pipes
PETROL

R CAR CO. LTD.
ENGLAND
K·L·G

one-piece bonnet and wings of the Cooper that hinged forwards to give good access to the mechanics. The body was built by Wakefield's of Byfleet and painted red.

It seems that this Cooper was not ready to race until the August Bank Holiday weekend and Risley-Prichard competed at Davidstow in Cornwall on the Saturday and Thruxton on the Monday. The Thruxton meeting proved disastrous, as in the 1500 cc race Risley-Prichard damaged the bodywork when he collided with another car and then shortly before the finish the Riley engine threw a rod; a fuel line was severed, the car caught fire and whilst Risley-Prichard abandoned ship and suffered only minor injuries, the Cooper ran off course and was quite badly fire-damaged.

Apart from the fact that this Cooper was badly under-braked, Risley-Prichard was well pleased with the concept of the 'Disco Volante'. It was repaired for 1954 and a very expensive (and very powerful) Connaught 1484 cc engine was installed. The performance was transformed, although the braking was worse than ever, and throughout the year the car, now painted dark green, if this writer's memory is correct, proved itself one of the fastest cars in its class.

It first appeared in this form in the British Empire Trophy at Oulton Park in April and here Risley-Prichard took pole position on the grid of the 1500 cc heat with a time of 1 min 55 sec, that was faster than all but three of the cars in the 2000 cc heat and faster than six of the 12 starters in the unlimited heat. Over 16 laps he built up a lead of over 50 sec, but retired because of a broken universal joint on a drive-shaft. Incidentally, *Autosport* in their report of the race described the Copper-Connaught as 'the little black car', and although it was subsequently painted dark blue, that was later. At the *Daily Express* Trophy meeting at Silverstone in May, Risely-Prichard again showed a good turn of speed, but was put out of the running because the engine was reluctant to fire at the Le Mans start and he finished last. Risely-Prichard did rather better at the Grand Prix meeting at Silverstone in July; in practice for the 1500 cc race he was fourth fastest in 2 min 20 sec (pole-position man Herrmann with a 550 Porsche recorded 2 min 17 sec) and he finished sixth in the race after a long battle with McAlpine (Connaught).

By the Gold Cup meeting at Oulton Park in August, Risely-Prichard had acquired Rob Walker's 2-litre Connaught Formula 2 car. As with the 'Disco Volante' he ran it in the name of the Cornhill Racing Team (after the Cornhill Insurance Company, which at this time was controlled by Willis, Faber & Dumas), he retained the Scots blue colour of the Connaught and it seems that at around this time the Cooper-Connaught was repainted blue. Both cars were maintained by Rob Walker's garage at Dorking. Risely-Prichard was thinking of selling the Cooper-Connaught, but before it could be offered it was crashed and written off by a mechanic during a test run on the Leatherhead–Dorking road—a sad end for one of the more enterprising 'Specials' of the 1950s.

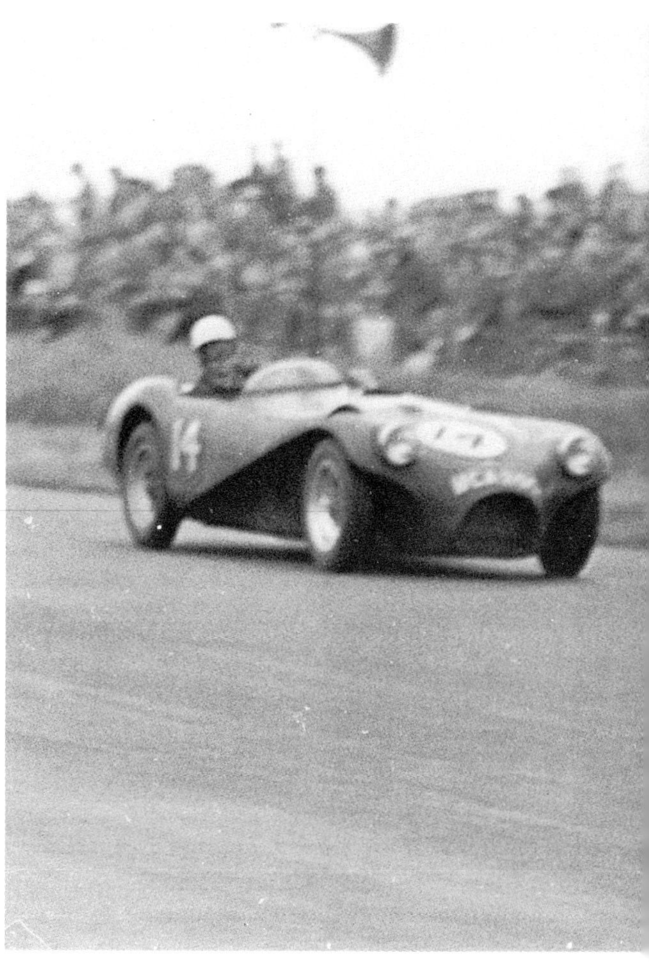

PREVIOUS PAGE *A superb paddock shot of Risely-Prichard's Cooper-Connaught at Silverstone in May 1954. Photographs such as this that capture the atmosphere of the period mean so much more than mere racing photographs (T. C. March)*

ABOVE *In the 1500 cc Sports Car race at Silverstone in July 1954 Risely-Prichard leads the works Connaught of McAlpine (T. C. March)*

RIGHT *Just for comparison—the original 1952 Alfa Romeo* Disco Volante

Cooper-Bristol

The Cooper company's first breakthrough into serious International racing (if one may be forgiven for not regarding Formula 3 as serious) was when the company announced a Bristol-powered Formula 2 contender for 1952. It achieved considerable success in single-seater racing and formed the basis of a very successful sports/racing car. The chassis was a direct development from the 1951 500 cc car and was based on two main members of light-gauge box-section, drilled for lightness. There were similar cross-members, tubular members ran parallel to the box-section members, two hooped-shape tubular members formed the scuttle, and there were other tubular members welded to the fabricated suspension bridges front and rear. Suspension, inevitably, was by transverse leaf springs, lower tubular wishbones and telescopic dampers. Steering was rack-and-pinion, and the wheels were the usual alloy Cooper cast with integral brake drums. Fuel capacity was a total of 28 gallons carried in three tanks, in the tail and on each side of the cockpit.

As fitted to the Formula 2 car, the Bristol engine developed around 140 bhp (but on modified versions such as used in Hawthorn's car this was increased to 155 bhp) and the Bristol 4-speed gearbox drove through a prop-shaft running slightly upwards to a spiral bevel final drive mounted on top of the rear suspension bridge. The final drive was soon changed for one of the hypoid bevel type. The body was a neat aluminium single-seater, undoubtedly inspired by Ferrari styling, and the complete car weighed fractionally over 9 cwt.

The prototype, which first appeared in January 1952, was sold to Archie Bryde, but the next three cars were undoubtedly the most successful. Young Mike Hawthorn at the wheel of a car bought by Bob Chase scored a phenomenal run of success in International racing that included fourth place in the Belgian Grand Prix, third in the British Grand Prix, fourth in the Dutch Grand Prix (results sufficient to give him fourth place in the World Championship) and four wins in British events. Both Alan Brown and Eric Brandon entered by Ecurie Richmond also enjoyed a good run of success in 1952. Three other cars were sold during the year, but none of these achieved much in the way of success.

For 1953 Cooper produced a Mk II version of the Cooper-Bristol with much lighter 16-gauge tubular frame. Other changes were a new magnesium final-drive casing and new wheels with separate 11 in. A1-fin light alloy drums. A combination of a new radiator design split into vertical sections with the oil cooler at the base to provide an opening between them for air to the carburettors, coupled with proper ducting of hot air from under the bonnet through the suspension cut-outs in the sides of the body, did away with the large bonnet-top scoops that had characterized the 1952 cars.

Mike Hawthorn was now a member of the works Ferrari team, so Cooper had lost their most successful customer. However, Mk II cars were raced with success by Ken Wharton (his car was run as a semi-works entry and was fitted with a preselector gearbox), Bob Gerard and Horace Gould. Including the works prototype, four other Mk II Cooper-Bristols were built; 2 cars were built to take Alta engines for Peter Whitehead and Tony Crook, Stirling Moss had two Cooper chassis (of which only the second was built in the works) and another chassis was fitted with a de Dion rear axle, Alfa Romeo engine and Ferrari-style body.

From these single-seaters a total of six sports/racing cars were built, and in addition there were two other sports/racing cars based on Cooper Formula 2 chassis frames and built from scratch for sports car racing. Once again it is easier to describe these cars by their registrations:

HPN 665

When Alan Brown raced for Bob Chase's Equipe Anglais with his own Mk I Cooper-Bristol Formula 2 car in 1953, the Mk I raced by Hawthorn for Chase in 1952 was surplus to requirements. Brown conceived the idea of converting it to a sports car and all the work was carried out by Bernie Rodger. A cage framework was welded up to carry the body which was built by Wakefield's of Byfleet, a firm very well known for sports/racing car bodies in the 1950s. Alan Brown is on record as saying that Wakefields were instructed to build a body of the 'Barchetta' style as fitted to Davis's Cooper-MG. In fact what emerged was a body almost identical to the 1952 Vignale-bodied Le Mans Tipo 340 Ferraris—complete with the same 'portholes' in the front wings and rubbing strips linking front and rear wheel arches. The car was shown to the press in March 1953 and at that stage it was stated that it would be raced with an Aston Martin 2.6-litre engine and that a second car with hard top was being built by the works for Ken Wharton to race. In fact the Chase Cooper appeared for the first time at the Members' meeting at Goodwood later in March 1953 with a Formula 2 Bristol engine, with lowered compression ratio and running on 100-

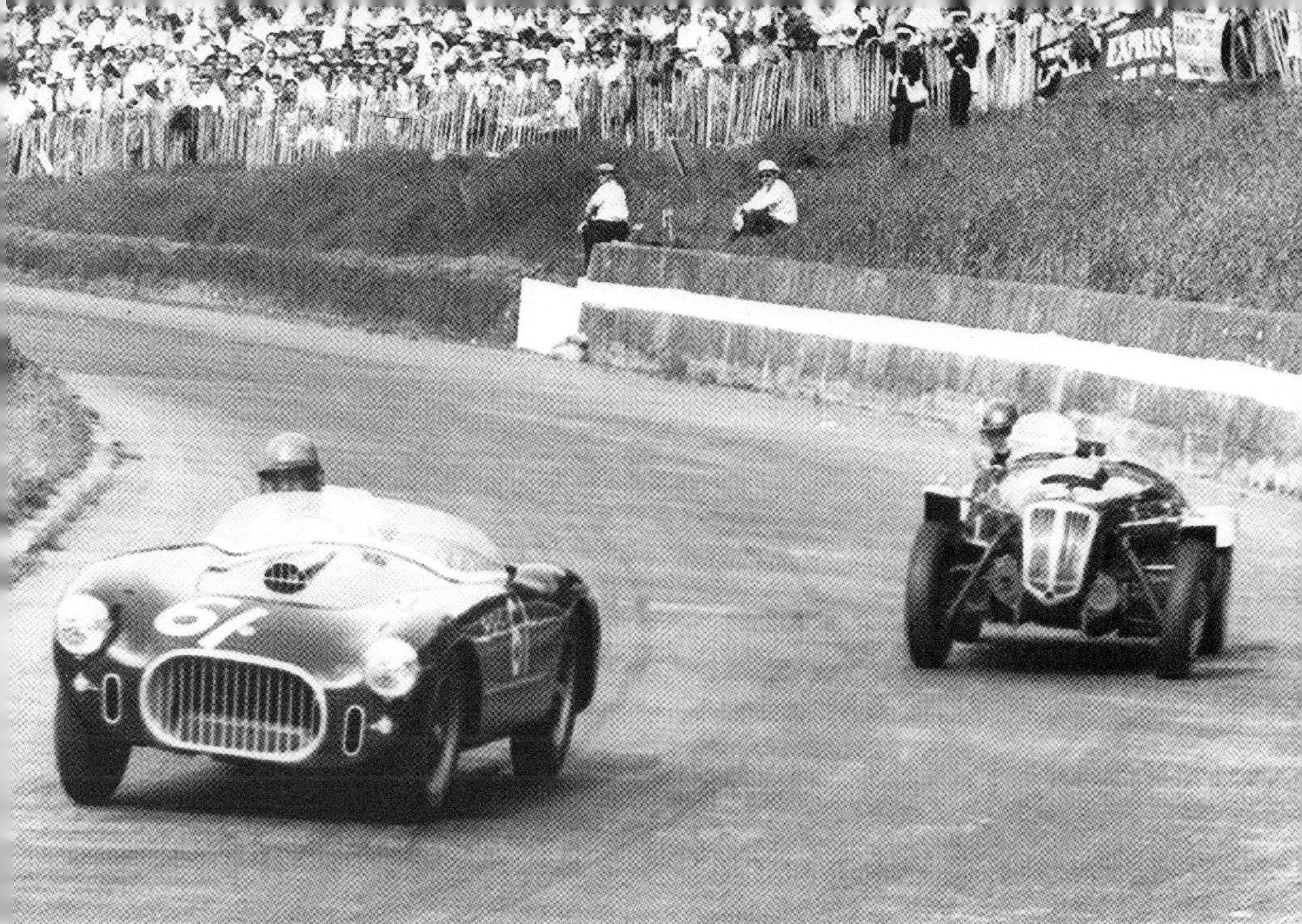

Alan Brown with the Bob Chase Cooper-Bristol leads Mitchell's Frazer Nash Le Mans Replica at the Crystal Palace in May 1953 (Guy Griffiths)

octane fuel, and it remained in this form for a couple of years.

Alan Brown enjoyed a superb run of success with this car, finishing eighth and winning his class in the Production Sports car race at Silverstone in May (at this time the BRDC had some very odd ideas as to what constituted a production car), and with Michael Currie as co-driver took seventh place and a class second in the 1953 Goodwood Nine Hours race. In 1954 Brown won outright the handicap British Empire Trophy at Oulton Park and took a class win at Zandvoort in August. In the early part of 1955 HPN 665 was driven for Chase by Michael Keen, and he finished fourth in the British Empire Trophy. Not long afterwards this Cooper was sold to Tony Everard and, as he had previously raced Aston Martin DB3 and DB3S cars, it was not surprising that he fitted a 2.6-litre Aston Martin engine. The car was maintained for Everard by Rob Walker's garage at Dorking and he raced it for a couple of years before it passed to Austen Nurse, a very keen, veteran driver in the Midlands, who at various times owned several other cars mentioned in this book. Today, the car is once again owned by Alan Brown, but just how much of the original Hawthorn car remains in it is very doubtful.

UPF 440

During 1953 Alan Brown had acquired the Mk II Formula 2 Cooper-Bristol delivered to Bobbie Baird, the enthusiastic Belfast newspaper proprietor who had been killed at the wheel of a 4.1-litre Ferrari in practice at Snetterton at the end of July. So Brown's Mk I also became surplus to requirements, and he and Rodger promptly rebuilt it as another Vignale-styled sports/racing car. In early 1954 this car was bought by David Watts, who used it to break the hill record at Trengwaiton in Devon and sold it very shortly afterwards to Tom Kyffin, who in 1955 raced both this car and the ex-Horace Gould Mk II Formula 2 car under the banner 'Equipe Devone'. Kyffin disposed of his Coopers when he bought Peter Collins' ex-works disc-braked, twin-plug Aston Martin DB3S in 1956.

UPA 261

The success of the original sports Cooper-Bristol built by Brown encouraged the works to have a go, and in August 1953 they announced the prototype of what was intended to be a production batch of 25 cars with a price tag of approximately £2000. In fact all the evidence supports the view that only the prototype car was completed. The Cooper works also used a Mk I Formula 2 box-section chassis with the important difference that the main side-members were undrilled. The suspension was exactly as for the Mk II, as were the 11 in. brakes. The body was again built by Wakefield's to the Vignale design, but there were a number of distinguishing features: the 'portholes' were missing from the wings, there was a very prominent bonnet-top air scoop and, whereas the Chase car had a full-width screen, the works car appeared with a small perspex screen and metal tonneau over the passenger side. It was also painted green with cream wheels, whereas the Chase car had green wheels. According to Cooper's press release, the Bristol engine developed 141 bhp at 5750 rpm (i.e., it was a standard BS4 unit). Having completed the car, the Cooper works, which was always under immense pressure, had no plans for racing it themselves and loaned it to John Coombs to drive in the Goodwood Nine Hours race with Tommy Sopwith as co-driver. The car was far too new to do well; it was plagued by brake trouble in practice, but ran quite well in the race until, less than an hour before the finish, Coombs spun on oil at St Mary's, went off into the ploughed field at the edge of the track and the Cooper cartwheeled. This Cooper returned to the factory in a very battered state, but was rebuilt with a new chassis (a standard Mk I chassis with drilled side-members), registered UPA 261 and sold to the Hon. Edward Greenall, who raced it in Club events in 1955. In 1956 Greenall acquired a Lotus Eleven and sold the Cooper-Bristol—with which he had enjoyed a fair measure of success in minor events—to The Chequered Flag, the well-known dealers in Chiswick High Road who turned over many of the delectable sports/racing cars of the 1950s.

TPD 1

This was the first of two Cooper-Bristol sports/racing cars owned by Tony Crook, then the foremost Bristol distributor and later Chairman of Bristol Cars Ltd. Crook had been racing Frazer Nash Le Mans Replicas since 1950 and he campaigned all the different Bristol production models—the writer remembers being overtaken in Dunstable High Street in May 1954 by Crook with his well-known Bristol 404 MHP 100 on his way to the MCC meeting at Silverstone. I arrived at the circuit rather later, as I was on my push-bike! For 1953 Crook had decided to take his motor racing very seriously and ordered from the Cooper works

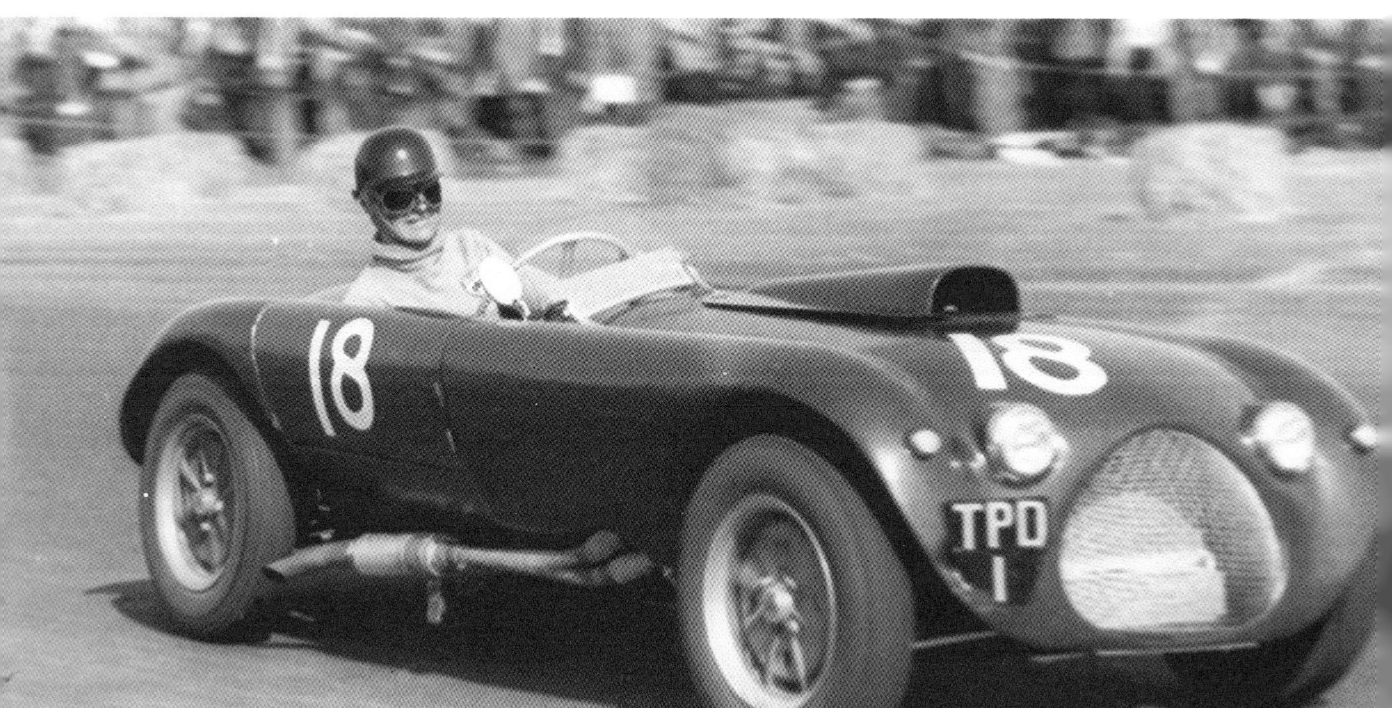

both a Mk II chassis to be powered by an Alta engine and a box-section Mk I chassis for building up into a Bristol-powered sports/racing car. Crook styled the body himself and had it built by a Bristol sub-contractor in Surrey. In its initial form it was very unattractive, with the body sides sloping inwards to leave the exhaust system on the right-hand side completely exposed, a simple mesh-type grille of a style vaguely similar to that of the Mk II Cooper-Bristol, a large and ugly scoop on the flat bonnet and a small, flat aero screen mounted on the scuttle. Like all Crook's cars, it was painted maroon and it was registered TPD 1. It made its debut in the Production Sports car race at Silverstone in May 1953 (where it seemed rather lacking in speed), but as the season progressed so the car was sorted. During the year a complete new, more stylish and sloping bonnet with Bristol-style grille, small bonnet scoop and much larger perspex aero screen was fitted. In the Goodwood Nine Hours race Crook was partnered by Guy Gale, and they finished tenth overall (fifth in the 2-litre class). Crook was never happy with TPD 1, and at certain events in 1953 continued to drive a Frazer Nash (possibly because it was a much more manageable proposition to drive on the road to race meetings).

For 1954 TPD 1 was sold to Bert Rogers, who had raced at Brooklands and had shown himself a dab hand in saloon car racing with a rather shabby Riley 2½-litre saloon. Rogers had immense fun with this Cooper-Bristol, which he nicknamed 'Mucky Pup', and although he raced it for two seasons, he was really out of his depth, the proverbial accident looking for somewhere to happen—and only too often it did. At the Crystal Palace in September 1954 he completely disrupted the field when, in second place, he spun on the first lap of the 2000 cc sports car race. He overturned the Cooper at the British Grand Prix meeting at Aintree in July 1955 and a month later rolled Crabbe's Tojeiro-Bristol in the Goodwood Nine Hours race. For 1956 Rogers switched to a Tojeiro-Bristol which he named the 'Sun-Pat Special' (he headed the Sun-Pat peanut butter business) and was killed when he rolled this ill-handling brute on its debut at the Easter Goodwood meeting.

LEFT *Tony Crook with his first Cooper-Bristol sports car, TPD 1, in its original form at Silverstone in May, 1953 (T. C. March)*

BELOW *Walton's very stark Cooper-Bristol competing at the Notts S.C.C. meeting at Silverstone in August 1954 (LAT)*

RUM 2

This was the first of two Mk II chassis built into sports/racing cars. It was built up by Northern enthusiast Jack Walton, who had the chassis in effect widened by bending the chassis tubes, fitting a longer cross-member and two seats. In this form

it looked just like a Formula 2 Cooper-Bristol with cycle wings and sidelights. As originally constructed it used a BMW as opposed to a Bristol-built engine and was raced from the middle of 1953 onwards by Walton and Peter Bolton. For 1955 RUM 2 was fitted with a full-width body featuring vestigial tail-fins by Williams & Pritchard, the well-known Edmonton bodybuilders, but by this time Jack Walton was seriously ill, and he died of cancer early in 1956.

Tony Crook's 1954 car

Crook's 1953 Cooper-Alta had been a disastrous failure, and for 1954 the chassis of this, too, had widened and fitted with two seats, cycle wings and side-lamps—because of Crook's connections with the Bristol factory he was able to have the work carried out at Filton. Crook's aim was to have a dual-purpose car that he could use in both sports car and single-seater events, and although he did race it in some single-seater events, the majority of its outings were in sports trim. During 1954 this Cooper-Bristol was one of the fastest cars in the 2-litre category in British races and Roy Salvadori, who was racing the very expensive 2-litre Maserati A6GCS 2-litre car, regarded Crook and Scott-Brown (with the Lister-Bristol) as his most serious opponents. During 1954 Brook finished second in his heat in the British Empire Trophy (he retired with engine trouble in the final), won outright victories in a 100-mile race at Silverstone in August and in a race at the Crystal Palace the following month, as well as scoring success in minor events at Snetterton, Brands Hatch and Silverstone. Crook also ran the car in supercharged form (probably the only time that a Bristol engine was supercharged) and at Shelsley Walsh Hill Climb was fastest sports car driver. At the end of 1954 Crook thought that he would retire from racing and sold the car to Dick Gibson. Crook co-drove the car in the 1955 Goodwood Nine Hours race, spun in the dark on oil dropped by another competitor and was rammed by the Porsche 550 of Stirling Moss. Crook subsequently bought the car back and still owns it today. It was never registered.

LBU 349

This was based on the ex-Alan Brown Mk II Cooper-Bristol which Alex McMillan had converted to a sports car, and it originally looked very similar to Walton's car as first raced. Not long after the car was bought it was fitted with a fibreglass aerodynamic body built by Rochdale Motor Panels and looked very smart in white with a broad black stripe. McMillan raced the car with great success in Club events, and when Rochdale Motor Panels advertised it for sale in *Autosport* in September 1955 they claimed that the car had scored 20 first places. The car was bought by Neil Campbell-Blair, who continued its run of successes in Club events until the Lancs and Cheshire CC meeting at Oulton Park in October 1956, when, after winning one race, he crashed badly hitting the bank very hard and being thrown out of the car. Campbell-

ABOVE *Alex McMillan's Cooper-Bristol in its original form in the Sports Car race at Silverstone, July 1954 (T. C. March)*

LEFT *In the rain-swept Sports Car race at Silverstone in May 1954 Tony Crook with his semi-single-seater Cooper-Bristol leads Horace Gould (Kieft-Bristol) (T. C. March)*

BELOW *The Golding-Cooper as rebuilt with right-hand drive bodywork and driven by Sir Clive Edwards at Prescott in May 1955 (T. C. March)*

Blair was largely unscathed, but the 'Bristol Barb', as the car known, was to all intents and purposes a write-off.

NXH 586

It would have been very convenient to close the Cooper-Bristol section of this book quietly forgetting the unsolved mysteries of the Golding-Cooper. This was a Bristol-powered car raced by

John Barber in 1953, probably based on the chassis of his Mk I Formula 2 car that he had crashed at Castle Combe in October 1952 and fitted with a very wide, flat streamlined body which, for some inexplicable reason, had left-hand drive. It seems that the car was built by Ron Golding of Barwell Engineering (hence the name) and it may have had a body that was originally intended for a car to be driven by Ken Wharton in the Mille Miglia, but this does not explain why it had left-hand drive (apart from anything else many continental sports/racing cars, including the works Lancias, still had right-hand drive). One theory is that Barber, who had raced in the Argentine at the beginning of 1953, was planning to compete in South American sports car races during the winter of 1953–54 (as did de Graffenried) and sell the car there afterwards. Barber raced the mysterious Golding-Cooper on its debut at Snetterton in June and then entered the British Empire Trophy in the Isle of Man. In this race he was closely following a Frazer Nash that crashed badly, the driver being thrown in the road and killed, and Barber, who believed initially that he had run the driver over, appeared again at Snetterton and then retired from racing. This car was later fitted with conventional bodywork, right-hand drive and driven by Sir Clive Edwards.

XEV 601

Not strictly one of the Cooper-Bristol line, but with much in common as far as the chassis was concerned, this was the Cooper-Maserati raced by the Gilby Engineering team in 1955. Gilby, headed by Sid Greene, had been running Roy Salvadori in a 2-litre Maserati A6GCS since late 1953 and in a 250F Grand Prix car since 1954. The A6GCS, by dint of very hard work by Roy, had been competitive in the 2-litre class in 1954, but it was a ruggedly built car more suitable for long-distance continental endurance races than British short-circuit events. For 1955 the decision was made to switch the A6GCS engine and gearbox to a lighter chassis and Cooper supplied a simple tubular chassis (having much in common with the design of the Mk II Formula 2 chassis) with the usual transverse leaf suspension and cast alloy wheels. The body was a very simple aluminium structure designed and built by Maurice Gomm. The Cooper-Maserati suffered from the most appalling understeer and Gilby had neither the time nor the facilities to develop the car—they were far too busy racing each weekend. The car's only real success was a win in a sports car race at Snetterton in August and a second place at Brands Hatch. At the end of the year the Maserati engine and gearbox were put back into the A6GCS, which was sold through The Chequered Flag, and the Cooper, less engine and gearbox, was sold abroad.

In the context of sports car racing of the time the Coopers have to be recognized as serious contenders only in British short-circuit races. If they had come up against the latest Ferraris and Maseratis in endurance racing, they would have been hopelessly outclassed, but they filled a niche in racing and filled it well.

BELOW *Roy Salvadori with the unsuccessful Cooper-Maserati at Snetterton in August 1955 (LAT)*

Ivor Bueb with the works 1100 cc Cooper-Climax leads Tony Brooks with the works lightweight Mk II Frazer Nash at Silverstone in May 1955 (T. C. March)

Cooper-Climax

During 1954 Cooper built the first three Cooper-Jaguar cars (and three more of the improved Mk II version followed in 1955) with the characteristic curved-tube chassis frames first seen on the 1954 Mk VIII Formula 3 car. Although cars of considerable interest, the Cooper-Jaguars were something of a 'blind alley' in the Cooper company's development, and in 1955 there appeared the first of a line of rear-engined cars that was to be developed until the Formula 1 version was driven to victory in the 1959 and 1960 World Championships by Jack Brabham.

The new car, subsequently typed the T39, was a rear-engined sports/racing car with the 1098 cc Coventry-Climax FWA single overhead camshaft engine, a chassis based on the design used for the company's latest Formula 3 car, and bodywork inspired by that developed in the Hawker wind-tunnel for the 1953 Cooper Formula 3 record-breaking car. It was to prove dramatically successful, sold in substantial numbers to private entrants at an initial price of £1350 and was to prove the only serious challenger to Lotus in the 1100 cc and 1500 cc sports car classes.

The basis of the new car was a chassis formed by four main tubular members of 1.5 in. 18-gauge steel, curving downwards and inwards at the front and rear with tubular bracing hoops extending to full body width immediately ahead and aft of the cockpit area. The driver's seat was on the centre-line of the car (a layout first used by Kieft on their sports/racing cars), with the passenger seat to the left. The weight of the chassis frame was a mere 65 lb. Front and rear suspension followed familiar Cooper practice—transverse leaf springs with single tubular lower wishbones and Armstrong telescopic dampers. These leaf springs were clamped between rollers at their outboard ends. Cooper rack-and-pinion steering was used and the first cars had the same tiny 8 in. brakes as fitted to the Cooper Formula 3 cars.

The Climax engine, developing 75 bhp at 6200 rpm, was mounted behind the rear bracing hoop on the centre-line of the car and drove through a hydraulically operated Borg & Beck 7¼ in. single dry-plate clutch and a French Citroën front-wheel-drive gearbox. This gearbox was turned about and used the special 4-speed close ratio gears and shafts made by ERSA, a Paris firm, as a conversion for production Citroëns. The gear-lever was mounted on a tube welded to the chassis tubing to the right of the cockpit and operated the gearbox through rods and levers. Drive to the rear wheels was by Hardy-Spicer shafts.

Although inspired by the record-breaking Formula 3 cars, the body was much stubbier, with a cut-off tail having a concave rear panel; the aerodynamic advantages of the cut-off tail had been advocated before the Second World War by Professor Kamm, and although this style of tail was usually known as the 'Kamm tail', the Coopers were more familiarly referred to as 'Manx-tail' or 'Bob-tail'. The rear of the Cooper body featured a combined headrest and sleek hump to clear the engine with a bulge for the carburettor intake on the left side of the hump. The whole of the rear of the body opened rearwards and the whole of the front, including the decking of the right-hand side of the cockpit, hinged forwards. To the left of the cockpit was a two-piece drop-down door, there was a wrap-round windscreen and a full-length undertray attached by Dzus fasteners. The radiator was in the nose of the car and hinged with it, but the header tank was bolted to the headrest above the engine. Standard fuel capacity was 8 gallons in an aluminium tank mounted just behind the right front wheel, but a 14-gallon tank could be substituted for longer races.

Race debut for the new Cooper came at the Easter Goodwood meeting, where Bueb finished third behind a brace of 1500 cc Connaughts in the 1500 cc race and at the *Daily Express* Trophy meeting at Silverstone in May, Bueb finished ninth overall in the Sports Car race, winning the 1500 cc class *and* defeating all the 2-litre cars. A second car had been completed for works driver Jim Russell and the first customer car was sold to Tommy Sopwith (who also raced a Cooper-Jaguar). Sopwith also ordered a second car, which was fitted with the 1484 cc Connaught engine.

For Le Mans a Cooper-Climax was entered by Edgar Wadsworth and John Brown and despite covering eight laps until the next permitted top-up with no water after a hose burst, the Cooper survived to finish 21st and last overall (third in its class behind a brace of Porsche 550s) at an average of 72.05 mph. Cooper successes continued in many National British events and another successful privateer was Peter Gammon, who raced the original works car registered XPG 2 with unpainted, polished bodywork. In the Goodwood Nine Hours race in August the works Cooper of Bueb/Russell finished second in the 1500 cc class to the Connaught of Scott-Brown/Leston. At the Tourist Trophy on the Dundrod circuit in September three Coopers were entered—works cars for Bueb/MacDowel and Russell/Dennis Taylor and a private car for Jim Mayers/Jack Brabham. The race was marred by an horrific multi-car crash that brought the use of the Dundrod circuit to an end. Mayers, struggling hard to pass the slow Mercedes-Benz 300SL of the Comte du Barry, lost control, hit a gate-post and the Cooper disintegrated in flames. Mayers died in the inferno and several cars plunged into the wreckage; Bill Smith was killed at the wheel of the works Connaught and Russell crashed with one of the works Coopers, but escaped unhurt. Bueb and MacDowel finished tenth overall and won the 1100 cc class.

There were three other rather different Cooper rear-engined sports cars raced in 1955; Jack Brabham had arrived in England, originally racing his ex-Whitehead Formula 2 Cooper-Alta, but he soon abandoned this in favour of a new rear-engined Cooper, which he built up himself in the Cooper works. This was a standard rear-engined sports car, but with the wheelbase increased by two inches to accommodate the long Bristol engine, with first gear removed from the Bristol gearbox (the power-to-weight ratio was such that first gear was superfluous) and without all the road-going sports equipment such as lighting.

Brabham entered his car in the British Grand

Prix at Aintree, but although it was supposed to have an enlarged 2.2-litre engine as fitted to Bob Gerard's front-engined Cooper-Bristol single-seater, it ran in 2-litre form (although appearing in the programme as a 2.2-litre). On the morning of the race the clutch failed and Brabham raced it clutchless until it expired through overheating. At Snetterton in August Brabham drove a fine race with the Cooper-Bristol in the Formula 1 event, battling with Stirling Moss's Maserati 250F for third place until he spun off, restarting to finish fourth. After running the car in other British events, Brabham took it to Australia, winning the Australian Grand Prix and finishing second in the South Pacific Road Race Championship. Brabham sold this car in Australia, and it still survives.

A second Bristol-powered Cooper in sports trim was built up by Bob Chase's firm, RJC Motors; this made its debut unpainted in the hands of Mike Keen at the August Bank Holiday Brands Hatch meeting, but Keen bashed the nose in a collision when leaving the paddock and was out of the results in the race. Three weeks later Keen and Mike Anthony drove this Cooper in the Goodwood Nine Hours race, but Keen was killed when the Cooper went off at Fordwater, rolled end over end and caught fire.

The third variant on the Cooper sports car theme was rather different. Pete Lovely, later better known for his Lotus connections, fitted a Porsche engine into the 1951 Cooper Mk V streamlined record breaking 500 cc car and scored considerable success in American sports car racing.

For 1956 Cooper developed a Mk II version of the sports car with 10 in. drum brakes (but some cars were fitted with Girling disc brakes), separate eight-spoke four-stud cast magnesium wheels, enlarged cockpit and duralumin body panels. There were three other very important developments. One was the appearance of the 1460 cc (76.2 × 80 mm) FWB Coventry-Climax engine, developing 100 bhp at 6000 rpm. The second was that Roy Salvadori, who had driven Sopwith's Cooper with great élan at a couple of races in 1955, joined the works Cooper team. Thirdly in 1956 Lotus introduced the very sophisticated Eleven model and this was eventually to prove superior to the Cooper in most respects.

Coopers were driven by a large number of drivers of different ability, including Ivor Bueb (who ran private Lotus and Cooper 1500 cc cars

A view of the engine installation, gearbox and rear suspension of the Cooper-Climax (T. C. March)

under the banner of Ecurie Demi-Litre), Stirling Moss (whose car was registered BPB 777), Les Leston (entered by the Willment Speed Shop) and Keith Greene (son of the Gilby Engineering entrant, running 1100 cc 30 FVX). Production of the rear-engined Cooper-Climax continued into 1957 and the total number built, including cars supplied in component form, was probably around 40.

In the Sebring 12 Hours race on 25 March, two 1100 cc cars ran in the name of the works, both in reality private entries; Cracraft/Byron finished well down the field in 21st place, but won the 1100 cc class, while Hugus/Bentley retired because of dynamo failure. The first outing for the works cars proper was at the Easter Goodwood meeting, where Roy Salvadori drove two different 1460 cc cars, one with drum brakes with which he won the Lavant Cup for cars up to 2000 cc from Bob Gerard's single-seater Cooper-Bristol and one with disc brakes with which he won the 1500 cc sports car race from Russell's works Cooper and Leston's private car. It was at this meeting that Stirling Moss tried Salvadori's car at the suggestion of John Cooper and as a result decided to order his own.

For the British Empire Trophy race at Oulton Park two weeks later Moss was entered by the works with RDG 474 (the 1100 cc car usually raced by MacDowel fitted with a 1460 cc engine) and Salvadori and Russell drove works cars. This race, run in three class heats and a final in which the 1500 cc cars were given a 40 sec advantage over the unlimited class, proved a magnificent Cooper versus Lotus dogfight. In the 1500 cc heat Chapman with his Lotus Eleven won from Salvadori, Mike Hawthorn (with Bueb's Lotus Eleven) and Moss, but it was a very different story in the final. Moss led until he was passed by Chapman, Chapman spun off and Stirling went on to win the race from Chapman, who had restarted, Salvadori and Hawthorn.

By the Aintree meeting on 21 April, Moss was racing his own Cooper, which was fitted with Weber carburettors (twin SUs were the usual equipment) and was found to handle atrociously. Hawthorn, with Bueb's Lotus won the 2000 cc sports car race from Salvadori's Cooper, with Moss way back in fifth place. A victory for Salvadori followed in the 1500 cc sports car race at the *Daily Express* meeting at Silverstone in May; second place went to Chapman's Lotus, but only after a stiff fight with Jack Brabham (deputizing for Russell), who was eliminated by gearbox trouble. Over the Whitsun weekend Brabham was beaten by the Lotus Elevens at both Brands Hatch and Goodwood, but at the Crystal Palace, Les Leston and Moss each won a 1500 cc sports car race with their private Coopers.

The handling problems of the Équipe Moss Cooper were eventually traced by his mechanic Alf Francis to a construction fault—the chassis had been misaligned in the jig and the front spring was bottoming against the damper backets. Francis faced a frantic rush to get the car ready to be driven by Stirling and Phil Hill in the 1500 cc Reims 12 Hours race at the end of June (Moss had been offered very attractive starting money), but the car was soon out of the race because of overheating, with the small consolation of a new class lap record of 112.16 mph. The following weekend it was rolled by Peter Jopp at Rouen. Alf Francis left Moss to look after Rob Walker's cars, while BPB 777 was repaired and sold.

Throughout 1956 the Cooper team very bravely tackled a number of continental races in which they faced strong opposition from both Porsche and Osca 1500 cc cars. Salvadori won the 148-mile City Cup at Porto in June from private Porsche 550 entries, but in subsequent races the opposition was rather tougher. In practice for the 1500 cc race at the German Grand Prix meeting at the beginning of August Salvadori badly bent his Cooper in a

RIGHT *In the 1956 British Empire Trophy at Oulton Park Jack Russell (Cooper-Climax) leads Mike Hawthorn (Lotus Eleven) through Deer's Leap (T. C. March)*

BELOW *The class-winning 1100 cc Cooper-Climax of Cracraft/Byron is passed by a D-type Jaguar at Sebring in 1956*

practice crash, but thanks to very hard work by John Cooper it was beaten back into shape for the race and he finished third behind Herrmann (Porsche) and Moss (works Maserati 150S). In the Berlin Grand Prix, on the incredibly bumpy banked Avus circuit, the Coopers were badly pounded and shaken, the suspension was deranged, the front wheels were fouling the bodywork and Brabham (now an accepted member of the works team) and Salvadori did well to finish fifth and sixth. In the Shell Grand Prix at Imola, where Salvadori battled with and bumped the leading Oscas of Musso and Castellotti until eliminated by distributor trouble, Brabham came through to split the Oscas and finish second. Cooper's final continental outing of the year was in the sports car Rome Grand Prix at Castelfusano; Salvadori led until eliminated by electrical trouble and the race was won by Musso's Osca.

In 1956 the Le Mans race was posponed until the end of July (from its usual mid-June date) for circuit improvements following the 1955 disaster, and Cooper entered a specially prepared 1100 cc car for American enthusiasts Ed Hugus and John Bentley. Because of a change in the race regulations proper two-seater bodywork was necessary and Cooper built a car with a stiffened cockpit centre-line, seats either side and full-width screen and painted American white and blue colours. Although beaten into second place in the 1100 cc class by a Lotus Eleven, Hugus and Bentley finished eighth overall, covering 2102 miles at an average of 87.61 mph.

A new 1500 cc Formula 2 single-seater category was due to come into force in 1957, but the first race of the new Formula was held at the British Grand Prix meeting in July, and with a field composed of sports cars, apart from the Cooper, Roy Salvadori scored a fine victory with the new single-seater Cooper that had been only too clearly inspired by the team's sports car design. Cooper were to become more and more preoccupied with single-seaters, entering Grand Prix with considerable success in 1957–58 and going on to race full 2.5-litre Climax-powered Grand Prix cars, with which Jack Brabham won the Drivers' World Championship in 1959 and 1960.

The result was that Cooper, while continuing to compete in sports car racing during the remainder of the 1956 season, had really lost interest in the category by the start of 1957 and ran works cars in only a couple of races before concentrating entirely on single-seaters.

In August 1956 Stirling Moss won *The Sporting Life* Trophy at Oulton Park with the Willment Cooper (deputizing for Les Leston), and Roy Salvadori with a works car pulled out of the race after one of the most frightening experiences in his long racing career. Roy was in second place when he was passed by Hawthorn with Bueb's Lotus at Knickerbrook. Hawthorn was driving much too fast, the back end broke away, the car mounted the bank and somersaulted, with parts of the

RIGHT *At Le Mans in 1956 this modified Cooper-Climax was driven into eighth place overall and second in the 1100 cc class by Hugus/Bentley*

BELOW *The works 1500 cc Cooper-Climax which Salvadori drove into third place at the Nürburgring in 1956. The body had been badly battered in a practice crash (LAT)*

disintegrating Lotus striking Salvadori and the Cooper. In the 1100 cc sports car race at Goodwood in September, MacDowel was beaten into second place by Keith Hall (Lotus).

At the end of the year Jack Brabham took both a single-seater and a sports car back home with him. With the sports car he finished second in the sports car race on the day of the New Zealand Grand Prix and won a sports car race at Christchurch before the car was sold to the McLaren family for young Bruce to race.

In 1957 Salvadori drove a sports Cooper in the 1500 cc Chichester Cup race at the Easter Goodwood meeting, but the engine went on to three cylinders and he finished at the tail of the field with the consolation of fastest lap of 89.07 mph. When Salvadori finished second to Chapman's Lotus in the 2000 cc race at the Whit Monday Crystal Palace meeting, it was to all intents and purposes the end of Cooper works participation in sports car racing. Jack Brabham and Ian Raby borrowed a sports Cooper from the recently formed Cooper Racing Drivers School to run at Le Mans, where they finished 15th overall and third in the 1100 cc class. Many private entrants continued to race the sports Coopers with great success; among other Cooper entrants Peter Gammon was still winning races with XPG 2, now painted British Racing Green, Sopwith's Équipe Endeavour were running a 1500 cc car with success and Chris Bristow with a Cooper 1100 was forging a career that was to take him into Formula 1.

Cooper Monaco

1959 Mk I Cars

Although Cooper had ceased production of the Manx-tailed sports/racing cars in 1957, by the end of 1958 the company had ready a new sports/racing car to meet the demand in this category of racing already supplied by Lister and Lotus. The new car was named the Monaco in celebration of Maurice Trintignant's victory in the 1958 Monaco Grand Prix at the wheel of Rob Walker's 2-litre Cooper-Climax, and its chassis design closely followed that of the single-seaters.

The chassis was based on four main $1\frac{1}{2}$ in. diameter tubular members sweeping outwards to form the two-seater cockpit area and with substantial cross-bracing. At the front, suspension was by coil springs and double wishbones, as on the 1958 single-seaters, and at the rear there was the familiar transverse leaf spring and single lower wishbones. Girling disc brakes were fitted front and rear and the wheels were Cooper cast magnesium eight-spoke with four-stud fixing. The car was designed to take the Coventry-Climax FPF twin-cam engine, available in 1.5 and 2-litre forms, and this was tilted 18 degrees to the right. Although the basic design of the ERSA gearbox remained, the casing was modified to Cooper requirements and the gears and shafts were specially made by Jack Knight. The right-hand gear-change was mounted on the lower chassis member. There was a 12-gallon welded aluminium fuel tank mounted on the left side of the chassis just ahead of the scuttle. The radiators for water and oil were mounted in the nose. The aluminium bodywork was not so very dissimilar from the earlier rear-engined Sports Coopers, but the lines were more rounded, with very small, curved, vestigial tail fins.

Cooper revealed the Monaco to the press in November 1958, and it seems that a total of eleven Mk I cars were built, including two built up by the Coombs organization to be driven by Roy Salvadori and Jack Brabham. Salvadori's car was particularly interesting, as it was powered by a 2.5-litre 4-cylinder Maserati engine. Coombs had realized that it would be virtually impossible to obtain a 2.5-litre Climax engine, as in their first year these would be reserved for the major Formula 1 teams, and the Maserati seemed a good substitute. Later in the year, however, Stirling Moss raced a Monaco with 2.5-litre Climax engine entered by Keele Engineering.

Salvadori enjoyed a fine run of successes with

RIGHT *Roy Salvadori with the Coombs' Cooper Monaco-Maserati in the wet at Oulton Park in April 1959. With this car Salvadori enjoyed a phenomenally successful season (T. C. March)*

BELOW RIGHT *The other Coombs' car in 1959 was this 2-litre Climax-powered Cooper Monaco seen here with Jack Brabham at the wheel on his way to third place at Aintree in July (T. C. March)*

Coombs' Cooper-Maserati, scoring wins at Aintree, the May Silverstone meeting (where he defeated Moss's Aston Martin DBR1, despite broken rear suspension) and the Crystal Palace. This car was sold at the end of the year to Brian Naylor, who replaced the engine with a 3-litre 4-cylinder Ferrari unit and continued to enjoy success in minor events.

Most of the remainder of the Monaco runners were out of luck. Right at the beginning of the season Percy Crabbe wrote off The Chequered Flag's Monaco in practice for the March Snetterton meeting, and Jim Russell scored a fine win with his car at Oulton Park, beating Salvadori into second place, but it seems that much of the credit for this success lay with Russell's choice of Continental tyres, which behaved better on a wet track than Salvadori's Dunlops. Russell ran this car at Le Mans with Bruce McLaren as co-driver, but although the Monaco showed an excellent turn of speed, it did not last long in the race. Russell hit oil at White House, collided with Whitehead's Aston Martin and was struck by a Stanguellini; the Cooper was destroyed in the ensuing fire and Russell was very badly burned. In August, Colin Davis with the Cooper Monaco-Maserati 2-litre owned by the Scuderia Centro-Sud, won the 186-mile Messina Sports car race, but only after the Ferrari Dino 196 of Giulio Cabianca had spun off and lost time.

1960 Mk II Cars

For the following year Cooper instructed the slightly improved Mk II version of the Monaco, but the changes were minor indeed and amounted to little more than improved front-end styling. Just how many Mk II cars were built is not known, but it seems to have only been about six. One of these was supplied to the Coombs' team, who fitted a 2495 cc FPF Climax engine, and Salvadori enjoyed another thoroughly successful season. He scored wins at the Easter Goodwood meeting, Aintree, Oulton Park, Silverstone in May and at

27

In 1961 Salvadori drove a Climax-powered Mk III Cooper Monaco for John Coombs. Here, with the car as yet unpainted, Salvadori is seen on his way to second place at the Silverstone Sports Car race in May 1961 (T. C. March)

Brands Hatch on August Bank Holiday Monday. It must be admitted, however, that there was not a great deal of opposition in the class. At the end of the year Salvadori drove the Ecurie Ecosse Cooper Monaco in two races in the United States. This car was normally driven by Tommy Dickson and before Salvadori could even get in it, 'Wilkie' Wilkinson had cut away part of the sheet metal round the cockpit. Salvadori finished third in the Watkins Glen Formule Libre Grand Prix, but could only manage sixth in the sports car Grand Prix at Riverside after he was nudged off at a corner, had difficulty in restarting and then had to fight his way back through the field.

Other Mk II Monacos were entered by Harry Zweifel (a Swiss driver who finished fourth in the European Mountain Championship), Jimmy Blumer (2-litre, but fitted with a 1.5-litre engine when he crashed fairly heavily at Spa in June) and Tony Marsh (2.5-litre).

1961 Mk III Cars

This was a much improved design, with the chassis based on the 1960 so-called 'Lowline' Formula 1 cars. The most obvious—and important—changes were that the chassis was constructed from straight tubes and there was double wishbone and coil spring rear suspension. The new Monaco had been designed to appeal to the American market and so two rather prominent tail fins were mandatory. Again, it is not clear how many Mk IIIs were built, but it is doubtful whether there were more than four or five. Coombs acquired one for Salvadori to drive and others were bought by Hap Sharp and Roger Penske in the United States and British private entrant Peter Berry.

At this time interest in sports car racing had faded in favour of GT cars, and in the rather thin sports car fields the Monacos faced stiff opposition from the Lotus 19s, three of which were run by the UDT-Laystall team. Salvadori first appeared with Coombs' as yet unpainted Mk III at the May Silverstone meeting and was beaten into second place by Moss with a Lotus 19. Salvadori then won at the Crystal Palace, with Blumer's Monaco second, but only after the 19s ran into problems with their new knock-off hubs. Ecurie Ecosse ran their older Monaco at Le Mans, but this was written off when Bruce Halford, unsighted in the

By 1963 Roy Salvadori was driving for Tommy Atkins and one of the team's cars was this Cooper Monaco-Climax T61M. Roy is seen at the Gold Cup meeting at Oulton Park where he convincingly won the Sports Car race (T. C. March)

wet, lost it at the Dunlop Bridge and crashed heavily.

In the autumn, McLaren drove the Peter Berry, Castrol-financed Mk III with 2.7-litre Climax engine at Riverside Raceway in the United States and finished second to Jack Brabham at the wheel of Sharp's Mk III, also powered by a 2.7-litre engine. Shortly afterwards he retired with piston failure at Laguna Seca. Berry's car, less engine, was sold to Briggs Cunningham. Cunningham sent this Monaco to Reventlow Automobiles, where it was fitted with a Buick V-8 engine; it did not prove successful.

1962 Mk IV Cars

The Mk IV was the next year's production model, incorporating only detail changes, and it seems that four of these cars were built for sale in the United States. The most interesting was the car supplied to Briggs Cunningham, as this was fitted with a Maserati 2.8-litre engine. Roger Penske and Bruce McLaren drove the Monaco-Maserati in the Sebring 12 Hours race and finished fifth, despite long delays caused by brake and electrical problems.

1963 Monaco T61M

This much improved version of the Monaco, given a new designation, first appeared in late 1962, and initially cars were built for Bruce McLaren and for export to the United States for Jack Hinkle. The chassis was a slightly modified version of that used for previous Monacos, but the suspension was the same as that on Cooper's 1962 Formula 1 cars; at the front by narrow-based double wishbones with partially inboard coil spring/damper units and at the rear by magnesium uprights, double wishbones and outboard coil spring/damper units mounted ahead of the axle line. The power unit was the 2.7-litre Climax mounted 30 degrees to the right and driving through a $7\frac{1}{4}$ in. twin-plate clutch to a Cooper-Knight C5S 5-speed gearbox and combined final drive unit as used on the 1960 Formula 1 Coopers. There were pannier fuel tanks with a total capacity of 28 gallons and the body was much smoother and more stylish, all-aluminium, and with the panels attached by Dzus fasteners. To comply with the Appendix C regulations there was a roomy 2-seater cockpit with full wrapround screen. On McLaren's car only the front wings were notched at the rear to permit a clean airflow past either side of the cockpit to the large intakes at the front of the rear wings. It was a feature that did not impress everybody and was dropped from subsequent cars. The T61M was the last works version of the Monaco and remained available until the end of 1964.

At Riverside Raceway McLaren was beaten into fourth place by Penske with the Zerex-Climax discussed later, Hall (Chaparral) and Gregory (Lotus 19). The following weekend at Laguna Seca he finished third overall. The T61M was simply too heavy and bulky to do well. Nevertheless C. T. 'Tommy' Atkins ordered a T61M, which was built up by Harry Pearce for Roy Salvadori in 1963 and painted in Atkins's usual metallic green and white colours. Partly because it was such a well-prepared car and partly because of Salvadori's superb driving, this T61M enjoyed a good run of success with a second at Snetterton in March followed by wins at Goodwood, Aintree, the May Silverstone meeting, the July Silverstone meeting, a second to Penske's Zerex at Brands Hatch on August Bank Holiday Monday and a win at Oulton Park in September.

Cooper-Zerex

American driver Roger Penske's racing reputation received its first real boost when he conceived and raced this fascinating 'Special'. The Zerex (named after a product of DuPont Chemicals, who were his sponsors) was based on the straightened chassis of the T53 Formula 1 car that Walt Hansgen had crashed in the 1961 United States Grand Prix; it retained its central-seat driving position and was fitted with outriggers to take minimal full-width sports body-work. The engine was the 2.7-litre Climax FPF used in Jack Brabham's 1961 Indianapolis car. It is said to have weighed complete a mere 1100 lb, and its performance was phenomenal.

After winning at Riverside in 1962, Penske was again the winner on the aggregate of two heats at Laguna Seca. He followed this up with another victory in Puerto Rico in November. At this stage the authorities stepped in and the Zerex was banned in December 1962 because it lacked two seats of equal size either side of the longitudinal axis of the car. Penske switched to the ex-McLaren T61M, which he had bought, but then sold both cars to John Mecom on the basis that he continued to drive them. The Zerex, now painted blue and white, reappeared in rebuilt form with curved main chassis members and full side-by-side seating. After finishing fourth at Mosport and retiring at Elkhart Lake, the Zerex was brought to England, and Penske drove it to a fine win in the Guards International Trophy at Brands Hatch on August Bank Holiday Monday.

RIGHT *Roger Penske with his Cooper Formula 1-based Zerex-Climax in 1963 (David Phipps)*

BELOW RIGHT *For 1964 the Zerex-Climax was sold to Bruce McLaren. Here McLaren is seen at the May Silverstone meeting where he won the Sports Car race by a substantial margin (T. C. March)*

For 1964, the Zerex was sold to Bruce McLaren complete with an Oldsmobile V-8 engine, which had been acquired by Mecom but not installed. McLaren ran the car with Climax engine and the mandatory and hastily installed boot and spare wheel at Oulton Park, but retired because of overheating. Wins followed at Aintree and Silverstone. McLaren then rebuilt the car with a much more rigid frame centre-section (Penske had simply cut away part of the frame and replaced it with curved tubing) and the Oldsmobile engine was installed together with a Colotti 5-speed gearbox. In this form the Zerex (now known as the Cooper-Oldsmobile in the interests of keeping the peace at Surbiton) won the Player '200' race at Mosport Park and the Guards Trophy at Brands Hatch. By this stage construction of the first McLaren-Oldsmobile was well under way and the Zerex had provided a sound learning curve for the small McLaren team.

King Cobra

By mid-1963 Carroll Shelby had production of the AC Ace-based Cobra well under way and his small team decided that the time had come to try their hand at sports car racing. There was not a great deal of choice for the basis of what was to be the team's 'Super-Snake'—it had to be either Lotus or Cooper. Shelby's team took the view that the Lotus 19 was already over-stressed with the Coventry-Climax 2.7-litre engine, and so Shelby made arrangements for Cooper to supply strengthened T61M chassis complete with bodies and running gear. Shelby installed Ford 289 (4.7-litre) engines with stack exhausts and Colotti 4-speed gear-box/final drive units. Revised 'Indianapolis'-style

DUNLOP
DUNLOP
41

exhausts emerging from the tail were soon substituted.

Two King Cobras made their debut at the Kent, Washington race in September 1963 in the hands of Dane MacDonald and Bob Holbert, but both cars succumbed to overheating. They were then entered in the *Los Angeles Times* Grand Prix at Riverside, and although Holbert again retired because of overheating, MacDonald scored a fine win from Penske's Zerex. Another victory for MacDonald followed at Laguna Seca and Holbert again retired because of overheating. The following month both cars retired with suspension problems in the Nassau Trophy race in the Bahamas.

For most of 1964 Shelby was too preoccupied in competing for the World GT Championship with the team's Cobra Daytona coupés to seriously develop or race the Cooper-based sports/racing cars. The cars were, however, fielded in a few races early in the year. Holbert crashed badly in practice at Kent with a King Cobra sold to a private entrant and suffered severe burns; MacDonald took over Holbert's car to win the race, but was killed at Indianapolis a matter of days afterwards.

The car previously raced by Holbert was driven by Ed Leslie in a few events, but it was not until the autumn that the Shelby team made a serious return to sports car racing with three works cars and a fourth car with sleeker bodywork designed by Pete Brock that had been sold to brewery heir Craig Lang for Ed Leslie to drive. Initially the works team consisted of R. Parnelli Jones, Bob Bondurant, Ronnie Bucknum and Richie Ginther, but Ginther left the team after a dispute at Laguna Seca. The results overall were very worthwhile, with a win by Parnelli Jones at Riverside and third place by Bondurant at Laguna Seca, but the Shelby works cars did not run again and were sold off in 1965. The Lang-entered car was run at a number of races in 1965.

There was one King Cobra built up in England. Despite his retirement from racing, Roy Salvadori had agreed to drive a King Cobra for John Wyer's Ford Advanced Vehicles. It was built up by the team's chief mechanic, Ermanno Cuoghi, and powered by a Shelby-prepared engine. Both chassis and engine were delivered late, there were a lot of changes to be made to the chassis to comply with European regulations and Wyer's commitments to Ford were such that there was really not time to spend on what could have been a very promising project. The car made its debut at the Senior Service '200' race at Silverstone at the end of March 1965, but there had not been time to fit an undershield, and in pouring rain Salvadori became so water-soaked that he had little alternative but to retire. This King Cobra used a ZF gearbox in place of the Colottis fitted to the Shelby cars, and at the Easter Goodwood meeting Salvadori pulled out of the sports car race on the grid because of difficulty in engaging the gears.

At this point Ford Advanced Vehicles abandoned the King Cobra project. This was rather a pity because sports car racing was regaining popularity with the emergence of the McLarens and the Lola T70s. If the King Cobra had achieved success, it could well have encouraged the Cooper company to continue building sports/racing cars. Instead they dropped this area of activity altogether and as a result lost the chance of exploiting lucrative dollar sales to the United States.

Atkins Cooper-Maserati

In the United States a number of Monaco chassis were re-engined with American V-8 'stock-block' power units, but the most powerful version built in the United Kingdom was C. T. Atkins's mighty Maserati-powered car raced by Salvadori in 1964. On this car, built up by Harry Pearce, the tubular frame was strengthened by a 20-gauge steel sheet undertray that was welded and riveted, and the front suspension was similar to that of the current Cooper Formula 1 car, save that the coil spring/damper units were mounted inboard. The Maserati V-8 4941 cc (94 × 89 mm) was said to develop 430 bhp at 7000 rpm and was used with a Colotti Type 37 gearbox. The flat Cooper nose was modified so that there was a large vented bulge that housed the spare wheel, and, although first raced unpainted, this Cooper was soon sprayed Atkins' usual metallic green and white colours.

Atkins and Salvadori were well aware that the Cooper-Maserati was unlikely to be the best-handling sports car on the circuits, but reckoned that the speed on the straights would compensate for handling deficiencies. When the engine was tested on the Coventry-Climax dynamometer, it was found that the power output was far less than Maserati had claimed and that valve bounce was setting in at 6000 rpm. With a very narrow power band between 4000 and 6000 rpm and with the power coming in very suddenly, the Cooper-Maserati was almost unmanageable in the wet, and in these conditions Salvadori used to switch off one of the two magnetos so as to slash the power.

Admittedly a brave failure, this car did achieve some measure of success, with second place to McLaren's Zerex at the May Silverstone meeting, a win at Goodwood at Whitsun and a third place in

An interesting, but largely unsuccessful effort was the Cooper Monaco with 4.9-litre Maserati engine that Salvadori drove for Tommy Atkins in 1964. Salvadori and the Cooper are seen in the paddock at the May Silverstone meeting when the car was still unpainted. The large bulge on the bonnet concealed the regulation spare wheel (T. C. March)

the Sports Car race at the British Grand Prix at Brands Hatch. Salvadori retired in the Guards trophy at Brands Hatch while holding second place, and in the *Autosport* Three Hours race at Snetterton. This Cooper still survives in a German car collection.

Elva

The Elva, designed and developed by Frank Nichols, was one of a whole series of British sports/racing cars of the 1950s and 1960s that enjoyed success on a substantial scale in Club and National events, but made no real impression Internationally and, eventually, quietly faded into obscurity.

Predecessor to the Elva was the CSM raced by Nichols in 1954. The CSM was a multi-tubular chassis frame built by Michael Chapman of Western Light Engineering of Hastings. CSM stood for Chapman Sports Motor. Nichols, who ran the London Road Garage in Bexhill, built up the car with independent front suspension by the familiar method of splitting a Ford axle to produce swing axles and suspending them on coil springs; at the rear a Ford rigid axle was suspended on coil springs and located by a Panhard rod. The engine was a Ford 1172 side-valve linered down to 1100 cc, extensively modified and used with a 3-speed Ford gearbox with Buckler constant mesh-gears. The body was a neat but stark two-seater with cycle front wings and the rear wings integral with the bodywork. The CSM was good for a little over 100 mph and during 1954 achieved a modest degree of success.

Originally Nichols was thinking of offering the CSM to home constructors as a kit of components. Instead he offered the CSM for sale for £550 in October 1954 and started work on a new sports/racing car that he called the Elva (supposedly derived from the French, 'elle va', and unlikely to have any other sensible derivation). The

Peter Gammon at Prescott in May 1955 with the prototype Ford-powered Elva (T. C. March)

new Elva featured a multi-tubular chassis that was simple, light and rigid; front suspenion was by wishbones and coil springs (Standard 8 components were used) and at the rear there was a Ford Anglia rigid rear axle suspended on coil springs. The engine was again the 1172 cc Ford side-valve linered down to 1098 cc (61.25 × 92.5 mm) and fitted with the LRG overhead inlet valve conversion devised by Nichols and also marketed separately; four Amal carburettors were used and there was a Lucas coil and distributor. A proprietary 4-speed gearbox was fitted. During 1955 Nichols built two of these cars, JPN 875, with a very simple aluminium body, and 300 EMX, with rather more shapely lines.

For a car of such modest specification, the Elva had an excellent performance with a top speed of around 110 mph and acceleration from 0–60 mph in around 9.5 secs. During 1955 the Elva was raced by a number of well-known drivers, including Peter Gammon, Robin Mackenzie Low, Les Leston and Stuart Lewis-Evans. It performed well and it performed reliably, with the result that Nichols found quite a demand for the basic component kit of chassis, less engine, gearbox and body for £350. At this stage there was no provision for the supply of bodies, so that the cars that were raced appeared in a number of different forms.

In 1956 the Elva was available with the Coventry-Climax FWA 1098 cc single-cam engine and the usual body fitted was a fibreglass two-seater by Ashley Laminates. Cars were exported to Canada and the United States and one was driven in British events by Alex McMillan. After Brian Lister had withdrawn the new Formula 2 Lister from the Gold Cup race at Oulton Park in September, Archie Scott-Brown drove the works Elva, KDY 68; apart from the fact that this simple 1100 cc sports car was outclassed in an event dominated by the 1500 cc single-seater Coopers, Scott-Brown had to make two pit stops and he finished at the tail of the field. Shortly afterwards he drove this Elva in a 10-lap handicap for fibreglass-bodied cars at Brands Hatch and won the race from Lewis-Evans's 500 cc Cooper on scratch.

During the year the company, now known as Elva Engineering, had developed an improved car

An Elva with fibreglass body by Ashley Laminates at Mallory Park in 1957 (T. C. March)

with a simpler, lighter chassis frame with a fabricated cross-member at the front (instead of the Standard 8 pressed steel cross-member usually used), Cooper rack-and-pinion steering, de Dion axle located by radius arms and a channel and sliding block and inboard rear brakes. This formed the basis of the 1957 Mk II model, and as a result of his drives for Elva in 1956, it was agreed that Archie Scott-Brown should handle the car entered by the Butterworth Engineering Co.

Archie Butterworth had been working on designs for horizontally opposed air-cooled 4-cylinder engines since 1950, and two cars with these engines in 2-litre form had been raced in Formula 2 events in 1952 as the Aston-Butterworth (one was later rebuilt as a sports/racing car with Climax FWA engine and known as the Aston-Climax). There had been many problems with these engines, but Butterworth had persevered. The 1496 cc (76 × 82.5 mm) Butterworth engine featured a very stiff aluminium alloy crankcase, cast-iron cylinder barrels and light alloy cylinder heads; there was a single camshaft per bank of cylinders, with Butterworth patent swinging inlet valves and conventional exhaust valves. Four Amal carburettors were fitted and the power output was reckoned to be 125 bhp at 6200 rpm. This Elva had a very streamlined body, with enclosed front and rear wheels, full metal tonneau and prominent headrest, but above all distinguished by two bulges in the bonnet housing the ram pipes for the carburettors—which led to the nickname 'Sabrina' (after the very curvacious young lady seen on television at the time).

The Elva-Butterworth was not ready to race until the August Bank Holiday meeting at Brands Hatch and in the 1500 cc sports car race Scott-Brown built up a tremendous lead before retiring with valve trouble. It was the same story for the rest of the year—the car was fast in practice, led away at the start of the race and was eliminated by trouble, not with the swinging inlet valves, but the conventional exhaust valves. The Elva-Butterworth was a magnificent sight on full song and it did win at least one race; at Brands Hatch in October the writer saw Scott-Brown pull out a 40-sec lead in a 10-lap race and set fastest lap (a class

record) at 73.9 mph. After 1957 the Elva-Butterworth was abandoned.

During 1957, both Scott-Brown and Mackenzie-Low drove works Elvas with Climax engines, and private owners included Dennis Taylor and Ian Raby. Neil Campbell-Blair raced the car driven by McMillan in 1956, MBU 309, with Rochdale body and colour finish similar to the 'Bristol Barb' Cooper-Bristol, LBU 349, raced by both Macmillan and Campbell-Blair.

In 1958 Elva produced the much improved Mk III car directly developed from the car raced by Scott-Brown in 1957. The multi-tubular frame was lighter, with fabricated tubular wishbones and coil spring/damper units at the front, and rear suspension once more by a de Dion axle located by twin trailing arms and coil spring/damper units. The brakes were usually Lockheed two leading shoe, with Al-fin drums, 10 in. at the front and 9 in. mounted inboard at the rear. Disc brakes could be fitted if required. The engine was the Coventry-Climax FWA, used with an MG gearbox fitted with special close ratios. The body, panelled in light alloy, was a refined version of that fitted to the Butterworth-powered car in 1957, with proper provision for headlamps, spotlamps (for endurance racing) and full-width screen and hood to comply with international regulations. The wheelbase was 7 ft $1\frac{1}{2}$ in., track 4 ft 0 in. and weight around 8 cwt.

The first of the new cars were shipped out to compete in the Sebring 12 Hours race, but were out of luck. Elva were planning to run at Le Mans, but this never happened. In British events Mk III cars were raced by Ian Raby, Chris Bristow and Mackenzie-Low, but although a few places were gained in the 1100 cc class, the Elvas were no real

match for the Lotus opposition. During the same year Elva went into production with the Courier sports car, for road use, with ladder chassis and MGA engine and gearbox.

For 1959 Elva developed the Mk IV, broadly similar to the 1958 Mk III, with multi-tubular frame, wishbone front suspension and Climax FWA engine, but there was now independent rear suspension by lower wishbones, links and coil spring/damper units with the drive-shaft acting as the top wishbone. The body was a neat, low two-seater with rather more angular lines than its predecessors. The first cars were again shipped to the United States for private owners to race in the Sebring 12 Hours event and, although far down the field, Baptista/Tweedale/Wallace and Jordan/Dietrich/Martin took the first two places in the 1100 cc class. The sports/racing Elvas rarely figured in the results in 1959, despite Mike McKee's efforts with a new and very low Mk V car, partly because the 1100 cc class was now dominated by the Lolas

LEFT *Archie Scott-Brown with the Elva-Butterworth leads away at the start of the 1500 cc Sports Car race at Silverstone in September 1957. The Elva-Butterworth retired after only one lap. To Scott-Brown's right is the Elva of Ian Raby. Although he was slow away from the Le Mans start No. 39, Ron Flockhart, was the eventual winner with Coombs' twin-cam Climax-powered Lotus Eleven (T. C. March)*

BELOW *In the Silverstone race Ian Raby was involved in a collision at Copse with Tomaso's Osca and McMillan's Lotus. He is seen here rejoining the race, but was later black-flagged (T. C. March)*

ABOVE *The new Elva Mk 6 that first appeared driven by Chris Ashmore at the Boxing Day Brands Hatch meeting in 1961*

LEFT *At Silverstone in May 1959 Tommy Dickson drove this Elva Mk IV into third place in the 1100 cc Sports Car race (T. C. March)*

BELOW LEFT *Chuck Daigh at Silverstone in July 1960 with the Mk V Elva-Climax (T. C. March)*

and partly because Elva were increasingly preoccupied with the Formula Junior single-seater category for which they had built, initially, very successful front-engined cars, powered by DKW and BMC engines. For 1961 Elva followed the trend set by the Lotus 18 and built rear-engined Formula Junior cars.

In 1961 Elva went into liquidation. The company had been shipping considerable numbers of Couriers and Formula Junior cars to the United States, but they had not received payment and the final blow came when the importer was arrested. The company was re-formed as Elva Cars (1961) Ltd and continued to operate on a smaller scale in part of the old works. In December 1961 Elva announced a completely new sports/racing car, the Mk 6, of exceptionally low construction and with rear-mounted engine. The chassis was a fully triangulated multi-tubular space-frame constructed of 1 in. 18-gauge and 20-gauge .75 in. steel tube, with duralumin floor incorporated as a stressed member and complete with brackets and fittings weighing only 73 lb. At the front, suspension was by double wishbones, coil spring/damper units and anti-roll bar, while at the rear there were lower wishbones, fixed-length drive-shafts which formed the upper links, twin parallel trailing arms and coil spring/damper units. Rack-and-pinion steering was fitted, there were Elva 15 in. cast magnesium wheels and Lockheed brakes with 9 in. drums mounted outboard at the front and inboard at the rear. The spare wheel was mounted horizontally at the front of the car, with to each side of it the divided cross-flow radiators linked by pipe. The engine was the familiar FWA Climax in Stage 3 tune used with a modified Volkswagen 4-speed gearbox. The body, in fibreglass, was strikingly sleek and low and measured only 2 ft 2 in. to the top of the windscreen.

The new Elva made its debut at the Boxing Day Brands Hatch meeting in the hands of Chris Ashmore. In the race for unlimited capacity sports/racing cars the Elva went magnificently, and Ashmore finished second to Graham Hill's Ferrari 'Testa Rossa' entered by Scuderia Serenissima. During 1962 a works car was driven in a few events by Paddy Gaston, while Chris Ashmore, Bill Moss and Tony Lanfranchi drove their private cars. One of the best performances of the year was a win by Ashmore/Robin Carnegie in the 2000 cc class of the Nürburgring 1000 Km race, but they were well down the field overall. In addition Addicott won the 1300 cc class and finished sixth overall in the Guards Trophy at Brands Hatch on August Bank Holiday Monday.

During 1962 Elva moved to new premises at Rye, manufacture of Formula Junior cars was stopped (a new and promising model had appeared in December 1961) and the production of the Courier was resumed by the Trojan Group at Purley in

Considerable success was achieved by the Elva-BMW. Keith St. John is seen at the wheel of his Radio London-sponsored car at Silverstone in May 1965 (T. C. March)

Surrey. One of the strengths of Elva had always been that far more cars were exported than had ever been sold in Britain, and export demand—and overseas racing successes—was considerable.

In 1963 Nichols opened up negotiations with BMW for the supply of 2-litre engines (as later used by Chevron) and a number of Elvas were supplied to the United States with Porsche engines. One of these cars was driven by Mike Beckwith at Brands Hatch on Boxing Day 1963, but finished a poor fifth. The most successful car in British events in 1963 was that entered by Team Crostune and driven by Tony Lanfranchi, and this scored a considerable number of wins and places in mainly minor races.

The 1964 Elva sports/racing car, known as the Mk 7, was powered by either the BMW 2-litre engine or a Porsche engine. A works BMW-powered car was fielded during the year for Tony Lanfranchi and he scored four wins, three second places and two thirds, as well as winning the *Autosport* Championship. Another success during the year was second place in the European Hill Climb Championship by Herbert Müller with an Elva powered by a Porsche 2-litre flat-8 engine.

There were a large number of changes at Elva in 1964. Early in the year it was announced that the company had been taken over by the Lambretta-Trojan Group, the GT160 coupé powered by a 2-litre BMW engine was announced, but production abandoned, and Elva commenced manufacture of the production McLaren Group 7 sports/racing cars. The beautiful GT160 styled by Fiore and built by Fissore was burdened with an excessively heavy body and, it was realized, would simply be uneconomic to produce. The arrangement to build McLaren Group 7 cars lasted until 1971 when McLaren withdrew from this class of racing. Frank Nichols, who had held the post of technical director, resigned and the final sports/racing Elvas were the BMW-powered Mk 8 of 1965 and Mk 8S of 1966.

Emeryson-Climax

Paul Emery was a well-established figure on the motor racing scene, building and racing his own design of front-engined fwd 500 cc cars from 1950 onwards, and in 1953 constructing his own 2-litre Formula 2 car with an Alta engine, which was subsequently enlarged to 2500 cc for the Grand Prix Formula of 1954 onwards. All Emery's early projects were self-financed and run on the proverbial 'shoestring' finance.

It seemed that all this would change in 1960, when Emeryson Cars Ltd. was formed with finance from Alan Brown, and Emery moved from his

Doreen Fielding at the wheel of husband Ray's Emeryson at Bo'ness in 1961

small workshop at Twickenham to Connaught Cars (1959) Ltd on the Portsmouth Road at Send near Ripley in Surrey. Connaught was no longer of course a racing car constructor (the team had retired from racing in May 1957), but a garage business run by Brown.

Here Emery built a 1500 cc Formula 2 single-seater that was very typical of design practice of the time. It featured a multi-tubular space-frame with the lower members constructed from 16-gauge $1\frac{1}{4}$ in. tubing and the upper members from 1 in. tubing. At the front there was double wishbone and coil spring suspension and the rear suspension was the equally conventional layout of single lower wishbones, unsplined drive-shafts, parallel trailing radius arms and coil spring/damper units. Transmission was by a 5-speed Colotti gearbox with a hinged flap to prevent accidental engagement of first and reverse gears. The Emeryson was fitted with handsome six-spoke cast magnesium-alloy wheels and there were 11 in. disc brakes mounted outboard front and rear. A number of parts for the Emeryson were manufactured by Lister, and former Vanwall team manager David Yorke became responsible for the entries of the works team.

This first car made a couple of appearances in 1960, driven by Ron Flockhart at Brands Hatch and John Turner at Montlhéry, and the team entered into a deal with the Équipe Nationale Belge to supply them with three 1500 cc chassis for Formula 1 (the 1500 cc Grand Prix Formula started in 1961), to be powered by Maserati engines, and a Formula Junior car to the same basic design. ENB's racing efforts proved disastrous, but the works managed rather better. Mike Spence drove a Formula Junior car to victory in the Commander Yorke Trophy at Silverstone and then graduated to the works Mk 2 Formula 1 car with shallower, wider frame and smoother body lines. At the end of 1961 Emeryson was taken over by American Hugh Powell and two cars were driven in 1962 by John Campbell-Jones and Tony Settember. By 1963 the team was known as Scirocco-Powell (Racing Cars) and was running a pair of BRM V-8-powered cars of basic Emery design and usually driven by Settember and Ian Burgess. The Scirocco team withdrew from racing at the end of 1963.

From this rather confused background there emerged in 1961 a very interesting and very special sports/racing car to the order of successful hill-climb campaigner Roy Fielding and registered HSD 77. Fielding's car featured very handsome 2-seater aluminium-alloy bodywork with distinctive sloping nose, full wrapround perspex windscreen blending into the neat tail and with rear wings forming vestigial tail fins—not unlike the Cooper Monaco. The power unit was the 1460 cc

Coventry-Climax FWB single-cam engine. Mechanically the specification was similar to that of the single-seaters. Fielding enjoyed an immensely successful year, consistently winning 1500 cc Sports class at hillclimbs, winning the RAC Championship climbs at Craigantlet and finishing sixth in the Championship overall.

This Emeryson continued a successful hill-climbing career in the hands of Gerry Tyack and, later, in 1966–67, the delightful Georgina Baillie-Hill. When I was competing in hillclimbs—in a rather slower class—we greatly admired Georgina and not merely for her considerable driving ability! In 1971 the Emeryson was acquired by Richard Falconer and it remains in his ownership.

Felday-BRM

Peter Westbury, who ran Felday Enginnering from a garage at Forest Green, to the south of Dorking in Surrey, was a keen hillclimbing enthusiast. Westbury, still a student at Engineering college, had started his hillclimbing career in 1959 with a Special which he called the MGW, based on Buckler chassis, MGA engine and Falcon fibreglass body. From this he progressed to an elderly Formula 2 Cooper-Climax, with which he competed in 1960, and he used this car the following year with a supercharged Daimler V-8 2.5-litre engine. The car was progressively modified and developed over the next two years; a space-frame chassis was built, a Lotus gearbox and final drive unit were fitted and in due course this car, which Westbury drove to victory in the 1963 RAC Hill Climb Championship, became known as the Felday-Daimler or F.1.

For 1964 Westbury started work on a 2-seater Felday F.2, which was intended for use in the European Hill Climb Championship. At the end of 1963 Ferguson Research suggested that he use the Ferguson P99 four-wheel-drive ex-Formula 1 car to make some demonstration runs at Wiscombe Park hillclimb. It was subsequently agreed that Westbury could use the P99 in hillclimbs in 1964 until the F.2 was ready. In fact Westbury soon abandoned the F.2 and started work on the F.3, which was another space-frame two-seater, but powered by a BRM V-8 1880 cc engine. By this time he was doing so well with the P99 that it seemed he was set for another victory in the RAC Hill Climb Championship, so he continued to drive this car and duly won. Westbury was still anxious to run in the European Championship, which was restricted to two-seaters, so he bought a Lotus 23B in which the BRM engine was installed. His outings in Europe with this car were dismally unsuccessful.

The next step in Felday development was the design and construction of the F.4, a new sports/racing car with Ferguson four-wheel-drive and using the BRM engine that had been fitted to the Lotus. Although this car was exhibited in chassis form at the Racing Car Show at Olympia in January 1965, Westbury was very occupied running his business, and also working with Ferguson and BRM on the experimental four-wheel drive Formula 1 car that had appeared in 1964. As a result, the new Felday was not ready until the end of the year and made its debut at the Boxing Day Brands Hatch meeting.

For the Felday 4, Westbury switched to monocoque construction because, with space-frame construction, it was impossible to combine a sufficiently wide footwell area to comply with prototype regulations with a track of the width that Westbury had chosen; this was caused by the space required for the front transmission. The monocoque was constructed of a mixture of steel and aluminium sheets and sections, with the main backbone of the monocoque and the bulkhead constructed of steel and most of the outer panels in aluminium. At the front Westbury used a suspension layout that differed from normal practice; there were double wishbones, but the springs ran transversely and operated horizontally against the tops of the Austin 1800 suspension uprights, while the dampers linked the chassis and the bottom of the suspension uprights. At the rear the suspension was more conventional: lower wishbones, twin radius arms, single upper links and coil spring/damper units together with Brabham uprights.

The engine was the 1880 cc BRM V-8 (subsequently increased in capacity to 1930 cc) mounted back to front in the chassis. A short prop-shaft took the drive to the front-mounted 6-speed BRM gearbox, ahead of which was the control unit (through which the distribution of torque to front and rear wheels was adjusted) and the front differential. The drive from the gearbox back to the rear differential ran alongside the input shaft. The Felday ran on 13 in. Brabham wheels with 8 in. rims front and rear—the rims were the same width because of the four-wheel-drive. Front and rear there were 10½ in. disc brakes. The body was a neat, low aluminium structure with four head-lamps and with a transparent centre-section between the wheelarches and running back to the scuttle, which doubled as the windscreen and gave

Mac Daghorn with the four-wheel-drive Felday-BRM in the 1966 Tourist Trophy at Oulton Park (T. C. March)

both excellent forward vision and protection from wind turbulence.

At Brands Hatch on Boxing Day the Felday performed magnificently. It won the Formule Libre race in the hands of Mac Daghorn, who worked for Westbury, and Westbury himself drove the car into second place in the Unlimited Sports Car race behind Coundley's McLaren.

In the April 1966 issue of *Motor Racing*, John Blunsden reported on a short drive at Brands Hatch in the Felday and commented:

'. . . it was not until the second session that I really began to identify the difference in feel between the Felday and a two-wheel-drive sports car. It all boils down to the fact that until you start to tramp on, there is just no noticeable difference, at least none that you can pinpoint as being specifically a function of the transmission, and not merely the sort of minor difference you get as a matter of course between one car and another.

'The first thing I noticed concerned the braking. You get more help from the engine overrun, and consequently you find yourself braking too early for a corner . . . .

'But it is travelling through and away from corners where the advantages of four-wheel-drive show up most of all. The Felday 4 has quite considerable understeer, to the point where you have to make a definite effort to hold the car in on a tight line through Clearways. Just tightening up the lock has little or no effect and to kill it you have to back off. The point is, you can back off and induce a rear-end "twitch" at moments when to do so in a two-wheel-drive car is to invite trouble.

'As might be expected from a car displaying considerable understeer, the switch to oversteer when the power comes off is quite marked and virtually instantaneous. But the slide is killed with almost uncanny certainty immediately the power is reapplied, so that far from being an embarrassment the power-off oversteer is in fact an asset to help you round the corner. The magnitude of the slide, of course, is governed to a considerable extent by the amount of excess lock being applied to counter understeer at the moment the right foot is lifted—the more lock the more the reverse slide. Therefore, unless you *really* want to hang the back out, to get you round a hairpin, it is better (or so I thought), not to have too much positive lock on when you take your foot off.'

The experimental 7-litre Ford-powered Felday 5, Mac Daghorn at the wheel, in the Guards Trophy at Brands Hatch, 1966 (LAT)

Westbury's plans had now advanced to a much more powerful car, and the Felday 4 was offered for sale, eventually being acquired by John McCartney, who competed with it in 1968. The new Felday 5 was a development of the existing design, but with a number of significant changes. For chassis construction Westbury had reverted to a multi-tubular space-frame of square and round tubes. The power unit was the 7-litre Ford Galaxie modified by Holman and Moody and converted by Felday to dry sump lubrication. The latest Ferguson transmission was fitted with four or five forward gears and the gearbox was mounted behind the engine in the same housing as the final drive with the control unit and transfer gears immediately to the rear of the gearbox. The Ford engine could now be installed in the normal fore and aft position. The prop-shaft running to the front passed along the right-hand side of the engine, with a universal joint at the centre of the car, passing through the cockpit between the seats. The bodywork was similar to that of the Felday 4, but the front and rear body sections were in fibreglass.

At Brands Hatch on August Bank Holiday Monday the Felday 5 was driven by Mac Daghorn, while the Felday 4, at this stage still owned by the company, was driven by Jim Clark. Clark was driving the car because of Colin Chapman's interest in the possibility of building a four-wheel-drive car. Neither car featured prominently in the race. The Felday 5 was later used by Felday Engineering and Ferguson Research as a test vehicle. It was not until after Lotus, McLaren and Matra had all raced Formula 1 cars with four-wheel-drive in 1969 that it was decided that the deficiencies of the system outweighed its advantages in racing. There was one other Felday that should be mentioned, the F.6, a single-seater with drive to the rear wheels only and 4.7-litre Ford engine, built in 1966 for Tony Griffiths to use in hillclimbs.

Ford P68 and P69

This view of the Ford P68, Bruce McLaren at the wheel, on the grid for the start of the 1968 BOAC 500 race, displays the 3-litre Prototype's gull-wing doors and very clean lines (Guy Griffiths)

After the American Ford company withdrew from Prototype racing at the end of 1967, a further project was sanctioned by Ford in England, an exciting and promising design that complied with the new three-litre capacity limit for prototypes in International racing. The new car, designated the P68 F3L, was designed by Len Bailey, who had worked on the GT40 project and developed the Mirage coupés raced in 1967 by the JW Automotive team. The new cars were constructed in Alan Mann's workshops at Byfleet, and Mann, who had previously run a team of Ford GT40s, was to be responsible for race preparation.

Bailey designed a very elaborate monocoque structure made up of riveted and bonded light alloy panels; apart from the nose and the tail, the outside skin of the car was made from malleable aircraft alloy of a thickness of only one-thirtieth of an inch. The P68 was a low, sleek coupé with a long tail that was vortex-creating—it had the same aerodynamic effect as a much longer car. The suspension followed Formula 1 practice with double wishbones and coil spring/damper units at the front and, at the rear, lower reversed wishbones, upper straight tubular links, twin radius arms and coil spring/damper units. The power unit was the Ford-Cosworth DFV V-8 2993 cc (85.7 × 64.8 mm) with twin overhead camshafts per bank of cylinders and developed 420 bhp at 9000 rpm. The engine was in exactly the same tune as used in Lotus, McLaren and Matra Formula 1 cars. It seemed unlikely that it could last a 24-hour race and it was only later that Cosworth developed 'endurance' versions of the DFV. Transmission was by a ZF 5-speed or Hewland DG300 5-speed gearbox and combined final drive unit.

The wheelbase of the P68 was only 7 ft 3 in.—shorter than that of any of the Formula 1 cars using the Cosworth engine, and one result of this was a

ABOVE *The Ford P68 entered for Dickie Attwood/David Hobbs in the 1968 Nürburgring 1000 Km race (LAT)*

LEFT *The Ford P68 with enormous rear aerofoil driven by Gardner/Hulme in the 1969 BOAC 500 race at Brands Hatch. The car had not been running long when the aerofoil had worked loose and the oil pressure had plummeted (Guy Griffiths)*

very cramped and claustrophobic cockpit. When the second car was built, the wheelbase was increased slightly to give more cockpit room. The cars were finished in Alan Mann's very distinctive red with a central gold stripe.

It seems that when the P68 was first raced, there had been little time for testing, and the 1968 season would be regarded as a year of testing and development with a view to fielding a full team in 1969. In fact the early performances were so disappointing that the cars were rapidly withdrawn from the racing scene. The P68s made their racing debut at Brands Hatch in the BOAC '500' race on 7 April, 1968, and since they had first been shown to the press, the uncluttered lines of the P68 had been marred by the addition of a rear spoiler. The writer was present at this race, and the P68s looked and sounded very impressive, but what is most memorable about that race is that it took place on the day that Jim Clark was killed at Hockenheim, and that overshadows all other memories. Originally Clark and Graham Hill were to have driven the longer-wheelbase car with a Hewland gearbox, but at a late stage their places were taken by Bruce McLaren and Denis Hulme. The new car broke its engine in practice and so the only starter was the original P68 with ZF gearbox driven by Bruce McLaren/Mike Spence. In practice they were second fastest to the Porsche 907 of Siffert/Herrmann. After falling back at the start of the race because of loss of fuel pressure, McLaren came through to battle with the leading 907s and was in third place when he handed over to Spence at the first refuelling stop after an hour-and-a-half's racing. Very soon afterwards Spence came to a halt opposite the pits; the inner drive shaft coupling on the left-hand side had broken and had wrecked the exhaust system and damaged the rear chassis bulkhead.

This was a very promising but delusive start to the P68's racing career. Alan Mann Racing missed the Monza race and the Targa Florio and next ran two cars in the Nürburgring 1000 Km race. A newly

The P69 with enormous front and rear aerofoils that ran in practice only at the 1969 BOAC race at Brands Hatch (LAT)

built car was driven by Pedro Rodriguez/Chris Irwin, and the Brands Hatch runner was entered for Frank Gardner/Richard Attwood. Practice was marred by bad weather and on the Friday Irwin, trying really hard on a damp track, lost control over the bump at the Flugplatz, the car rolled over and over and came to rest in the ditch with the engine still running. Irwin suffered dreadful head injuries and received emergency brain surgery at Bonn hospital. He eventually made a good recovery, but never raced again. In the race, with Attwood at the wheel, the surviving P68 shed the complete right-hand brake caliper on the first lap, on its second lap the driver's door blew open and was distorted by air pressure *and* a rear tyre punctured. The car was eventually got back into the race, but it was not long before the P68 was out with engine failure.

At the Spa 1000 Km race, one P68 was entered for Frank Gardner/Hubert Hahne, and Gardner was fastest in practice with an impressive lap in 3 min. 46.3 sec (144.04 mph). The race started in heavy rain (typical Ardennes weather!) and the P68 pulled into the pits at the end of the first lap in tenth place with completely waterlogged electrics. The mechanics tried without success to dry out the engine, but the car was retired.

By this stage Ford's patience was exhausted and the team withdrew from racing until 1969. By then Len Bailey had produced the P69, an open car to take advantage of the relaxed racing regulations relating to minimum windscreen height, cockpit width and weight. The open body was fifteen inches shorter than the coupé, the complete car, apart from a small cockpit area, was encased in light alloy panels and there was a very sophisticated system of spoilers, inspired by the American Chaparral team, with interconnected spoilers mounted in the nose and across the tail; these were actuated mechanically and hydraulically with the pitch angle adjusted by wind pressure. When the P69 was tested it proved unstable both on the straight and when cornering. As a result it appeared at the BOAC '500' race at Brands Hatch with enormous front and rear suspension-mounted aerofoils. The P68, now with larger brakes and rear suspension-mounted aerofoil, was also entered at Brands Hatch. The P69 broke its engine in practice and non-started, while the P68 was driven by Gardner/Hulme. After less than half an hour's racing the P68, its aerofoil loose and flapping, was withdrawn because of low oil pressure.

With the exception of one appearance by the P68 at the Martini Trophy at Silverstone, the cars were not raced again. Their withdrawal was blamed on the ban on aerodynamic aids imposed by the CSI at Monaco in 1969. Certainly the P69 could not have been raced again without a major redesign, but the same arguments could not be applied to the P68, which had been evolved as a clean smooth coupé and raced in 1969 with an aerofoil only as an afterthought. Inevitably the decision not to race the cars must have been a desire not to waste further money on a project that could not be seen as leading to success.

Frazer Nash

Distinctive in name and distinguished by its chain-drive transmission, the Frazer Nash marque was acquired by H. J. Aldington when he bought the shares of AFN Limited from Archie Frazer-Nash in 1929. Production of the chain-drive cars continued on a small scale at the premises occupied by AFN Limited in London Road, Isleworth. In 1934 AFN became British BMW agents.

In 1936 BMW development took a significant step forward with the introduction of the 328 sports car powered by a 6-cylinder 1971 cc (66 × 96 mm) engine featuring a new aluminium cylinder head with inclined valves in hemispherical combustion chambers. BMW cleverly avoided the cost and complexity of twin overhead camshafts by the use of a set of transverse pushrods to operate the exhaust valves. The 328 was a full-blooded sports car, possessing a high performance and considerable character, and it scored many competition successes, including class wins in the 1938 Mille Miglia and 1939 Le Mans races.

After the war the Bristol Aeroplane Company decided to market an improved version of the BMW in collaboration with the Aldingtons to be known as the Frazer Nash-Bristol. In addition the Aldingtons would use Bristol components to build Frazer Nash sports cars at Isleworth. By the time Bristol were ready to exhibit their production 400 saloon at the 1947 Geneva Motor Show, they had decided to scrap the agreement with Frazer Nash and market the cars under their own name.

Bristol were still willing to supply engines and gearboxes to Frazer Nash, but while the Aldingtons were anxious to exhibit under the Frazer Nash name, they had nothing readily available. The answer was a 1940 streamlined 328, one of the Brescia Grand Prix team cars, that the Aldingtons had imported for development purposes soon after the war ended. This was resprayed, fitted with a new grille and Frazer Nash badges and shown to the press in November 1947 as the Frazer Nash Grand Prix. Later this car was registered LTC 9 and sold to Gillie Tyrer, who raced it with great success in British sports car races.

New Frazer Nash models proper followed in 1948. At Geneva the Company exhibited the Fast Touring model with Superleggera Touring two-seater roadster body, and immediately after the show this car was shipped to the Shah of Persia. Much more significant was the High Speed model that appeared at the London Show. Both cars featured a simple 8 ft wheel-base, large-diameter tubular chassis with BMW-type front suspension by wishbones and a transverse leaf spring and rear suspension by a rigid axle sprung on longitudinal torsion bars and located by an A-bracket with the apex pivoted on top of the differential housing and the base pivoted on the side members of the chassis. Hydraulic brakes were fitted, with two-leading shoes at the front, and the wheels were of the centre-lock disc-type used by BMW.

The High Speed was a traditional competition sports car with narrow 2-seater body, cycle wings, a canvas tonneau over the rear-mounted spare wheel (a metal tonneau was substituted in 1950) and the headlamps mounted low down in nacelles on either side of the nose. Early in 1949, tubular shock absorbers were added at the front and the headlamps raised to positions on either side of the top of the nose. As initially used by Frazer Nash, the Bristol-built 1971 cc engine developed 120 bhp at 5500 rpm. The High Speed cost £2250, which the double purchase tax imposed at the time increased to a swingeing £3501 10s. od.

In the spring of 1949, AFN loaned a High Speed to Count Johnny Lurani's Scuderia Ambrosiana for Dorino Serafini to drive in the Tour of Sicily. The Frazer Nash led for more than half-distance, but was eliminated when Serafini hit a kerb and damaged the steering. Not long afterwards two cars ran in the Mille Miglia, but no success was achieved.

The 1949 Le Mans race brought the post-war Frazer Nash to motor racing prominence. At the wheel of his private High Speed, Norman Culpan, partnered by H. J. Aldington, took third place overall (but not a class win as a 2-litre Ferrari finished first) and covered 1884.87 miles at an average of 78.54 mph. For this race the High Speed was fitted with supplementary fuel tanks, a lower 3.75:1 axle ratio (the usual ratio was 3.55:1) and engine speed was restricted to 5000 rpm, which gave 110 mph in top gear. As a result of this success the High Speed was renamed the Le Mans Replica at the 1949 London Show. Another success followed in August, when Culpan drove his car into third place behind two Jaguar XK120s in the Production Car race at the International Silverstone meeting.

Despite its high price the Le Mans Replica soon became a popular choice for keen private owners and their chances of success were increased by the fact that AFN did not run a works team. The Aldingtons much preferred to encourage the bill-paying customers and lent the company's name to entries at Le Mans and elsewhere. With an exceptional performance and, by the standards of the time, superlative roadholding, the Le Mans Replica was beatable in the 2-litre class of long-distance International racing only by the Tipo 166 V-12 Ferrari. The Le Mans Replica also dominated its class in British short-circuit events until the lightweight breed of Bristol-powered Coopers, Tojeiros and Listers appeared in 1953–54.

Two new touring cars appeared in 1949 (neither advanced beyond the prototype stage), and in addition Frazer Nash introduced a new competition sports car at the London Show, the Mille Miglia, mechanically similar to the Le Mans Replica, but with aerodynamic full-width bodywork. An unusual feature was the mounting of the spare wheel behind a panel in the left front wing (a similar arrangement was later adopted by Bristol). Frazer Nash cars were now available with power output ranging from 80 bhp at 5500 rpm, and close ratio gears could be obtained for competition work. Increased production of the Le Mans Replica had led to a reduction in the basic price to £1750, while the Mille Miglia cost a basic £2250.

The results of the 1950 racing season reflected the growing power of the Frazer Nash as a competition car. Initially there was disappointment, when Serafini, holding second place in the Tour of Sicily with a new Le Mans Replica owned by the Scuderia Ambrosiana, was forced to retire with a split fuel tank. This was more than compensated for when Franco Cortese drove the same car to sixth place overall and second in class in the gruelling Mille Miglia road race held shortly afterwards. At Le Mans the Mille Miglia of T. A. S. O. Mathieson and Dickie Stoop took ninth place and a class win despite brake trouble, and covered 1972.68 miles at 82.20 mph.

On the British racing scene the Le Mans Replica was well to the fore; in June, Culpan drove his much-raced car into third place in the Manx Cup and in the One Hour Production Car race at Silverstone in August, Jack Newton, Tony Crook and Culpan were classified third, fourth and fifth on handicap behind the works Tipo 166 Ferraris of Ascari and Serafini. In September, Bob Gerard drove his Le Mans Replica, HBC 1, into third place on handicap in the rain-soaked Tourist Trophy on the Dundrod circuit.

Even greater success was achieved by Frazer Nash in 1951. Franco Cortese with an Ambrosiana-entered car made a brilliant start to the year by finishing fourth overall and winning the 2-litre class in the Tour of Sicily. Subsequently he scored an outright win in the Circuit of Enna and took eighth

RIGHT *John Newton with the prototype Frazer Nash Le Mans Replica at Silverstone in 1950. This car was distinguished by the ribbing running horizontally along the lower part of the bodywork (Guy Griffiths)*

BELOW *Tony Crook and his famous maroon Le Mans Replica at Goodwood in April 1951 (Guy Griffiths)*

ABOVE *This green Le Mans Replica was raced by Bob Gerard for many years. He is seen in the 1952 Goodwood Nine Hours in which, with David Clarke as co-driver, he finished fourth overall (Louis Klementaski)*

RIGHT *The Le Mans fhc Frazer Nash driven by Ken Wharton in the Production Sports Car race at Silverstone in May 1953 (LAT)*

place and a class second in the Mille Miglia. Le Mans Replicas dominated the 2-litre Production Car race at Silverstone in May; Tony Crook with PPG 1 crossed the line in first place at 83.63 mph, ahead of four other examples of the model and with Tyrer's BMW sixth.

In May 1951, John Bolster tested a Le Mans Replica for *Autosport*. The car was fitted with a 3.9:1 axle ratio (giving a theoretical maximum speed of 109.12 mph at 5500 rpm) and an engine said to develop 117 bhp at 5200 rpm. Bolster achieved 0–60 mph in 8.8 seconds, covered a standing quarter-mile in 17 seconds and attained 85 mph in third gear. Maximum speed was estimated at '110 plus mph', but Bolster mentioned that short bursts approaching 115 mph were possible on this axle ratio. Fuel consumption was 20 mpg.

This car, registered WMC 181, was destined to gain fame a bare month later when, entered by Sid Greene of Gilby Engineering and driven by Stirling Moss, it scored a fine victory in the British Empire Trophy in the Isle of Man from Bob Gerard with HBC 1. Oddly enough, WMC 181 also featured in *The Autocar*'s 'Used Cars on the Road' series in the issue of 26 March, 1954. It was on offer at Performance Cars (who are still in business on London's Great West Road) with an odometer reading of 19,773 miles and a price tag of £1395. By this time WMC 181 had been fitted with 'an engine for which a claim of 141 bhp was made by its manufacturers' (presumably Bristol's Type BS1 Mk 3 unit). The testers had nothing but praise for this fine but ageing warrior. 'On several quite brief but open stretches 5500 rpm was seen on top gear, representing a speed of about 115 mph', despite wheelspin 0–60 mph was covered in 7.9 seconds, fuel consumption was 19–22 mpg and oil was burnt at about 1200 mpg. WMC 181 is now preserved in the AFN showrooms at London Road, Isleworth.

Frazer Nash was out of luck at Le Mans in 1951 and the best performance was fourteenth place by Eric Winterbottom and John Marshall at the wheel of Le Mans Replica WHX 225, soundly beaten in the 2-litre class by the Lancia Aurelia GT of Lurani and Bracco. Not long afterwards, Winterbottom, now partnered by George Duff, won a Coupe des Alpes in the Alpine Rally for a penalty-free run and finished first in the 2-litre class—convincing evidence of the versatility of the Le Mans Replica.

In September 1951 the Le Mans Replica achieved two important successes. Cortese with the Ambrosiana car won the Targa Florio outright and Bob Gerard was third overall (and first in the 2-litre class) behind the works C-type Jaguars in the Tourist Trophy. To round off a successful year

Tony Crook went record-breaking at Montlhéry and in November broke the Class E record for 200 miles with a speed of 120.13 mph, after putting 123.5 miles into the first hour.

For 1952 Frazer Nash developed both a single-seater Formula 2 car and a Mk II version of the Le Mans Replica intended purely for competition work. The Formula 2 car was no match for the much lighter Cooper-Bristol that appeared the same year, but a works-prepared example driven by Ken Wharton took third place in the Eifelrennen and fourth in the Swiss Grand Prix.

The Mk II Le Mans Replica featured a lower and lighter body, very abbreviated cycle wings, lighter pressed-steel bolt-on wheels and an extractor exhaust system that terminated just ahead of the offside rear wheel. Instead of merely encouraging private owners, AFN now entered a works development Mk II with Ken Wharton at the wheel. Wharton drove this Mk II to a stirring second place behind Ian Stewart's Ecurie Ecosse C-type in the Jersey Road Race and won a 100-mile race for 2-litre cars at Boreham from Salvadori (Mk I) and Crook (Mk II). Crook also finished third with his Mk II in the 65-lap Prix de Monaco for 2-litre sports cars.

The older cars continued to perform well in 1952. Mike Hawthorn drove Len Potter's Mille Miglia, LUF 956, into third place on handicap in the British Empire Trophy in the Isle of Man and Bob Gerard/David Clarke brought their Mk I across the line in fourth place in the Goodwood Nine Hours race. At Le Mans the 2-litre class was dominated by the Lancias, but Peacock and Ruddock finished tenth overall and third in their class with their Mk I. An unexpected success was the victory early in the year in the Sebring 12 Hours race by a brand-new and completely standard Mk I Le Mans Replica driven by Kulok and Grey. On the rallying front O'Hara Moore and Leavens enjoyed a penalty-free run in the Rallye Soleil-Cannes and were clear outright winners; over a flying kilometre during the rally their Mk I was timed at 120.83 mph.

For 1953 cycle wings were banned in International sports car racing and so the Mk Is had to be fitted with valances between the wings and the body, which increased drag. In British short-circuit events the Le Mans Replicas were usually outpaced by Bob Chase's Cooper-Bristol, driven by Alan Brown, and Cliff Davis's famous Tojeiro-Bristol, LOY 500. Bristol themselves contested Le Mans and the Reims 12 Hours race with their new, technically and aerodynamically advanced 450 coupés. All these designs were far removed from the sort of car that Frazer Nash built, and Isleworth's new model, the Le Mans fixed head coupé, was in the marque's traditional mould of a

LEFT *This view of Bob Gerard's Le Mans Replica in the 1953 Tourist Trophy shows clearly the valances linking the front wings with the bodywork so as to comply with International Sports Car regulations. Gerard and co-driver Clarke finished seventh (Louis Klementaski)*

sports car suitable for both road and competition use. Although the design was virtually identical to that of the well-established open cars, the body was delectably handsome and characterized by a lozenge-shaped air intake with horizontal bars.

Ken Wharton drove the Le Mans fhc on its debut in the Production Sports Car race at Silverstone in May 1953, but trailed round to finish a poor seventeenth. Prospects of success at Le Mans were slim, but both of the new Bristol 450s retired with engine problems and the fhc with standard 132 bhp engine was driven by Wharton and Mitchell to an easy victory in the 2-litre class (thirteenth overall) at 88.30 mph and was timed at 121.47 mph on the Mulsanne Straight.

The Le Mans Replica fared well in tougher British events. Ken Wharton drove the works Mk II to a fine second place to Parnell's Aston Martin DB3S in the handicap British Empire Trophy on the Isle of Man and the old Mk I of Bob Gerard and David Clarke took a good sixth place and class victory in the Goodwood Nine Hours race. At the Tourist Trophy the works fielded a much modified Mk II with restyled rear end, flared front wings, a de Dion rear axle and cast iron (instead of the usual light alloy Al-fin) brake drums. This Mk II was driven with gusto by Wharton and Ernie Robb to take third place on handicap (sixth on scratch) and win its class.

By 1954 Frazer Nash was in decline in competition and as a production car, for the Aldingtons' energies were directed elsewhere. AFN was now Porsche concessionaire, as well as representing BMW and DKW. At Le Mans the fhc of Gatsonides and Becquart finished eleventh, but the first three places in the 2-litre class went to the Bristol 450s. Tony Brooks (already an accomplished performer in British events with Hely's Mk II) drove what was described as the new Sebring, registered 548 BMU, into a poor fourteenth place in the Sports Car race at the British Grand Prix meeting in July. The Sebring was in effect an open version of the Le Mans fhc with optional de Dion rear axle, and the first example, 7834 H, had been

BELOW *This Frazer Nash Sebring was driven into tenth place at Le Mans in 1955 by Stoop/Becquart (T. C. March)*

registered as long ago as September 1953. AFN had hoped that the Sebring would attract orders from the United States, but it represented very poor value at a basic price of £2500 and only three were built.

The last Le Mans Replica was built in 1954, and in July O'Hara Moore and Gott drove their veteran Mk I, XMX 4, to a Coupe des Alpes and a 2-litre class victory in the Alpine Rally. As late as April 1955 *The Autocar* road-tested a Targa Florio Fast Roadster, the final version of a limited production touring car that had appeared in 1952, and this neat 2-seater with a basic price of £1650 achieved a best maximum speed of 114 mph. The last appearance of the works developed Mk II was in the 1955 Tourist Trophy. The car was destroyed in the multi-car crash that cost the lives of several drivers, but Wharton was lucky to escape unscathed.

Dickie Stoop raced the first Sebring, 7834 H, until 1961, finishing tenth at Le Mans in 1955 with Marcel Becquart as co-driver (but only fourth in class behind a trio of the now open Bristol 450s) and retiring at Le Mans in both 1956 and 1957. Along with several Le Mans Replica owners Stoop contested the *Autosport* Championship for production cars and in 1959 he was not only joint overall winner of the Championship (equal on points with Bob Gerard who raced a Turner), but finished second on scratch to Jim Clark's Lotus Elite in the 3-hour Championship final at Snetterton.

Among the last Frazer Nash products was a prototype powered by the 3.4-litre Armstrong Siddeley Sapphire engine and the BMW-powered Continental model. The first Continental was exhibited in chassis form at Earls Court in 1956, but the following year there appeared a second car with stylish coupé body that incorporated Porsche 356 roof and doors. The 1956 chassis was sold to a private owner and fitted with an aerodynamic coupé designed by Peter Kirwan-Taylor, who had been responsible for the styling of the original Lotus Elite. There were plans to run this car at Le Mans with a BMW engine linered down to 2.5 litres, but these came to nothing.

Frazer Nash exhibited their Continental coupé for the last time at Earls Court in 1958, and although this was listed for several years afterwards, production of the marque was in reality at an end. Between 1948 and 1957, total Frazer Nash production amounted to about 85 cars (plus a number of rebuilds) and of these around 31 were Le Mans Replicas, the epitome of the road-going competition sports cars of the 1950s.

Gilby-Climax

For many years Sid Greene of Gilby Engineering had been an enthusiastic motor racing entrant, fielding a Frazer Nash Le Mans Replica and then Maserati A6GCS Sports and 250F Grand Prix cars for Roy Salvadori to drive. In 1955, Sid Greene ordered a new Cooper-Climax for his 17-year-old son Keith. Delivery was late and so Keith drove a works-loaned car at Stapleford in October 1955 and first raced his own car, 30 FVX, in 1956. From the Cooper, Keith Greene graduated to a Lotus Eleven, then in 1959 to a Lotus 17, and for 1960 the Gilby team commissioned its own sports/racing car known as the 'A' type.

The new car was the work of designer Len Terry and featured a neat, compact multi-tubular space-frame with front suspension by double wishbones and coil spring/damper units and rear suspension by low-pivot wide-based wishbones, with the half-shafts acting as upper wishbones. The engine was the 1100 cc Climax FWA in Stage 3 form. The steering was Morris Mini rack-and-pinion, there were disc brakes front and rear (inboard at the rear) and Lotus 13 in. magnesium alloy wheels were fitted in August (originally Sprite rims with wider and lighter rims were used). The aluminium body was very slippery and low, with very flat nose, with the air intake beneath a pronounced lip, bonnet hump, pronounced front wings and cockpit well to the rear of the car, with very full and enclosing perspex windscreen. Allegedly the style of the front of the body was copied from a record-breaking Abarth and the rear was based on the 1959 Lister. This body was designed by Len Terry and built by Williams and Pritchard Ltd.

Behind the design of the Gilby there were two principal aims: to produce a successful sports/racing car without the faults of the Lotus that Greene had raced in 1959 and to gain construction and development experience for the production of a Formula 1 car. The Gilby made its debut, as yet unpainted and completely untested, at Goodwood on Easter Monday 1960, and ran second in the 1100 cc class until an oil seal failed. At this time the 1100 cc class was completely dominated by the Lolas and so Greene had to work really hard to achieve any success. A fortnight after Goodwood Greene finished third in the 1100 cc class at Aintree.

At the May Silverstone meeting disaster struck. At Abbey Curve, Greene was in collision with an Elva and a Lola while travelling at well over 100 mph; the Gilby skated along the ditch, turned upside down and continued for some distance before coming to rest with Greene trapped under the car. The car was a terrible mess with the chassis bent (but no tubes had broken—a testimony to its inherent strength) and the nose section and windscreen smashed.

A new chassis and body front section were made and the Gilby reappeared at Snetterton in July, where it was driven to second place by Peter Arundell to Bekaert's Lister-Jaguar in the Un-

The very successful Gilby-Climax seen on its debut in the hands of Keith Green at the Easter Meeting at Goodwood in 1960

limited Sports Car race. Later in the day, on a rain-soaked track, Arundell won the Formule Libre race against some very formidable machinery. At the British Grand Prix meeting at Silverstone, Arundell finished second to Ashdown's Lola in the 1500 cc class of the sports car race. In August, Greene, who was not always able to drive the Gilby himself because he was also driving the team's Formula 1 Cooper-Maserati, reappeared at Brands Hatch, where he was third in the 1100 cc class, and at Snetterton, winning the 1100 cc sports car race and finishing fifth in the Formule Libre event. A second in the 1100 cc class followed at Mallory Park in September and Greene rounded off the season with a class second at Silverstone and a fine win from Alan Rees's Lola at Brands Hatch. Out of 15 starts during the year the Gilby gained five wins, two seconds, four thirds, a fifth and only two retirements.

By 1961 Gilby was committed to running their Formula 1 programme, at first with a Climax 4-cylinder-powered car, but switching to BRM V-8 power in 1962. Early in 1963 the complete Gilby Formula 1 équipe was sold to Ian Raby and the team withdrew from racing. Keith Greene remained a very familiar face on the motor racing scene and is established as the leading team manager in endurance racing with experience that has encompassed the Rondeau team, the Ford C100 project, and, most recently, managing a Porsche 956 team for Richard Lloyd.

Ginetta

The origins of the Ginetta lie in an agricultural and constructional engineering business near Woodbridge in Suffolk run by the Walklett brothers—Bob (to become managing director of Ginetta), Ivor (responsible for design), Trevor (responsible for the chassis) and Douglas (works manager). In the 1950s Ivor Walklett constructed a special based on a prewar Wolseley Hornet (this later became known as the G1) and in 1958 the brothers put into production a sports two-seater not so very different in appearance from the Lotus 7, known as the G2.

There followed in 1960 the G3, with fibreglass full-width body, and the G4 of 1961 onwards, which was another sports two-seater with fibreglass body and Ford Anglia 997 cc engine suitable for both road use and Club racing, production of which was transferred to new premises at Witham near Chelmsford in 1962. The G4s were widely raced in British events with success. There were a number of variations of the design, including the G5 with Ford Cortina engine (to avoid confusion the designation was soon dropped and this version continued to be known as the G4), the G6 to take the DKW 850 cc two-stroke engine and the prototype G7 with gearbox in unit with the final drive to improve weight distribution. Over 500 of these cars were built. The G8 was a single-seater for Formula 3 and the G9 was a Formula 2 car that was never built. The next stage in development was the production of the G10 coupé and convertible with Ford V-8 engine, both sophisticated road-going sporting cars of which the later G11 derivative with MGB engine sold in considerable quantities. There followed in 1966 the first Ginetta two-seater built solely for competition use.

G12

When the G12 was introduced in 1966, it was claimed to be the first British mid-engined GT car. It was certainly a very advanced and very competitive car of sound design in accordance with contemporary racing practice. There was a multi-tubular space-frame, with the cockpit and centre part of the body bonded to the chassis. At the front the Walkletts used double wishbones and coil spring/damper units with anti-roll bar and Triumph suspension uprights. The rear suspension consisted of lower reversed wishbones, single upper transverse, twin radius arms, adjustable anti-roll bar and coil spring/damper units. The wheels were Minilite 13 in. cast magnesium, and Girling 9.5 in. disc brakes from the Triumph Spitfire were mounted outboard and front and rear. The body was a neat fibreglass coupé and the usual power unit was the Cosworth-Ford SCA of 997 cc used with a Hewland gearbox/final drive unit.

The G12 proved an immediate success, and at a price in component form of £1200 it was in great demand, and over a three-year period more than 50 of these cars were sold. The most successful Ginetta driver in 1966 was Willie Green, a comparative novice, who swept all before him in, admittedly minor, British races in 1966, scoring eleven victories and breaking the class lap record on five occasions. At the end of 1966 Green disposed of his 997 cc Ginetta, advertising it with the slogan 'You can't beat it, so buy it'. For the following year Green acquired a new G12 with a 1594 cc Ford twin-cam engine; Green's old car was raced by Keith Jupp, *Motoring News* ran their own car for editor Mike Twite and Ian Tee, the Worcestershire Racing Association fielded G12s with Cosworth twin-cam engine for Paul Bamford

and a 997 cc SCA-powered car for Paul Ridgway, and other G12s were raced by Paul Byran, John Creasey and Bob Eva. John Burton raced a car fitted with a Martin V-8 2-litre engine said to develop 200 bhp, but it was unreliable, developed far less power than its makers expected and towards the end of the year he switched to an SCA-powered version.

It would be unrealistic to suggest that the G12s did not achieve a measure of success in 1967, but they were no match for the new Ford twin-cam-powered Chevrons in their class and suffered handling limitations compared to the Chevrons because the maximum rim width that could be used was 7 in. G12s continued to be raced in 1968, certain examples with Ford twin-cams 1594 cc engines, but to all intents and purposes their day was over and they had been superseded by the G16 model.

G16

The designation G13 was not used for the usual reasons of superstition, the G14 was a planned sports car that was never built and the G15 was the immensely successful Imp-powered road car that was in production from 1968 to 1974 and resumed production again in 1981. Directly derived from the G12, the G16 was an open Group 6 Prototype introduced in 1968. The first cars were supplied to the Worcestershire Racing Association to be driven by John Bamford and John Burton, and this team in effect took control of racing development—mainly because of the Walkletts' preoccupation with getting the G15 into production. The result was that development did not progress as smoothly as the Walkletts would have liked, and although the cars were consistently raced, not much in the way of success was gained. Jeremy Richardson raced a G16 with Coventry-Climax 2-litre engine and Bamford's car was raced from time to time with a 2-litre BMW unit.

For 1969 the company introduced an improved version of the G16 with the large windscreen replaced by a very small perspex screen (this was said to reduce frontal area by 30 per cent), changes to the spring rates, stronger drive-shafts and, if required, a fibreglass tonneau to cover the passenger side of the cockpit. In addition Ginetta developed the G16A with 2-litre BRM V-8 engine. One of the G16As was retained by the works and the other was acquired by Ian Tee, but neither achieved much in the way of success. Brian Alexander used a G16 with Buick V-8 engine in hill-climbs and sprints and Gerry Tyrack bought the ex-Bamford G16, which he also used with great success in hillclimbs and sprints. In all only eight G16s were built.

Ginetta diversified into single-seaters, without much success, and work was started, but abandoned, on a Formula 1 car to be powered by the BRM V-12 engine. Next came the G21 sports coupé with 1725 cc Chrysler engine, which was built in small quantities until 1978, and despite the economic pressures of recent years the company survives as a small-scale manufacturer of road cars.

ABOVE LEFT *In 1966 Willie Green enjoyed a phenomenal run of success with his Cosworth SCA-powered Ginetta G12*

LEFT *The Ginetta G16A with 2-litre BRM engine driven by Ian Tee/Willie Green in the 1969 BOAC 500 race at Brands Hatch (LAT)*

Halseylec

The widespread availability of the Coventry-Climax FWA 1098 cc engine encouraged many drivers and entrants to have a go at constructing their own cars, and Eric Brandon's Halseylec was one of the more successful efforts. Brandon, long-time friend of John Cooper, had raced Cooper 500 cc cars and Cooper-Bristol Formula 2 cars with considerable success. In 1954 he decided to put in hand construction of his own car, which was largely the work of his mechanic 'Ginger' Devlin, and it was substantially Cooper-inspired. Devlin used a simple tubular chassis with front and rear suspension by the standard Cooper layout of transverse leaf springs and lower wishbones, but with the major difference that the engine was front-mounted. Cooper wheels with integral brake drums were fitted and the Climax FWA engine drove through a Bristol gearbox. The body was said to be Ferrari-inspired, but while bearing no recognizable features in common with Ferrari models, it had a very sleek, slippery shape with low, sloping bonnet, metal tonneau over the passenger side of the cockpit and very shapely tail. It was also lighter, smaller and lower than many of its rivals—when it raced against Porsche 550s, they towered above it. Brandon called the new car the Halseylec, which was the telegraphic address of his family electrical wholesaling business.

Brandon drove the Halseylec, registered WPK 6, on its debut in the British Empire Trophy at Oulton Park on 2 April, 1955, finishing fifth in the 1500 cc

ABOVE *Eric Brandon's Halseylec was a very sleek and slippery design. Brandon is at the wheel on the car's debut in the 1955 British Empire Trophy at Oulton Park (LAT)*

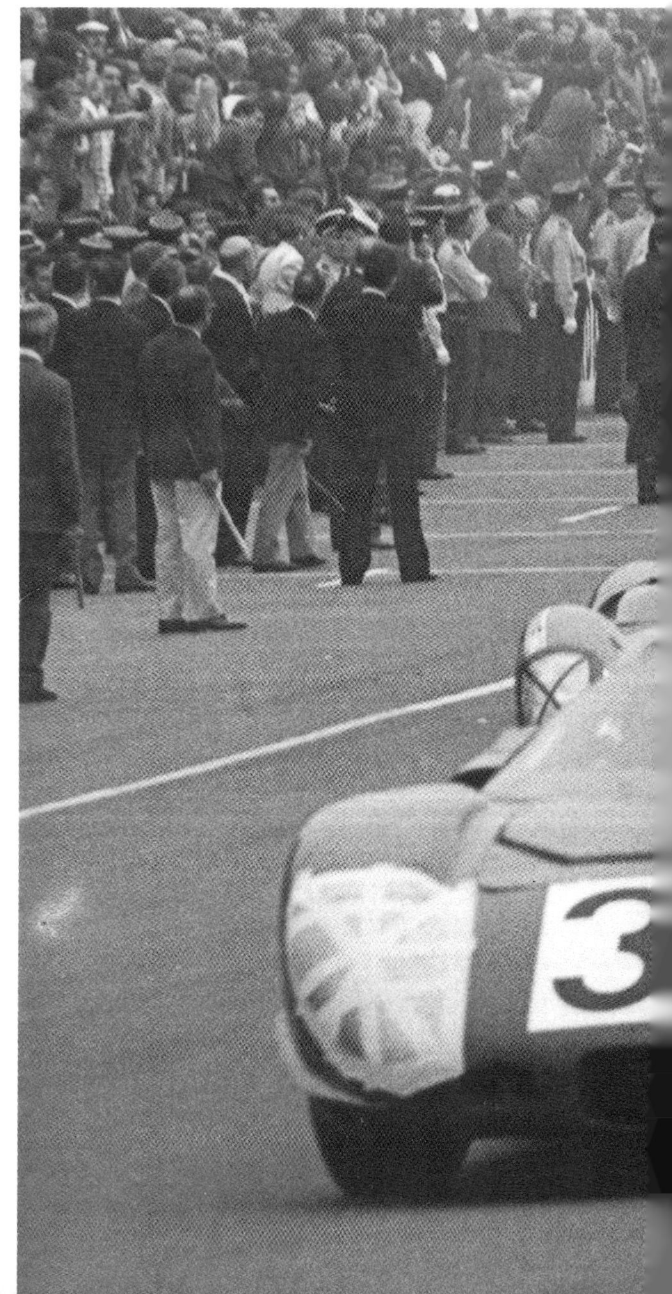

heat behind two Connaughts, an Osca and a Porsche, and sixth in the handicap final (second in the 1500 cc class). The Halseylec was raced regularly throughout the year and scored a long list of fine performances that included a fifth at Goodwood on Easter Monday (second in the 1100 cc class), at Davidstow on Whit Monday he won the 1300 cc race and finished second in the 2750 cc event and at Elaintarharnajo Park in Finland he won a 2000 cc race and finished third in the Unlimited capacity event.

For 1956 Brandon built a second Halseylec, which was registered 7 BPA, and both cars were entered at Goodwood on Easter Monday, to be driven by Brandon and Alan Brown/Peter Jopp—but both non-started. Brandon drove one of the cars in the British Empire Trophy at Oulton Park a couple of weeks later, but the Halseylec had been overtaken by Cooper and Lotus developments and he finished twelfth in the 1500 cc heat, retiring in the final. The cars were raced from time to time, not achieving much in the way of success, and Brandon was losing interest in motor racing. The cars were entered in the Television Trophy at Brands Hatch on August Bank Holiday Monday for George Wicken and Peter Jopp, but failed to feature in the results of this 1500 cc sports car race. In October, Les Leston and Jopp drove the cars again in a 1200 cc sports car race at Brands Hatch, finishing fourth and fifth.

At the end of the year the cars were sold. David Latchford bought the first car, WPK 6, and raced it regularly through 1957–58 taking in a good number of continental races. The one real success attained was a class third with Cyril Scott-McArthur in the Messina 10 Hours Night race in Sicily in 1958. For some obscure reason the car was entered as a Cooper. After the race Scott-McArthur commented, 'The Halseylec Cooper ran throughout the race without missing a beat, but caused slight consternation with overheating, due to the fact that two spotlights had been set in the air intake.' This Halseylec was then sold to John Anstice-Brown, who in 1959 won the *Motor Sport* Trophy at the North Staffs MC meeting at Silverstone. In 1960 it was sold in Ireland, where it was raced by Denis Kingham as the Cliden. Although the second car, 7 BPA, survives, there is no record of it having been raced once it was sold by Brandon.

Healey SR

In the years between the end of production of the Austin-Healey 3000 and the introduction of the new Jensen-Healey in 1972, the Warwick Company, anxious to keep the Healey name in the public eye, built a prototype purely for Le Mans and this was raced at the Sarthe circuit in three successive years.

This prototype, designated the SR (which apparently stood for 'sub rosa'), was based on a fairly elaborate sheet steel centre-section platform

The Healey SR driven by Baker/Harris accelerates away at the start of the 1969 Le Mans race (LAT)

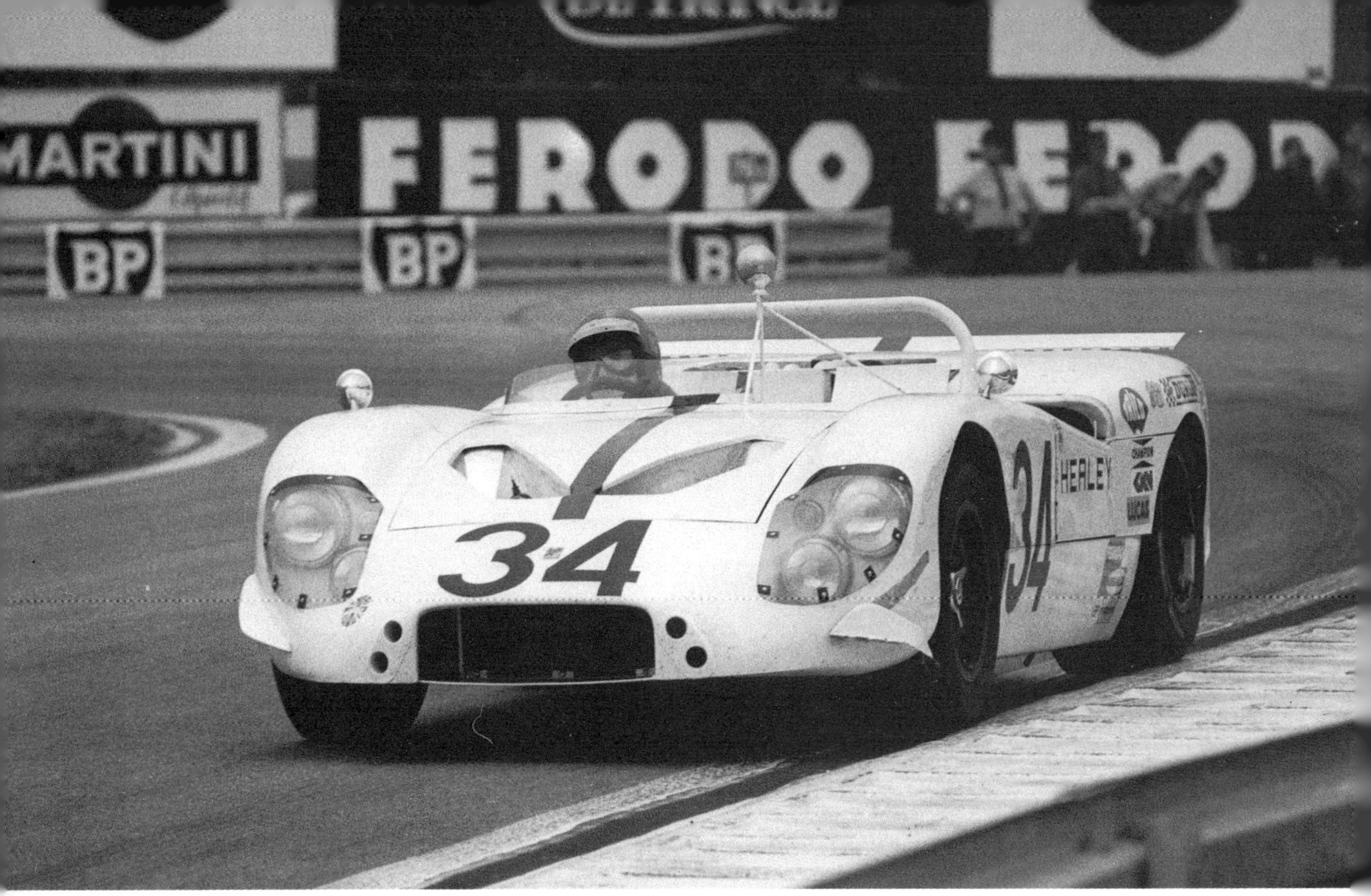
MARTINI
FERODO
BP
BP
34
34
HERLEY

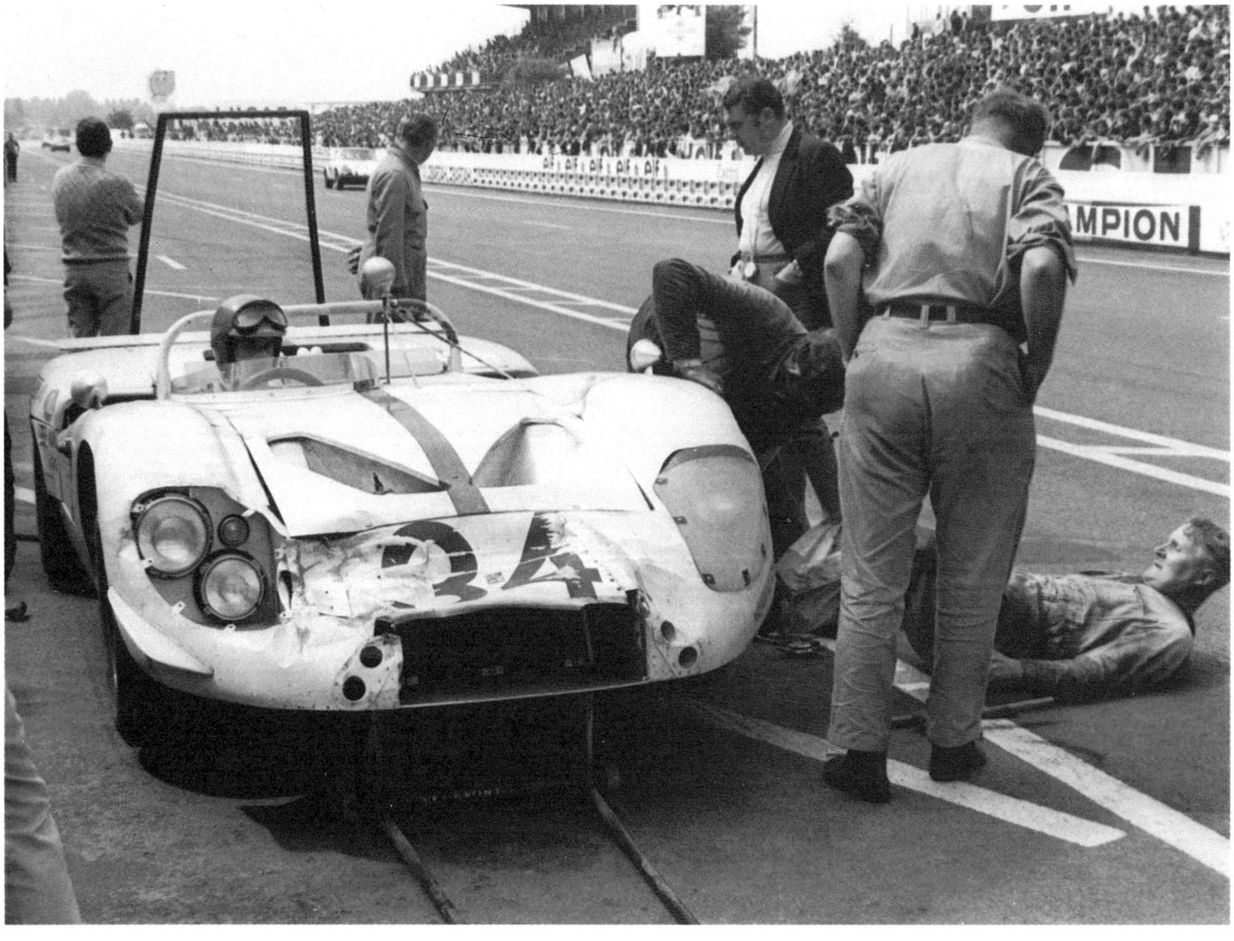
34

frame with sponsons to house flexible fuel bags and with built in roll-bars. It was the work of Geoffrey Healey and Barrie Bilbie and built in accordance with Donald Healey's edict that the design should be of a type with which the company was familiar and which might form the basis of a production car. At the front, suspension was by double wishbones and coil springs and at the back Healey adopted links, radius arms and coil spring/damper units. Rack-and-pinion steering based on modified MG components was used, the brakes were Girling disc, and Dunlop light alloy centre-lock wheels were fitted. The power unit was the Coventry-Climax FWMV in 2-litre form developing 240 bhp at 9000 rpm, and this was used with a Hewland DG300 5-speed gearbox and final drive unit. Styling of the alloy coupé body was very much in the contemporary idiom, with deep, sloping windscreen, curved cockpit roof, cut-off tail and large intakes either side ahead of the rear wheels to take air to the twin rear-mounted radiators. The oil cooler and 2-gallon oil tank were mounted immediately behind the nose cowling, and fuel capacity was 21 gallons. It was a very purposeful, well-designed car, but decidedly overweight for its engine size and unfortunately destined not to achieve success. Maximum speed in top gear was estimated at 180 mph in favourable conditions.

There was a frantic rush to get the new Healey ready for the 1968 Le Mans race, which was postponed until the end of September. At Le Mans the drivers were Clive Baker and Andrew Hedges and the Healey ran steadily until the clutch jammed in the 'out' position because of bearing failure. The Healey SR reappeared at Le Mans in 1969 driven by Clive Baker and John Harris. On the first lap of the race John Woolfe crashed his Porsche 917 with fatal results at White House, completely blocking the road, and all the following cars had to wait until the track was cleared. Among these was the Healey SR, which overheated, causing a water leak to develop and the car's early retirement.

For the 1970 Le Mans race the Healey SR was rebuilt with open bodywork and a Repco Formula 1 3-litre single cam per bank engine developing 330 bhp at 8800 rpm. It was driven by Andrew Hedges and Roger Enever. Early in the race the car was involved in a collision that wrecked the front of the body; it was delayed by stops for body repairs and to rebuild the clutch and with only 20 minutes of the race to run it expired out on the circuit with ignition problems.

The Healey SR was an interesting project, but vastly overweight and with no realistic prospects of achieving any success in a major international race such as Le Mans.

ABOVE *For 1970 the SR was rebuilt in open form and powered by a Repco 3-litre engine. It was driven at Le Mans by Enever/Hedges (LAT)*

BELOW *Frantic work in the pits on the SR in the 1970 Le Mans race after the front end of the car had been damaged in a collision (LAT)*

HRG

Uncompromisingly 'vintage' in style, character and performance, the HRG was a delightful traditional sports car built in small numbers at Tolworth in Surrey by a company formed by Halford, Robins and Godfrey (the last-named having been the 'G' of GN). The first cars were powered by the 1.5-litre Meadows 4ED engine. In 1938 HRG moved to Singer power and all post-war cars used Singer 1100 and 1500 cc engines. HRGs had enjoyed wide use and considerable success in prewar competitions, including a class second at Le Mans in 1938 and a class win there the following year, so it was inevitable that HRGs should be widely raced and rallied in post-war days, when competition cars were hard to come by.

Right at the end of the war, HRG had announced the 'Aerodynamic' two-seater with all-enveloping aluminium bodywork, and both these and the original and more popular 'square-rigged' model were raced extensively. For 1949 three Aerodynamic cars were completely rebuilt at Monaco Motors at Watford under the supervision of John Wyer, for Peter Clark, John Scott and Eric Thompson. The bodies were removed and replaced by much lighter, stark, slim bodies with cycle wings; the engines were modified with raised compression ratio of 9:1 and sodium-cooled valves and were carefully tuned and developed; larger 18 in. wire wheels were fitted at the back. The whole emphasis of the work carried out by Wyer was on careful preparation and reliability so that the cars would have staying power for 24-hour races, as well as improved performance.

At the first post-war Le Mans race in 1949 the three cars were driven by Clark/Morris-Goodall (eliminated by radiator trouble), Scott/Gee (eliminated by engine problems) and Thompson/Fairman, who finished eighth overall and won the 1500 cc class. Interestingly the winning Ferrari was co-driven by Lord Selsdon, a director of HRG. Of the closing stages of the race Jack Fairman wrote,

ABOVE *Peter Clark with a streamlined HRG leads a similar car in the 1948 Manx Cup in the Isle of Man. Clark was radio-controlled from the pits and the radio aerial mounted on the tail can just be seen in this photograph (Guy Griffiths)*

BELOW *Eric Thompson with the lightweight 'Le Mans' HRG at Goodwood in August 1949. This was the car that won its class in the 24 Hours race that year (Guy Griffiths)*

RIGHT *Another view of a lightweight HRG leading a Riley at Goodwood in 1951 (Guy Griffiths)*

'With an hour and a half to go, the full realization that the gallant Hurg might make the grade after all was quite overwhelming, and I was petrified that I might make some idiotic mistake and mess up the show right at the end. At this stage I think I watched the oil and water gauges more than the road ahead, and my ears were positively flapping with the effort to detect any unusual noises.'

Two weeks later the same three cars ran in the Spa 24 Hours race, but Cecil Gee's place in the team had been taken by André Pilette. In addition, Ray Barrington Brock had entered his coupé HRG, a conversion of an Aerodynamic, with Bob Freeman-Wright as co-driver. All four HRGs finished the race, taking the first four places in the 1500 cc class, and Thompson/Fairman were again the class winners, at an average of 64.50 mph. None of the cars was in the healthiest of conditions at the end and the Clark/Goodall entry had been merely completing a lap an hour so that it still counted as a runner!

Private owners were racing their HRGs with success in Club events throughout the 1950s and the last of the original square-rigged cars did not leave the HRG works until 1956. Although with the passing of the years HRG had turned more and more to other engineering work, the company had been carrying out development work on the Singer engine and produced a twin overhead camshaft cylinder head. David Blakely raced one of the ex-Le Mans cars fitted with one of these engines and he installed it in his Emperor-HRG. The Emperor featured a tubular chassis, Volkswagen front suspension, de Dion rear end and full-width aerodynamic bodywork with prominent headrest. Blakely had driven this car into second place in the 1500 cc race at the Boxing Day Brands Hatch meeting in 1954; it was a car of some promise and was being prepared for a full 1955 season at the time Blakely was murdered.

In 1955, HRG introduced their own twin-cam sports car of very modern concept. There was a tubular ladder-type frame constructed from 16-gauge 3.75 in. tubing with two cross-members of the same diameter and two other cross-members with an inverted 'U'-shaped member at the rear. Suspension was independent front and rear with, at the front, double wishbones, a very wide low-mounted transverse leaf spring and coil spring/damper units. At the rear there was a similar arrangement save that the transverse leaf spring was high-mounted. The power unit was the Singer SM1500 1497 cc 4-cylinder engine, but with chain-driven twin overhead camshafts, together with new crankshaft, rods and pistons. With two twin-choke Solex carburettors the claimed power output was 108 bhp at 5800 rpm. A Singer 4-speed gearbox was fitted. The wheels consisted of steel rims bolted on to 6-spoke cast magnesium spiders. One of the most interesting features of the car was the brakes, which were the company's own HRG-Palmer disc brakes, as fitted to Cooper IX Formula 3 cars. On

VPH 188

SHELL X-100 MOTOR OIL
SHELL X-100 MOTOR OIL
SHELL X-100 MOTOR OIL
8
3
2
33

LEFT *The 1955 prototype twin-cam HRG (LAT)*

BELOW LEFT *In the 1955 Goodwood Nine Hours race the twin-cam HRG of Calvert/Green holds up the Aston Martin DB3S of Peter Collins, Harry Schell's Ferrari Monza and Peter Walker's DB3S (LAT)*

the Cooper a single brake acted on the rear axle, but on the HRG the brakes were mounted at the wheels in the usual way. The body was a full-width aluminium design with hinged front and rear sections. The dry weight was around 14½ cwt. Originally HRG planned to market the cars at about £1800 including purchase tax, but in fact only four were built.

In the Goodwood Nine Hours race one of these cars was entered by D. J. Calvert for himself and Green, and although they finished the race, they were plagued by problems and finished last, many laps behind the class winner. In 1956, Calvert drove his car in the *Autosport* Production Sports Car Championship and finished third overall.

The Singer company had plans to market their own Hunter saloon with the twin-cam engine, but these came to nothing after the Rootes takeover. Although HRG later built a Vauxhall-powered prototype, the make was to all intents and purposes dead in 1956.

HWM-Alta

In early post-war days there was no greater contribution to the growth of British power in International motor racing than that of John Heath and George Abecassis. For four years they raced their Alta-powered HWMs (Hersham and Walton Motors was the meaning of the initials and the company was HW Motors Ltd, in 2-litre Formula 2 races all over Europe, picking up starting and prize money to keep the team going, giving breaks to young drivers of potential (the list included Stirling Moss, Lance Macklin and Peter Collins) and thoroughly enjoying their racing. In 1953 HWM withdrew from serious single-seater racing and for the next four years competed with Jaguar-powered sports/racing cars of the same basic chassis design.

Abecassis had raced an Alta single-seater in prewar days and in the 1940s acquired a new Grand Prix Alta, while Heath raced a streamlined Alta sports/racing car. For 1949 Heath built a new dual-purpose car for both Formula 2 (still known as Formula B at this time) and sports car racing with offset driving position, detachable wings and lights. There was a simple tubular chassis with three welded cross-members, front suspension by lower wishbones and transverse leaf spring (incorporating proprietary uprights and stub axles) and rear suspension by a rigid axle from a Lagonda Rapier suspended on quarter-elliptic springs with single torque arm. The power unit was the 4-cylinder 1960 cc (79 × 100 mm) twin overhead camshaft Alta from the streamliner used with an ENV Wilson-type preselector gearbox and ENV differential. The stark but neat body was built by Leacroft of Egham and the car was known as the HW-Alta.

During 1949 Heath raced this car extensively, winning the Manx Cup on the Douglas circuit after the retirement of Moss's Cooper-JAP 1000, finishing fifth in the Coupe des Petites Cylindrées at Reims against strong Formula B opposition and finishing second to Pozzi's 4.5-litre Delahaye in the French Grand Prix run as a sports car race at Comminges.

The success of the HW-Alta encouraged Heath and Abecassis to build four new cars for Formula B for 1950. Because there was the possibility of running at Le Mans, the dual-purpose arrangement was retained. Likewise, the basic chassis layout of the 1949 car remained unchanged, but Heath adopted independent rear suspension by a transverse leaf spring and lower wishbones and the preselector gearbox was of Armstrong-Siddeley manufacture. Once again the bodies were by Leacroft.

One of the four cars was sold to A. A. Baring, a friend of Abecassis, but the other three were raced throughout the year, gaining a good measure of success; what they lacked in power (power output was only about 115 bhp) they compensated for with excellent handling. They never managed to beat the V-12 Ferraris, but they were usually good for a place. With starting money (which rose as the team's reputation spread) and prize money, the team also enjoyed a financially successful year.

At the end of 1950 the three 1950 works cars were sold and the HWM team built new single-seater Formula 2 cars for 1951. All three 1950 cars were used for sports car racing. One car was sold to Swiss enthusiast Count Jacques de Wurstemberger (who competed under the pseudonym 'Herve') and was apparently burnt out during the filming of 'Such Men Are Dangerous'. The others were sold to Tom Meyer and Oscar Moore. Meyer's car, registered MXK 727, was rebodied with a very

H.W.M. 2-LITRE

This car, the property of Mr. T. M. MEYER, was specially converted, having been one of the original 1950 team cars. Body is now of full width and complies with F.I.A. regulations. High compression ALTA engine runs on petrol-benzole or 80 octane. Whole car specially prepared for long distance sports-car racing, and is in perfect condition throughout and ready for any event. Specification includes 4 wheel independent suspension, Armstrong self-change gearbox, alloy wheels, Alfin drums, dry-sump lubrication, enclosed spare wheel.

All enquiries to H. W. MOTORS, LTD.
Walton-on-Thames 2404-5-6

ABOVE *At a BARC Members' meeting at Goodwood in August 1953, Oscar Moore with his HWM, by this time Jaguar-powered, leads Michael Head's Jaguar XK120 (LAT)*

LEFT *Tom Meyer's HWM-Alta advertised for sale by HW Motors in September 1952*

handsome, slim, pencil body with integral wings, but was never raced a great deal, and Meyer sold it through HW Motors in the autumn of 1952. Throughout 1951 Moore, a North London motor dealer, raced his HWM, registered XMC 34, but was plagued by problems that included a constantly disintegrating exhaust system and a loss of a wheel *twice* at one meeting at the Nürburgring. For 1952 Moore replaced the Alta engine with a Jaguar unit and raced XMC 34 in this form for another couple of years.

JBW

Brian Naylor was a director of six companies—all in the motor trade—and during his motor racing career extending from 1953 to 1960 raced a diverse selection of cars, all of which were prepared at his Wellington Road South, Stockport, premises. He started his competition career with a Bristol-engined Alta in 1953, the following year he raced 500 cc Cooper-Norton and sports Cooper-MG cars and in 1955 was seen at the wheel of two different Lotus Mk 8s, an MG 1467 cc-powered car and the ex-Coombs car with Connaught engine. In British Club events that year he scored 13 first places and seven seconds.

Towards the end of 1955 Naylor imported a new Maserati 150S sports-racing car, a potent piece of machinery with a 1484 cc twin overhead camshaft engine (in simple terms a version of the 250F Grand Prix engine minus two cylinders). The Maserati was a substantially built car aimed at continental endurance racing, and in British short-circuit events it proved too heavy to beat the Lotus and Cooper opposition in 1956 (and its roadholding was inferior). During the early part of the 1956 season Naylor's mechanic transferred the Maserati engine and gearbox to a Lotus Eleven chassis. After early problems with the oil pump and drive-shaft failures (attributed to the extra torque of the Maserati engine compared with the usual Climax) Naylor enjoyed an exceptionally successful season, scoring 27 firsts in British events and a class win in the Leinster Trophy. He competed abroad at Imola, where he retired with brake failure, and at Rome, where he finished fourth overall, taking a class second.

In 1957 he moved on to a Lotus Eleven powered by a Maserati 200S 2-litre engine and his run of successes continued, including class wins in the Spa Grand Prix and in the Sports Car race at the British Grand Prix at Silverstone. At the September Goodwood meeting a weld attaching the lower left-hand front wishbone failed, Naylor lost control and crashed; the Lotus was a write-off and Naylor suffered a broken leg. Accordingly Naylor and Wilkinson decided to build their own car for 1958 to which they transferred the engine and gearbox from the crashed Lotus.

Fred Wilkinson's chassis design closely followed that of the Lotus Eleven, but the Eleven was a notoriously fragile design, and so the JBW, in the words of Naylor, 'was of much stronger tubing to take the power and weight of the 2-litre Maserati

Brian Naylor at the wheel of the immensely successful JBW-Maserati built after he had crashed his Lotus-Maserati

engine'. In fact the main tubing was 16-gauge. While the suspension was basically Lotus, there were a number of modifications: new front wishbones were fabricated with the anti-roll bar attached to the lower wishbone (on the Lotus it was attached to the upper wishbone; there was a new, longer A-bracket at the rear located nearer the chassis centre; there were new and stronger de Dion hub castings; and the camber and caster angles were adjustable. The engine was mounted some 6 in. further back in the frame and this substantially reduced the understeer characteristics which Naylor had found excessive on his 1957 Lotus. Front and rear brakes were Girling disc, 10.75 in. at the front (turned down from 11.5 in.) and 9.5 in. at the rear. Dunlop wire knock-on wheels were fitted. Cooling was by an ex-Connaught aluminium radiator and there were two fuel tanks, of 16 gallons and 14 gallons, mounted in the sides of the car. Naylor reckoned that the removal of the tanks from the tail of the car permitted a much better flow of air to the inboard rear brakes.

The intention was that the body styling should combine the 'better parts' of Lotus and Ferrari 'Testa Rossa' with Aston Martin DB3S frontal treatment. In fact the bodywork looked rather odd, with a low nose having the air intake angled downwards, and high front wings. This body of 20-gauge aluminium was built by the Gainsborough Engineering Company of Oldham and was painted green with a red stripe. Dry weight was claimed to be 10.25 cwt and with a power output of 190 bhp at 7500 rpm the performance was formidable.

Naylor drove the JBW-Maserati on its debut in the British Empire Trophy at Oulton Park, finishing third in the 2000 cc heat to a brace of Lotus 15s and taking fifth place in the final. The following weekend Naylor crashed his Formula 2 Cooper at Aintree after the right-hand universal joint had broken and the drive-shaft smashed through the suspension. He missed racing for a few weeks, but returned to win the Grand Prix des Frontières at Chimay at Whitsun, and at Snetterton at the beginning of June he won the 1500 cc sports race with the JBW fitted with the 1484 cc Maserati unit. Later that month he took two second places at Oulton Park and another overseas success followed in the Prix de Paris at Montlhéry, where he won the Sports category from a 2-litre Ferrari.

By the end of July Naylor had taken delivery of a replacement Cooper Formula 2 car and so racing activities were divided between two categories and the JBW did not make so many appearances during the remainder of the year. Naylor entered the JBW in August at the Roskilde Ring in Denmark. This was a series of races held over two days. In the first of the Saturday races Moss's Maserati broke a con-rod and he took over the JBW for the second race of the day, coming through from the back of the grid to win. By the Sunday a replacement engine had been fitted to Moss's Maserati and he appeared at the wheel of this once more for the remainder of the races, finishing second overall in the 2000 cc class to Carlsson (Ferrari). At the end of August at Silverstone, Naylor ran up an expensive bill when the 2-litre engine of the JBW poked a con-rod through the side of the crankcase. Nevertheless Naylor had the car racing again within a week and won the 2750 cc category of the sports car race at the Scott-Brown Memorial Trophy meeting at Snetterton. Naylor rounded off the season with a win in the sports car race at Innsbruck in Austria in October. In all during the year Naylor had entered 21 races, of which he had won 14 and gained two seconds and two thirds.

For 1959 Naylor sold the JBW-Maserati with 1500 cc engine to Colin Murray, and Fred Wilkinson built two new cars. One of these was a Formula 1 single-seater and the other a new sports/racing car powered by a 3-litre 4-cylinder Ferrari engine that had been used by Peter Whitehead in a single-seater Tasman Ferrari. The new sports/racing JBW closely followed the design of the 1958 car, but there was modified rear suspension incorporating a Watts linkage, the rear brakes were mounted outboard, apparently, an ERA combined 4-speed all-synchromesh gearbox and final drive unit were used and there were tail fins on the rear wings. The JBW-Ferrari made its debut at Oulton Park in April, but retired because of transmission problems. Naylor ran the car again at Aintree later in the month, but could manage no better than eighth in the Unlimited Sports Car race. At Mallory Park on Whit Monday Naylor won the Unlimited Sports Car race from John Dalton's now very dated Aston Martin DB3S. Colin Murray was also having some success with the JBW-Maserati and finished second on scratch to Bekaert's Lister-Jaguar in the Leinster Trophy run on the Dunboyne circuit in County Meath.

Apart from the fact that Naylor devoted much of his efforts in 1959 to racing his Formula 1 JBW, there was no doubt that the JBW-Ferrari failed to fulfil expectations and was no real match for the Cooper Monacos that were beginning to dominate the Unlimited category of British sports car racing. At the end of the year Naylor bought the Cooper-Maserati that Roy Salvadori had been racing for John Coombs and installed the Ferrari engine in this chassis. Minus engine the JBW-Ferrari survives today in the ownership of John Evetts of EMK Aeroplane—but John has a V-12 Ferrari engine which he hopes to install one day. An odd feature of the car now is that it lacks the cut-outs in the wings for the headlamps that were fitted when Naylor was racing the car.

Kieft

That Kieft was a company with many diverse projects and three different owners makes the telling of its history both complicated and, in some areas, uncertain. Kieft was formed by Cyril Kieft, who ran forging and electrical manufacturing businesses, and the first car, a 500 cc Formula 3 single-seater, was constructed at Bridgend in 1950. It was too heavy in the face of Cooper opposition, but later a JAP 1100 cc twin-cylinder engine was fitted, and in this form it was driven with limited success in hillclimbs by Michael Christie, one of the leading hillclimbers of the 1950s. Apparently five 'production' 500 cc cars followed. In addition Kieft built a road-going 2-seater powered by a BSA 650 cc vertical twin engine to the order of a customer in Germany.

At the end of 1950 the Kieft works were transferred to Reliance Works, Derry Street, Wolverhampton, and it was at around that time that Kieft took over a much improved 500 cc project created by Ray Martin with assistance from Dean Delamont and John Cooper (sports editor of *The Autocar*). This design, originated by Stirling Moss and Ken Gregory, was based on a multi-tubular frame, wishbone front suspension, swing axles at the rear and rubber suspension. Stirling Moss raced the first car built in 1951 with considerable success and this design was put into limited production. There are no precise records as to the number built, but it seems to be a total of around 15 during 1952–53. The 1954 version featured tubular wishbone and coil spring front suspension, but probably only a couple of these cars were built.

It is a matter of history that Cooper dominated Formula 3 and that their very success contributed, in the long-term, to its downfall. Nevertheless the Kiefts did enjoy substantial success and in 1953–54 were always regarded as the 'number two marque'. Moss switched to Coopers in Formula 3 after the end of 1952, but other drivers continued to race Kiefts with success, notably Don Parker, whose maroon car was always immaculately turned out and a potential race-winner (Parker switched to R. R. Jackson-entered Coopers after 1955), and Tommy Bridger. Model designation meant that the C52 was the 1952 model and the C53 was the 1953 version. In 1953 the price was £545 less engine and gearbox and the C53 was available as a kit for £445.

Towards the end of 1951 Gordon Bedson (designer of the promising Mackson Formula 3 car) joined the staff of Cyril Kieft & Co. Ltd. Bedson's brief was to design a Bristol-powered Formula 2 car, but this was never completed and instead the same basic design was adapted as a sports/racing car. The basis of the sports Kieft was a multi-tubular chassis (at the time it was described as a 'space-frame', but such a description would no longer be acceptable) with the then unconventional feature that the central seat of the proposed Formula 2 car was retained with the intention that there should be small seats on either side of the driver outside the main chassis frame; thus it was, strictly speaking, a 3-seater and complied with International regulations, although in practice the seat to the right of the driver was usually removed. There were unequal-length tubular wishbones front and rear with coil spring/damper units at the front and a transverse leaf spring at the rear mounted on top of the Elektron housing for the final drive. Kieft used a form of wheel and brake inspired by Cooper practice so that the ribbed Elektron drums for the Lockheed brakes also formed the wheel centres and were bolted to detachable steel 15 in. rims. There was full width 'aerodynamic' bodywork constructed in aluminium, with front and rear body sections hinged to give excellent accessibility, a passenger door on the left (getting into the driver's seat was a bit of a scramble!) and metal tonneau over the right-hand side of the cockpit. Prices quoted were £750 (less engine and gearbox), £1125 (MG engine and gearbox) and £1365 (Bristol engine and gearbox).

According to Kieft, eight cars were built in 1953 and early 1954 and were registered consecutively LDA 1 to LDA 8. If an attempt is made to trace these numbers through illustrations in magazines and photographs of the period, it is not possible to trace them all. However, early in the year arrangements were for three cars to be raced by 'The Monkey Stable' and these were registered LDA 1 to LDA 3. Originally The Monkey Stable were to have four cars, but it seems that only three were delivered. According to Cyril Kieft the cars were leased, but on the face of things this was not correct; two cars were advertised for sale by Peter Avern, The Monkey Stable Racing Manager, in October 1953, whereas if they were leased they would presumably have been returned to Kieft. It may be—and this is speculation—that the cars were originally sold, but a replacement supplied later in the year was on lease. The Monkey Stable cars used MG 1467 cc engines and MG TC gearboxes and the engines were tuned by team drivers Jim Mayers and Ian Wilson. Of the remaining cars built, it appears that one (supplied to a private owner for road use) was MG-powered and the remaining four were all fitted with Bristol 2-litre engines and gearboxes.

In 1953 The Monkey Stable was very pro-

LEFT *Centre-drive sports car—the Monkey Stable Kieft-MG driven by Pat Griffith. It seems that this photograph was taken in practice for this Silverstone meeting in May 1953 (LAT)*

ABOVE *Horace Gould (Kieft-Bristol) looks over his shoulder at Alan Brown (Cooper-Bristol) in the very wet Sports Car race at Silverstone in May 1954 (T. C. March)*

fessionally organized and tackled a full season of International races with some success. The full team of three cars was entered in the Production Sports Car race at Silverstone, and although they were beaten in the 1500 cc class by Cliff Davis's Cooper-MG they finished second and third in the class in the order Mayers and Griffith, but Keen was right at the tail of the field after mechanical problems. In this race Michael Christie drove the first of the Bristol-powered cars entered by 'Kieft Cars', but he was never in serious contention in his class. The Kiefts were again beaten by Davis's Cooper in the 1500 cc heat of the British Empire Trophy on the Douglas circuit, but in the handicap final, although Mayers non-started because of clutch trouble, Griffith came through to win the class at 63.80 mph after the Cooper broke a half-shaft. On 26 July The Monkey Stable competed in the Lisbon Jubilee Sports Car Grand Prix; the race was won by Bonetto's Lancia with Moss (works Jaguar) second, and the Kieft-MGs won the 2000 cc class in the order Mayers, Line.

The Monkey Stable transporter with two Kieft-MGs was driven direct to Nürburgring so that the team could compete in the 7-lap Sports Car race prior to the German Grand Prix. The third car for Mike Keen came direct from England. On the way the transporter was wrecked and the cars badly damaged. David Blakely was to have driven one of the cars, but was now a non-starter, and Alan Brown took over a car that Kieft was about to sell to a private customer. In the race Brown was right out of the picture because of engine trouble, but Keen finished fifth in the face of strong local opposition from Porsche, Borgward and EMW.

Because of the problems encountered abroad,

The Monkey Stable missed the Goodwood Nine Hours race, although a 2-litre Bristol-powered car was driven by Hazleton/Thompson; it was plagued by an engine misfire and retired because of a blown gasket. A week later The Monkey Stable ran their trio of cars in the Nürburgring 1000 Km race, but the sole finisher was the car of Mayers/Griffith, fifth and last in its class. Line over-revved his engine on the first lap and Keen led his class, but retired out on the circuit because of a broken wheel rim. In the Tourist Trophy on the Dundrod circuit a trio of Kieft-Bristols was entered under the name of Kieft Cars, but at least two of these belonged to private owners. None finished and two of the three were eliminated by accidents. Mayers wound up The Monkey Stable's season by winning the 1500 cc sports car race at Castle Combe in October and setting a new class lap record of 78.85 mph.

At the end of 1953 The Monkey Stable temporarily pulled out of racing and most of the Kiefts changed hands. Horace Gould acquired one of the Bristol-powered cars to replace his Cooper-MG, but even with his very press-on driving (not for nothing was he known as 'the Gonzalez of the West Country') could he achieve success. Probably his best performance was a class second at the May Silverstone International meeting. In British events the 1953 Kiefts scored nothing apart from a class win by Byrnes with a Bristol-powered car at Shelsley Walsh, but early in the year the Kieft-Bristol owned by Paul Ceresole and driven by Carpenter/van Driel finished sixth and won its class in the Sebring 12 Hours race. By the end of 1953, Cyril Kieft had his mind on a host of new projects, despite the comparative failure of these early projects.

During 1954 Kieft delivered a new sports/racing car to Erwin Goldschmidt in the United States. This was a conventional right-hand-drive car with tubular chassis, suspension similar to the 1953 cars and in chassis design generally followed the design of a Formula 1 single-seater that Kieft had started to build but never completed. This car, with aluminium bodywork, closely styled on that of the Cunningham CR-4, was powered by a Chrysler 'Firedome' 5.5-litre V-8 engine used in conjunction with a Jaguar gearbox. There is nothing to suggest that this 'monster' achieved anything in the way of competition success.

The main thrust of Kieft activities in 1954 was on production of a new 1100 cc sports/racing car and on their own air-cooled flat-four 1500 cc engine based on the AJB and fitted with Norton cylinder heads. There were severe overheating problems with this engine and although it was exhibited at the 1954 Earls Court show, development was abandoned. Another project was a 500 cc sports car which was to be powered by a 4-cylinder engine designed by John Turner. There were ambitious plans to lay down a line of 25 of these cars, but they came to nothing.

Much more serious and, potentially, much more successful was Kieft's new 1100 sports/racing car. This was based on a simple twin-tubular chassis with two main 3 in. steel members and the familiar suspension arrangement of wishbones and coil spring/damper units at the front and transverse leaf spring and wishbones at the rear. It was the first car to use the new Coventry-Climax FWA single overhead camshaft 1098 cc engine developing 72 bhp at 6300 rpm. Transmission was by a Moss 4-speed gearbox. It also featured neat, streamlined fibreglass bodywork. As events were to prove, its competition potential was limited, but it had good prospects as a production sports car.

At Le Mans a car was entered for Rippon/Black, and although it was no match for the Duntov/Oliver 1100 cc Porsche 550, it ran steadily until the back axle failed in the eleventh hour. Don Parker drove one of these cars in the 1500 cc sports car race at Silverstone in July, finishing well down the field, but lasting the distance to take third place in the 1100 cc class behind von Hanstein (Porsche) and Reece (Osca). At the Tourist Trophy on the Dundrod circuit two 1100 cc cars were entered by Kieft Cars Ltd. (in fact the company was still known as Cyril Kieft & Co. Ltd.) for Ferguson/Rippon and Parker/Boshier-Jones, and the private 1953 MG-powered car of Westcott/Bridger also ran as a member of the works team. Byrnes entered his 2-litre car for himself and Adams. Ferguson/Rippon were the sole finishers in the 1100 cc class, in twentieth place. Parker was at the wheel of the car he was sharing with Rippon when the front suspension broke and poked through the bodywork, while the Westcott/Bridger car was eliminated by a broken gearbox and the Byrnes/Adams entry was compulsorily retired because of body damage after striking a bank.

Kieft exhibited two 1100s, one in racing trim, at Earls Court in 1954 and in January 1955 John Bolster tested one of these cars for *Autosport*. The performance figures encompassed a maximum speed of 104.5 mph, 0–60 mph in 12.6 sec (quite respectable in those days), a standing quarter-mile in 18.2 sec and a fuel consumption of 30 mpg or thereabouts.

Bolster wrote:

'The 1100 cc Kieft is two cars in one. First of all, it is a smooth, quiet and tractable sports model, with perfect road manners. Fitted with the standard full-width screen, it would be quite practical as an everyday conveyance, and the remarkable resistance to impact possessed by fibre-glass bodies might well prove valuable on our grossly overcrowded roads. . . .

'Secondly, it is a competition model, designed *ab initio* for this work. Thus it already has brakes, roadholding and steering that are quite adequate for racing, and requires no extra equipment for this purpose. The engine gave every sign that it will stand up to the most gruelling event, and this is the sort of car that may well win victories by going on motoring when the rest have stopped.'

In other words, a nice little Club racer that could be used as an everyday car as well.

But the clock was winding down and Cyril Kieft had lost vast sums of money on various projects that were not pursued. In 1955 it was agreed that Berwyn Baxter, a successful Club racer with a C-type Jaguar, could use the name for works entries. Baxter agreed that he would race one of the 1100 cc chassis powered by the Turner 1500 cc engine, similar to the Connaught in that it was Lea-Francis based, with SU indirect fuel injection and twin-plug alloy head. In the early part of 1955 Baxter drove this car, registered LDA 5 (the number was probably switched from one of those allotted to a 1953 car, but exported), in Club events and then ran it at Le Mans. For this race the fuel injection was replaced by special Solex carburettors which necessitated an enormous air scoop on the bonnet. Baxter co-drove with John Deeley (an Austin-Healey racer), but the Kieft retired because of overheating on the sixth lap. Baxter was now thoroughly fed up with the unreliability of the inadequately developed Turner and substituted an Austin A50 engine for the Tourist Trophy at Dundrod, where Baxter's co-driver was Max Trimble. An 1100 cc car was also entered for Lord Louth/Rippon. Both Kiefts actually finished, but right at the tail of the field.

A nice little car, but not a serious sports/racer. The Kieft-Climax driven by Don Parker at Silverstone in July 1954. Number 23 is E. C. Harewood's MG (T. C. March)

The Kieft-Climax of Rippon/Merrick at Le Mans in 1955. The exhaust system looks somewhat fragile (T. C. March)

According to recent statements Berwyn Baxter acquired the assets of Kieft later in 1955, but reports of the time indicate that it was early 1956. Initially the new company, known as Kieft Sports Car Co. Ltd., operated from Nixon's Garage, Soho Road, Handsworth, but it transferred shortly afterwards to new premises in Bordesley Road, Birmingham. The company undertook the preparation of competition cars in addition to Berwyn Baxter's own Aston Martin DB3S and Max Trimble's Jaguars (his Jaguar career came to an end when he crashed an ex-Ecurie Ecosse D-type heavily at Spa in 1957). Once again there were ambitious plans for marketing a production version of the 1100 cc sports car, but these came to nothing. Kieft quietly faded away until the spring of 1960, when John Turvey and Lionel Mayman bought the company and used the name for a new Formula Junior car of which a very small number were built in 1961.

Killeen MG

This 1500 cc car was simultaneously a very advanced design for its time and outdated compared with its contemporaries. It was the design of Tom Killeen and was commissioned by Jack Newton of Newton Oils (well known in the 1950s for their Notwen brand), who raced the prototype Frazer Nash Le Mans Replica with considerable success. Killeen was keen to promote the principles of aircraft monocoque construction in the car world and the Killeen K1 was one of the first monocoque racing cars. Work on the design started in 1950, the drawings were completed in 1951 and the car built by 1953. When work started the Cooper-MG was the latest machine in the 1500 cc category, and when the car was completed Colin Chapman was about to launch the space-frame, aerodynamic Lotus 8 on an unsuspecting world. At the time when Chapman was designing and building new and advanced cars in a matter of a few months, it was inevitable that a car that took three years from inception to completion should be outdated when it was raced.

In *Classic and Sportscar* for September 1983, Editor-at-large Mike McCarthy gave an admirably succinct description of the Killeen monocoque: 'The basis of the K1 (as it became known after Tom designed a few other cars) was a main frame built up from three hoop-like formers of $\frac{1}{8}$ in. T-section steel spaced at approximately equal intervals, on to which six top-hat section steel stringers (in effect, fore-and-aft beams) were attached. The 16 swg Hinduminium skin was then attached to this frame by snap-head rivets. The scuttle and cockpit surround was made up from additional tubular formers, which were also used to provide extra local bracing for the skin where required, such as at the rear spring attachment bracket. Cockpit bulkheads in front of and behind the driver consisted of suitably braced Plymax diaphragms attached to the webs of the second and third former. The complete front suspension was mounted on a detachable bridge-like bracket spanning the bottom two stringers, which projected forward from the first former. The complete front suspension was mounted on a detachable bridge-like bracket spanning the bottom two stringers, which projected forward from the first former. Thus the K1's chassis consisted of an outer skin braced by fore and aft stringers and assorted hoops: simple, light, strong, ingenious.'

At the front, suspension was by lower wishbones and a transverse leaf spring and at the rear Killeen used a de Dion axle with trailing arms and quarter-elliptic springs. The engine was the familiar MG XPAG bored out to 1467 cc. It has been suggested because of its capacity that this engine was one of a batch built by MG for use in George Eyston's EX-MG streamlined record-breaking car, but this seems unlikely, as so many XPAG engines were bored out for racing. An MG TD gearbox was used and the final drive incorporated a fabricated casing made by Killeen himself. In appearance the Killeen was a neat, slim two-seater with cycle wings.

Newton raced the car over a three-year period, mainly in Club events, but also important races, including the 1500 cc sports car race at Silverstone in July 1954. This was a significant race, in which Chapman came out the winner with the streamlined Lotus Mk 8, Peter Gammon finished second with the unstreamlined Lotus Mk 6 and Hans Herrmann finished third with the works Porsche 550. D. C. Pitt brought the Killeen across the line in

An advanced concept, but not competitive. The Killeen-MG seen here driven by D. C. Pitt at Silverstone in July 1954 (T. C. March)

15th place—by no means the last finisher—but it was a fair indication of just how uncompetitive this square-rigged little car was. The Killeen's real merit lay in advanced construction features, certain of which Tom Killeen was able to patent, and for many years he pressed manufacturers and constructors to adopt his design ideas. Although the 1954 D-type Jaguar possessed a monocoque centre-section (which Killeen reckoned infringed his patents) it was not until the appearance of the Lotus 25 in 1962 that another monocoque racing design was seen and the concept became established.

Landar

In March 1965, Landar Components Ltd. of Dartmouth Street, Birmingham, run by Clive and Peter Radnall (hence the company's name) announced their new sports/racing car designed to take the Mini-Cooper engine, gearbox and transmission mounted at the rear of the chassis. It featured very low, sleek bodywork (it was only 2 ft 7 in. high) and was intended to run in the 1000 and 1150 cc classes in British racing. The following January Landar exhibited their car at the Racing Car Show at Olympia and this is how they described the car, typed the R6, in their catalogue entry:

'The Landar 1000 cc Sports Racing car . . . has been designed and developed for competition use utlizing the successful BMC Mini-Cooper engine/gearbox/transmission units mounted in the rear of the ultra-light Landar-designed multi-tubular and monocoque frame assembly. The front suspension is fully independent, incorporating wide-based tubular wishbones of unequal length, adjustable for wheel camber angle, Armstrong spring damper units and an anti-roll bar. The rear suspension is also fully independent, using upper and lower links of unequal length, radius arms, rubber cones and Armstrong telescopic dampers. These lower links are also adjustable for wheel camber angle.

'Wheels are a 4J section width, as standard, but magnesium alloy wheels of extra wide section can also be supplied. Rack-and-pinion steering together with an adjustable steering column and seats mounted at a racing reclining angle, giving lateral support, ensure a very relaxed driving position. The pedals are adjustable and together with the seating trim being removable, individual driving positions are possible.

'With the various engine capacities and the wide range of tuning available a high power/weight ratio is obtained, thereby making the car suitable for various classes.'

RIGHT *This advertisement from the catalogue of the 1966 Racing Car Show at Olympia shows off the very low lines of the Landar—and its makers' high hopes!*

When announced, a price of £945 in component form was quoted. One of these cars was raced in British events in 1966 by Tim Dykes and was offered for sale by the works in early 1967 at a price of £1050, while a new 1100 cc car with magnesium wheels and limited slip differential was offered at £1450. The R7 was the later slightly modified version. In all, 35 of these cars were built, of which 26 were said to have been exported. A small number of Formula Vee cars were also built by this company, together with the R5 and R6 prototypes with rear-mounted Ford engines, which were constructed in 1967 and 1970.

Another interesting project of similar concept to the Landar was the Aurora-BMC, powered by a 1150 cc BMC engine, only 2 ft 5 in. high and said to be capable of 135 mph. It was built for Trevor Taylor and Anita Taylor to race. Yet another car, with 998 cc Mini-Cooper engine and transmission mounted at the rear of a multi-tubular chassis, was the Unipower GT, introduced at the 1966 Racing Car Show, primarily intended for road use. Unipower survived until 1970, by when something over 60 cars had been built.

Leonard-MG

In early post-war days Lionel Leonard competed with an MG 'Special' based on an N-type four-seater that he had bought in 1938. He had used it as a road car until 1942, but then removed the body and gradually developed the car. The engine was bored out to make the capacity 1408 cc, a Marshall Roots-type supercharger was fitted (initially Leonard fitted a Centric supercharger), the gearbox was an ENV pre-selector from a Lagonda Rapier in an MG K-type casing and there was a light alloy two-seater body built by Harry Lester. Few changes were made to the chassis apart from the fitting of Hartford shock-absorbers at the rear. With this car, Leonard, working on it and preparing it at home, scored a string of successes in hillclimbs and sprints.

By 1950 Leonard was a recognized tuner and developer of MG XPAG engines, and the following year he bought a Cooper-MG, which he built up with the first of the 'Barchetta'-style bodies copied from a Superleggera Touring design for Ferrari.

MEET US ON STAND 46

TO SEE

THE

FANTASTIC

1000C SPORTS RACING CAR

The Landar 1000C sports racing car has been designed and developed for competition use, utilizing the successful BMC Mini Cooper engine/gearbox/transmission unit mounted in the rear of the ultra light Landar designed multi-tubular and monocoque frame assembly. The car features fully independent adjustable suspension, and disc brakes on all 4 wheels, together with rack and pinion steering fitted with an adjustable column, and full enveloping body, the highest point being only 30″ (.76m) from the ground. Engine removal is easily facilitated in 10-15 minutes by wheeling the power unit together with all ancillaries mounted in a subframe from the remainder of the car. With various engine capacities and the wide range of tuning available, high power/weight ratio is obtained, thereby making the car suitable to various racing classes.

FOR FURTHER DETAILS OF THIS BRILLIANT NEW CAR WRITE FOR ILLUSTRATED BROCHURE TO

COMPONENTS LTD

4-14 DARTMOUTH ST., BIRMINGHAM 7, ENGLAND. Tel.: ASTon Cross 1341-2

Leonard ran this car in a number of events in 1951, including the British Empire Trophy on the Douglas circuit in the Isle of Man, but he was generally unhappy with its performance. At the last Goodwood meeting of the season Cliff Davis made him an offer for the car and Leonard gladly accepted. It was ironic, in view of Leonard's reputation, that following an engine rebuild the car ran superbly and Davis enjoyed two thoroughly successful seasons of racing with it in 1952–53. In 1952 Leonard acquired another Cooper-MG, registered KOY 500, which he raced with the standard narrow body and cycle wings. It has to be conceded that Leonard was not a fast driver and this car went much quicker in the hands of Horace Gould, who raced it in 1953.

Lionel Leonard and Cliff Davis both acquired cars from John Tojeiro in 1953. Davis's car was the famous Bristol-powered LOY 500, while Leonard's car, with similar 'Barchetta' body, was registered LOY 501 and entered as a Leonard-MG. By this time Leonard was established in the motor trade with premises at Morrish Road in the Tulse Hill area of South London, and he decided that in the main he would enter the car for other, faster drivers. It would seem that the first appearance of the Leonard-MG was in the British Empire Trophy on the Isle of Man. Leonard himself drove, finishing fifth in the 1500 cc heat and eleventh place in the handicap final. At Davidstow on August Bank Holiday Saturday, Eric Brandon was at the wheel, winning his heat and the final of the 1500 cc sports car race. At the Crystal Palace in September Brandon retired because of steering trouble.

For 1954 Leonard built a second car, which was registered MOY 500, and the team, as it could now properly be called, contested some of the year's important races. In the British Empire Trophy, now held at Oulton Park, a single Leonard was entered for Stirling Moss, who finished third in his heat and went well in the final until the MG engine broke its crankshaft. In the rain-soaked Sports Car race at the May Silverstone meeting a single Leonard was driven by Les Leston, but it finished at the tail of the field, outside the 1500 cc class results. David Blakely was at the wheel at Snetterton on Whit Sunday, finishing third in the 1500 cc race, and drove again in the 1500 cc race at Silverstone in July. The writer considers this to be one of the most important 1500 cc races, with a very large entry comprising just about every British car of the capacity racing at the time and two works Porsche 550s. The results were dominated by Lotus, with Herrmann's works Porsche third, and Leonard was eleventh—a result that made quite clear the lack of competitiveness of the Leonard (and for that matter most other traditional MG-powered cars).

At the International Sports Car race at Zandvoort in August, Blakely was again at the wheel, and the second car was driven by Leonard. Blakely's LOY 501 threw a rod and Leonard's MOY 500 ran its bearings. There was a 100-mile sports car race at Silverstone in September, won by Crook's Cooper-Bristol, but Blakely drove a good race with MOY 500 to finish fifth overall and second in the 1500 cc class to Jackson's ex-Davis Cooper-MG.

Leonard withdrew from racing at the end of the year, but stayed in business supplying components to other constructors. By 1956 he had given up his premises and in the early part of the year was building a new Leonard-MG in the garage belonging to Chris Bristow's father. Eighteen-year-old Chris was very taken with the Leonard and persuaded his father to buy it. He raced it throughout 1956 as the Bristow-MG, but by the following year had moved on to a Cooper-Climax. It had played an important role in the learning curve of a driver who was to earn a place at the wheel of a Formula 1 car.

ABOVE LEFT *Eric Brandon at the wheel of the unpainted Leonard-MG at the Cornish Davidstow circuit in August 1953*

LEFT *David Blakely with LOY 501 at Zandvoort in August 1954—the MG engine has just thrown a conrod*

Lester

Harry Lester ran a garage business on the Bath Road at Thatcham in Berkshire; he was involved with MG Midgets in the thirties, and in early post-war days modified MG PB 'Midgets' and built a special based on the MG TC. The borderline between the Lester-built 'Special' and the first of the Lester-MGs is a very narrow one. It seems, however, that the true first member of the breed was the car built by Lester in 1949 (KUR 4) and raced by him for two seasons.

The basis of the Lester was a very simple chassis based on two 16-gauge 3 in. diameter tubes upswept at the front, suitably cross-braced by two main cross-members and two rear members. Front suspension was independent by the MG Y-series (saloon) coil springs and wishbones, while at the rear there was a live axle and semi-elliptic springs. The MG rack-and-pinion steering was discarded in favour of a cam-type box. Lester used the MG TC engine linered down to give a capacity of 1087 cc

(62 × 90 mm). Transmission was by a standard MG TC gearbox to a TA rear axle. Morris Ten disc wheels were fitted. The body was a very functional light alloy 2-seater with streamlined nose cowl and cycle wings.

For 1950 a second car was built for Jim Mayers, in many ways less sophisticated than Lester's own car. This example used a standard MG TA chassis and a rather starker body from an earlier Lester project, but the engine was bored and stroked to give a capacity of what was said to be 1474 cc. With special Lester cylinder head, twin SUs on a special inlet manifold, 10:1 compression ratio and Scintilla Vertex magneto, its performance was pretty formidable by the standards of the time and it was good for over 100 mph. With this car, registered KJH 114, Mayers won the 1950 *Motor Sport* Brooklands Memorial Trophy, awarded on points scored at Goodwood Members' meetings during the year.

Mayers' car was replaced for 1951 by a new Lester (NNK 526) with tubular ifs chassis and much smoother body (but still retaining cycle wings), and a similar car was supplied to Pat Griffith (MG 6850). The Lesters first caught attention when Mayers' and Griffith's entries were accepted for the handicap British Empire Trophy Sports Car race held on the very difficult Douglas circuit in the Isle of Man. Despite limited racing experience, Griffith drove magnificently and with a 3-lap handicap advantage led until two laps before the finish, when his MG engine ran out of oil and seized up. In September Lester-MGs were entered

ABOVE *J. C. C. Mayers at Goodwood in 1950 with his first and rather primitive Lester-MG (LAT)*

ABOVE RIGHT *The Lester-MG of Mayers/Keen in the 1952 Goodwood Nine Hours race. They finished sixth overall and won their class (LAT)*

for Harry Lester and Jim Mayers in the Tourist Trophy on the Dundrod circuit in Northern Ireland, but both retired because of engine trouble. The following month Griffith and Threlfall took second and third places to Cliff Davis (Cooper-MG) at Castle Combe.

For 1952 Mayers, Griffith and Gerry Ruddock (previously an HRG driver) formed themselves into a team known as 'The Monkey Stable' to race a trio of Lester-MGs. The Monkey Stable made its debut at the Easter Goodwood meeting and raced throughout the year with consistent success in the 1500 cc class. At Ibsley in April, Mayers and Ruddock took first and third places in a 1500 cc sports car race, Ruddock finished second in the 1500 cc class of the Production Sports Car race at Silverstone in May (yes, the organizers would accept virtually anything as a production sports car!), Ruddock won his class at Prescott in May and then the team turned to serious road racing.

At the end of May, Pat Griffith made up for his misfortune in 1951 by winning the British Empire Trophy at an average of 64.20 mph from team-mate Ruddock. Six weeks later the team scored another fine success when Mayers and Griffith took

first and second places in the 1500 cc class of the Jersey International Road Race ahead of Cliff Davis's Cooper-MG. On 2 August another fine success followed at the International Boreham meeting, where Mayers and Griffith took first and third places in the 1500 cc class of the 100-mile sports car race for cars of up to 2000 cc—almost inevitably they were split by Cliff Davis and his Cooper-MG. In the Goodwood Nine Hours another fine success followed when Mayers/Keen (sixth overall), Ruddock/Peacock (seventh overall) and Leston/Line (tenth overall) took the first three places in the 1500 cc class, soundly trouncing Davis's Cooper-MG. In addition the Monkey Stable took the team prize. A bare week later Ruddock set a new class record at the Shelsley Walsh hillclimb. This was followed up by a class win in the Brighton Speed Trials by Lester himself, with Ruddock taking a class second. Of course, the Monkey Stable suffered some defeats during 1952, but their well-prepared and well-driven, basically very simple cars more than proved their worth in the more strenuous British events.

However, perhaps ambitious for greater success, the Monkey Stable switched to Kieft cars for 1953, whilst over the next two years Gerry Ruddock continued to race his Lester, fitting a one-section bonnet with more aerodynamic front wings for 1954 and still enjoying a fair measure of success. The writer recalls this very well-turned-out and neatly driven car winning its class at Westbrook Hay hillclimb in May 1954. Later in the year Ruddock set a new class record at Shelsley Walsh hillclimb. Ruddock was very much the keen amateur, competing for the pleasure of the sport and without any serious ambitions. In 1953 Harry Lester continued development on a small scale and his own car was a very neat Lester-MG coupé (HJB 790), apparently incorporating Fiat panels, which he raced in a few Club events in 1953. The Monkey Stable cars passed to other amateurs, who competed with some success, and when Cyril Wick, having just bought the ex-Whitehead Cooper-Jaguar, advertised his Lester-MG in April 1955, he wrote, 'A very high power/weight ratio and superb roadholding make this a most desirable fully equipped road car.' A fair summary of the qualities of one of the more successful of MG-powered sports/racing cars of the early 1950s.

For 1955 The Monkey Stable was re-formed with a team of drivers consisting of Jim Mayers, Mike Keen, Trevor Line and Mike Llewellyn. At the small Monkey Stable workshops in North London a new team of cars to Lester design was put in hand. Once again the chassis was based on twin-tubular members, of 3.5 in. diameter, but there was now independent suspension all round, at the front by very substantial unequal-length wishbones, coil springs and André telescopic friction-type dampers, whilst at the rear there was a transverse leaf spring, wishbones and André dampers. The plan was that the first car should have a 1467 cc MG XPAG engine and the next two cars would be powered by Coventry-Climax FWA 1098 cc engines. Lockheed brakes in 11.5 in. Al-fin drums were used. The most striking feature of the new

NPO20
12
5 EME

LEFT *Gerry Ruddock climbs Prescott with his Lester-MG in May 1954. This car had a modified front with the wings integral with the bonnet (T. C. March)*

BELOW LEFT *The unsuccessful Lester coupé with fibreglass body and MG engine driven by Jim Mayers at Silverstone in May 1955 (T. C. March)*

Lester was its smooth and shapely fibreglass coupé body with very pronounced tail fins.

Since 1953 the 1100 cc and 1500 cc classes had been transformed by the appearance of the technically advanced Lotus Mk 8, and 1955 saw the appearance of Cooper's very ingenious and quick Climax-powered rear-engined car. The new Lester was very much of the old school of design and it was, inevitably, hopelessly outclassed. It appears that in all three cars were completed, but the Monkey Stable raced them very little and the team was effectively destroyed by the deaths of Mike Keen with a Cooper-Bristol in the Goodwood Nine Hours race and Jim Mayers in the Tourist Trophy at Dundrod. Before the end of the season both Climax-powered cars had been sold, but Llewellyn continued to run one car in a few events without success.

Lister

Inspired by Brian Lister's motor racing enthusiasm and financed to publicize the products of George Lister & Sons Ltd. of Cambridge, Lister's racing fame rose quickly, and has been kept alive by the success of the Jaguar-powered cars in Historic Sports Car events. Brian Lister ran a Cooper-MG linered down to 1100 cc, and then in 1952 bought a Tojeiro, which he powered by a transversely mounted JAP V-twin air-cooled engine. Lister drove the cars himself until he was beaten in a sprint by Archie Scott-Brown with an MG TD. He was so impressed by Scott-Brown's driving that he invited him to handle the Tojeiro. Scott-Brown was sadly deformed, only five feet in height, with a right arm ending with only a thumb and part of a palm. His driving over the years proved that his physical handicaps were no handicap to him behind the wheel of both sports/racing cars and single-seaters, and he became an integral and inseparable part of the small Lister organization, and when he died as the result of burns suffered at Spa in 1958, the spirit of the Lister organization died with him. The third member of this successful team was Don Moore, who tuned the engines fitted to Lister cars and ran his own garage business in Cambridge.

Lister-MG

With Scott-Brown at the wheel the Tojeiro-JAP enjoyed a fabulous run of success in Club events and to Lister it seemed logical that the company should build its own car, as the potential for worthwhile publicity was immense. Lister drew up his own plans and construction went ahead in 1953 quickly enough for the new car to make its debut at Snetterton in April 1954.

The 7 ft 6 in. wheelbase chassis was constructed from two 3 in. steel tubular members at full body-width at the cockpit, where they were linked by a cross-member of the same diameter and tapering in towards the front and rear, where there were similar cross-members. At the front there was a fabricated mounting to carry the unequal-length wishbones and coil spring/damper units. Further fabricated mountings were used at the rear, linked by a tubular cross-member; there was de Dion rear suspension with the tube located by a vertical centre-slide and twin parallel radius arms; coil spring/damper units ran to the ends of the upper cross-member. Rack-and-pinion steering was fitted, there were Girling brakes in Al-fin drums, inboard at the rear, and the car (chassis BHL1) first appeared with pressed-steel disc wheels. Knock-on wire wheels were later fitted. The body was a very simple all-enveloping two-seater built by Wakefield's of Byfleet, but distinguished by detachable pointed covers over the headlamps and by its bright mid-green finish and yellow stripe. This first Lister, registered MER 303, was powered by an MG 1467 cc engine and fitted with an MG gearbox.

At Snetterton Scott-Brown won two races and then ran the following day in a sprint at Weathersfield, but plagued by fuel starvation problems could only manage third in the 1500 cc sports class. Next the car was entered in the British Empire Trophy race at Oulton Park, and in practice Scott-Brown was third fastest in the 1500 cc class. Prospects for the race seemed excellent until on the Friday morning the race stewards announced that Scott-Brown would not be allowed to compete because of his disability and his competition licence was revoked. It was a bitter blow, especially as Scott-Brown had already been competing for some while without any problems.

There was a fight on to get the licence back, but in the meanwhile Ken Wharton, who was without a

drive at Oulton Park, took over the Lister and held fourth place in the 1500 cc heat until the oil pressure dropped; after a brief pit stop he rejoined the race to finish eighth, which was not quite good enough to qualify for the final. Subsequently Brian Lister drove the Lister-MG at Brands Hatch, taking second place to Gammon's Lotus, Jack Sears was entered at Prescott hillclimb but was slowed by ignition problems, and was second at Snetterton on Whit Sunday on handicap to Brian Naylor's Cooper-MG. By Whit Monday 1954 Scott-Brown had regained his licence and was entered at Brands Hatch. He finished second to Peter Gammon's Lotus Mk 6-MG, was second again to Gammon at Oulton Park in June and took a second at Snetterton to Gammon.

Lister-Bristols

These results confirmed what Brian Lister had realized early in the season, that the Lister-MG was no match in terms of weight or cornering power for the Lotus opposition. He had already decided to move up a class and a Bristol-powered car was under construction. Engine and gearbox apart, the Lister-Bristol was virtually identical to the first car, but could be distinguished by a much broader yellow stripe. The Lister-Bristol (chassis BHL 2) made its debut at the British Grand Prix meeting at Silverstone in the Unlimited Sports Car race and the Lister-MG was also entered in the 1500 cc event. In a very strong field Scott-Brown could manage no better than seventh place in the 1500 cc race. It was a very different story in the Unlimited event, held on a damp, oil and rubber-soaked track; Scott-Brown finished fifth behind three works Aston Martins and the Lagonda, winning the 2000 cc class and making the C-type Jaguar drivers (including Ecurie Ecosse) look rather silly.

From now on in 1954 it was success all the way, and during the remainder of the season there were some fantastic scraps between Scott-Brown and Roy Salvadori at the wheel of the Gilby Engineering Maserati A6GCS, a difficult left-hand-drive car with lots of power and poor torque. Scott-Brown raced again a week after Silverstone at the Fairwood aerodrome circuit near Swansea, finishing second with the Lister-MG in the 1500 cc Sports Car race to Chapman's streamlined Mk 8 Lotus-MG and winning the 2500 cc race from Chapman. In addition he finished second in the Unlimited race to Michael Head's well-driven C-type Jaguar. On August Bank Holiday Monday Scott-Brown was out again with the Lister-MG, winning his heat of the 1500 cc National Sports car from Champman and finishing second in the final to Alan Brown's Connaught. In the Formule Libre Rochester Cup he drove the Lister-Bristol, rather outpaced by the faster single-seaters, but finishing fifth on the aggregate of two heats behind a quartet of Connaughts.

At the International Snetterton meeting in August there was the first of the series of magnificent duels between Scott-Brown and Salvadori. *Autosport* commented, 'The Lister-Bristol was a revelation on corners, going round as if on rails; Salvadori pulled out all the stops, but that tantalizing green and yellow machine would not be caught. . . . Archie lapped in 1 min. 53 sec. (85.41 mph), a cracking pace for a 2-litre . . . Brian Lister's face was one huge grin when he welcomed his winning driver, and he also patted Jack Sears on the back for a fine third place with the $1\frac{1}{2}$-litre car.' Sears was of course at the wheel of the Lister-MG and took third place in the 1500 cc class behind McAlpine (Connaught) and Coombs (Lotus-Connaught).

In *Autosport* for 27 August, 1954, John Bolster road-tested the Lister-Bristol and the results speak for themselves:

ABOVE LEFT *Jack Sears with the Lister-MG at Prescott in May 1954. He was out of the running in the 1500 cc Sports Car class because of ignition problems (T. C. March)*

BELOW *On the debut of the Lister-Bristol at Silverstone in July 1954 Scott-Brown harries Manussis' C-type Jaguar. Behind him is Davis's Tojeiro-Bristol (T. C. March)*

TEST PILOT: Archie Scott-Brown winning his heat at the recent Daily Telegraph *Brands Hatch meeting.*

All of us will long remember Archie Scott-Brown's performance in the sports car race at the Silverstone Grand Prix meeting. He not only won the 2-litre class, but soundly trounced the $3\frac{1}{2}$-litre brigade. The Lister-Bristol which he drove on that occasion has been prominent on many circuits this year, and so it was a great privilege for me to take over the car for a few days recently.

The Lister is now in production, and several orders have already been accepted. For various reasons, it has been found preferable to let the customer supply his own engine, and body panelling is also carried out by any chosen coachbuilder. Similarly, the tyres are the owner's responsibility, because he is usually a racing driver who can get them at a specially reduced rate. The machine will generally be sold in chassis form, therefore, but as "my" Lister was a complete car I shall treat the rest of this report as a normal road test.

JOHN BOLSTER TESTS

THE LISTER - BRISTOL

Cambridge-built Competition 2-litre a stable and tractable 130 m.p.h. Sports Car

The basis of the vehicle is a tubular frame, of which the two main members swell outwards at the centre. They approach each other again at either end, where they join the fabricated uprights that carry the suspension units. In front, there are equal length wishbones, and at the rear, a de Dion axle. Suspension all round is by helical springs and telescopic dampers. The rear brakes are inboard mounted and the hypoid unit is a Salisbury.

The engine is set well back in the frame, and, since the wheelbase is only 7 ft. 6 ins., this means that the rear of the crankcase must come alongside the driver's feet. As the body is wide, this is of no consequence, and it makes possible the use of a delightfully short and rigid lever, mounted directly in the lid of the gearbox. The radiator block is a Morris Oxford unit, carried very low and with a small separate header tank. There is also an oil radiator.

The power unit is the competition version of the 2-litre Bristol. This is called the BS4, and has a camshaft with considerable overlap, driven by gears instead of the usual chain. The running is somewhat bumpy below 3,000 r.p.m., but from that speed onwards the engine "takes hold" in a most refreshing manner. In racing, 6,000 r.p.m. is frequently employed, but I contented myself with 5,500 r.p.m. throughout my tests, except when timing the maximum speed, which entailed something in the region of 5,800 r.p.m. in top gear.

During the time that I had the car I covered a considerable mileage. London was crossed from end to end twice, Oulton Park was visited and lapped, and the usual timed tests were also made. On the road, the machine is reasonably quiet at moderate revolutions, and I had no trouble with noise, over-heating, or oiling up. This competition car makes a perfectly good hack, in fact, though the engine is obviously happier when it is allowed to turn over briskly.

This is a small car, and only weighs 12 cwt. Yet it is entirely stable at the very high speeds of which it is capable. I felt no qualms in driving at 130 m.p.h. with one hand while operating the stop watch with the other, which proves that the steering and suspension are about right. The springing is not hard, but the dampers have a fairly firm setting. Even at maximum speed the car rides perfectly level, and it is unaffected by gusts of wind, which cannot be said of many modern "all-enveloping" jobs.

The driving position is curious. One sits very low down and the body comes up almost to one's shoulders. Yet there is none of the difficulty in placing the car that one might expect. The steering is very light, and corners can be taken fast without any sawing at the wheel. This is very much a machine for the more advanced driver. It is like the modern racing car, inasmuch as it has extremely high cornering power but does not, by rolling, screaming of tyres, or other signs of distress, give warning that the limit is being approached. Yet one seems to develop a sixth sense—to get in the groove, so to speak—and corners can then be taken at very high speed in absolute safety and certainty. I admit that I spun off the new banked bend at Oulton while acquiring the technique, but that is another story!

I was warned that the brakes were due for servicing after several hard-fought races, but they remained powerful throughout my test, albeit with increased pedal travel. Only an occasional suspicion of judder confirmed that attention would soon be required. No fading was ever experienced, a most essential requirement if that tremendous performance were to be exploited in safety.

The gearbox is an absolute delight. Although there is effective synchromesh in the three upper ratios, this does not prevent the very quickest changes being made. The acceleration figures speak for themselves, and it will be seen that the graph goes up like a lift. I would say

COMPACT dimensions, with a 7 ft. 6 ins. wheelbase, and 4 ft. $2\frac{1}{2}$ ins. track, feature in the Lister tubular chassis, which utilizes helical spring suspension all round with de Dion rear end.

FRONT END, showing the fabricated vertical members supporting the upper suspension wishbones and the helical spring for each wheel.

REAR END, detailing the Lister's de Dion layout, the helical spring suspension, the inboard brakes and Salisbury hypoid drive unit.

that the racing successes of this car stem almost as much from its acceleration as from its exceptionally fast cornering.

The de Dion axle is a very obvious asset. It has parallel radius rods each side, and a sliding block looks after the lateral location. Once one has driven a car like this, one does not wish to return to the conventional axle with its many disadvantages. It is of considerable interest that equal length wishbones have been adopted for the front suspension, and that there is no anti-roll bar. The car is so low, however, that the adoption of a system with a roll centre at ground level has no apparent penalty, and the freedom from gyroscopic manifestations must be beneficial.

It is often alleged these days that the cars in sports car races are merely "specials", and of no use for serious touring. I disproved this with the Lister, for I drove it about like a normal saloon (only much faster!). It starts instantly at all times, and although no hood was fitted, the body deflected the wind over my head, and most of the rain was carried away. A fair amount of engine heat is retained inside the shell, and I seldom wore an overcoat even in cold weather. If the general standard of comfort met with my approval, one exception was the seat. We have heard of the queen with Calais printed on her heart, but I am sure that I shall have Lister printed on my posterior for many weeks to come!

The accessibility of the mechanical components is first-class. The whole of the front of the body forms the bonnet, and when it is swung open the engine is entirely free of obstructions. A large door in the rear of the body renders the de Dion assembly equally easy to service. This is of immense value for racing, but it would be of advantage even under the more leisurely conditions of normal use.

The Lister is a well-built competition car of superb handling qualities and very high performance. With a cover over the

ACCELERATION GRAPH OF THE LISTER-BRISTOL

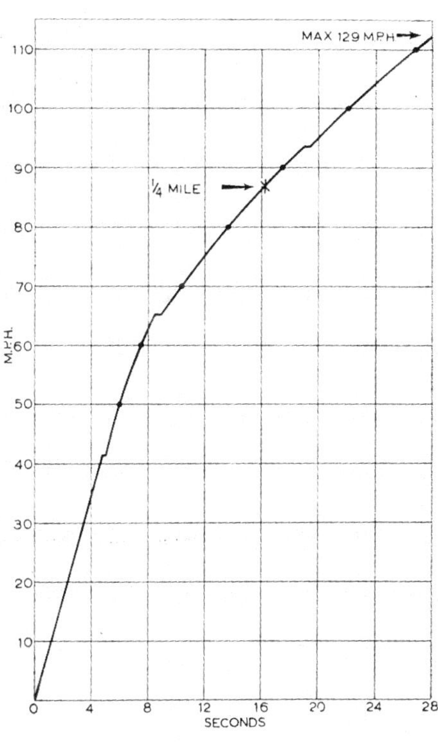

THROUGH SCOTT-BROWN'S VIZOR: (Above) The view forward from the driver's seat showing the stubby gear-change lever. A fuel tank is seen on the left.

POWER - PACK: The BS4 competition-type 2-litre Bristol engine is set well back in the Lister frame.

The Lister-Bristol—*continued*

passenger's seat, and some attention to the air intake, I feel that something like 140 m.p.h. would be available. Even in its present undeveloped form it reaches 130 m.p.h. with a couple of hundred revs. in hand, which is terrific motoring for a 2-litre. Messrs. George Lister & Sons, of Cambridge, have certainly produced a very fine little motor.

SPECIFICATION AND PERFORMANCE DATA

Car Tested: Lister-Bristol sports two-seater. Price, chassis only, less engine, gearbox, tyres and tubes, £465, plus tax.

Engine: Six cylinders in line, 66 mm. x 96 mm. (1,971 c.c.). Pushrod operated inclined valves in light alloy head. 142 b.h.p. at 5,750 r.p.m. 9 to 1 compression ratio. Three downdraught Solex carburetters. Delco Remy distributor, Lucas coil.

Transmission: Borg and Beck single dry plate clutch. Four-speed gearbox with short central lever. Ratios: 3.73, 4.8, 6.7, and 10.7 to 1. (Alternative final drive ratios of 4.1 and 4.56 also available.) Salisbury hypoid differential unit, driving rear hubs through Hardy Spicer universally jointed half shafts.

Chassis: Three-inch T.45 seamless drawn steel tubing with fabricated uprights. Independent front suspension by equal length wishbones with long threaded king pins. Forward mounted rack and pinion steering. De Dion tube rear axle, located by sliding block and parallel radius rods. Helical springs all-round, embracing Woodhead-Monroe telescopic dampers. Dunlop racing wire wheels with knock-on caps, fitted 5.50 in. x 16 in. racing tyres. Girling hydraulic brakes with 11 in. x 1¼ in. Al-Fin drums, 2LS in front, inboard mounted at rear.

Equipment: 12-volt lighting and starting. Speedometer, rev. counter, oil pressure gauge, oil and water temperature gauges.

Dimensions: Wheelbase, 7 ft. 6 ins.; track, front 4 ft. 2½ ins., rear 4 ft. 2 ins. Weight of complete car without fuel or oil, 12 cwt.

Performance: Maximum speed, 129 m.p.h. Speeds in gears: 3rd 94 m.p.h., 2nd 66 m.p.h., 1st 41 m.p.h. Standing quarter mile, 16.2 secs. Acceleration: 0-50 m.p.h. 6 secs., 0-60 m.p.h. 7.6 secs., 0-70 m.p.h. 10.4 secs., 0-80 m.p.h. 13.8 secs., 0-90 m.p.h. 17.4 secs., 0-100 m.p.h. 21.8 secs., 0-110 m.p.h. 26.6 secs.

Fuel Consumption: 22 m.p.g. (approx.).

A fortnight later it was Scott-Brown versus Salvadori again in the Unlimited Sports Car race at Castle Combe and Salvadori won by two-fifths of a second. To quote *Autosport* again, '. . . the cars were so close sometimes that they almost became a Maserlister—or would it be a Listerati?'—unconscious prescience on the part of Cyril Posthumus? In Roy Salvadori's long racing career the highlights for him were his drives for the works Aston Martin team and his many dices with Archie. Roy trusted Archie's driving implicitly and knew that he would never put a wheel wrong to the detriment of another driver. At Castle Combe Scott-Brown also drove the Lister-MG, but the engine was misfiring badly.

At the Brighton Speed Trials Scott-Brown finished second in the 2000 cc sports class and the following day competed with both Listers at Brands Hatch. He was narrowly beaten into second place in the 1500 cc Sports Car race by Coombs' Lotus-Connaught and in the 2000 cc sports car race by Crook's Cooper-Bristol—Crook's *quasi*-single seater was another immensely fast car of the period and when his car lasted the distance he was never beaten by either Archie or Salvadori. At the Crystal Palace Archie was again second in the 1500 cc race to Chapman's Lotus, but he made a rare mistake in the 2000 cc race, spun and rejoined the race to finish fifth. Stirling Moss drove the Lister-Bristol at the September Goodwood meeting, allegedly because the BARC would not accept Scott-Brown's entry, and was very narrowly beaten by Salvadori. Some critics have regarded Salvadori's win as a pointer that the Lister was not quite a match for the Maserati, but Roy reckons that it was because Moss did not have time in practice to get the Lister set up to his liking. At Aintree, Scott-Brown was beaten into second place in the 2000 cc class of the Sports Car race by Tony Crook. Scott-Brown won the 2500 cc race at the last Snetterton meeting of the year from Salvadori. In the final race of the day, a handicap, Chapman spun the Mk 8 Lotus in front of Scott-Brown and Lotus and Lister went off the course and into the wooden hurdles.

In December 1954 there was an interesting exchange in the correspondence columns of *Austosport* about the Lister-Bristol and the potential of a Bristol-engined Lotus (at this time it was not publicly known that Lotus were planning the Bristol-engined Mk 10). Keith Fuller's letter appeared in the issue of 10 December:

'I have been considering which sports car to race next season, and the test report on the 85 bhp Lotus-MG enabled me to compare it with the 142 bhp Lister-Bristol, and I observed the following: from a standing start and using maximum acceleration, after the quarter mile the Lotus is 0.7 sec (*i.e.*, about 30 ft) ahead of the Lister and keeps in the lead until about 90 mph is reached, where the Lister begins to pull away. Their top speeds are 121 mph and 129 mph, respectively.

'Suppose we now consider a Lotus-Bristol. The bhp needed to propel a car at its maximum velocity is proportional to something between the square and the cube of the maximum velocity, depending on the efficiency of the aerodynamics. This means that a Lotus-Bristol would have a top speed of 144 mph to 156 mph with acceleration to match. Add disc brakes to this, and surely it would be unbeatable in the 2-litre class.

'My choice is, therefore, decided and my next step is to find somebody to provide me with a Lotus-Bristol in exchange for my motor-cycle.'

Mr. M. A. E. Manning replied in the issue of 17 December:

'Once again we are faced with an odious comparison between cars in different classes.

'Does Mr. Fuller expect to substitute the 140 bhp Bristol engine for the MG in the Lotus chassis without a serious weight penalty and reshuffle of gear ratios?

'The Lotus-MG relies on its low weight, axle ratio

Regardless of their aerodynamic efficiency, the lines of the Thom Lucas-designed Lister-Bristol were exceptionally distinctive

and admirable lack of wheelspin to create its standing start times. It is not at all certain that a Bristol-engined Lotus with its altered weight distribution and an axle ratio chosen for a maximum speed of 150 mph would accelerate as well as the MG-engined car.

'What a fine, and above all, consistent, performance Archie Scott-Brown put up last season in a new and undeveloped car, with, let's face it, an apology for bodywork. I expect next year's Lister Bristol to have better performance and give Mr. Fuller, or any other conductor in any 2-litre combination what they like, a first-class run for his money.

'Incidentally, what is this fabulous motor-cycle Mr. Fuller has for exchange?'

Miaow!

It is of course a matter of history that the Lotus Mk 10 with Bristol engine was simply no match for the Lister.

For 1955 Scott-Brown continued to race the 1954 Lister-Bristol, while the Lister-MG was dismantled. In response to demand throughout the latter part of 1954 Lister decided to go ahead with a small number of production chassis. There were a number of mechanical changes; the rear coil spring/damper units now ran at an angle from the ends of the de Dion tube to a tall, vertical bridge; the Morris Minor rack-and-pinion steering rack was raised from the front cross-member to a mounting at hub height on a vertical frame; and there were new drum brakes with very large 12 × 2.25 in. finned drums.

The most significant change was the completely new body designed by Thom Lucas, a Bristol-based aerodynamacist, with a very low nose line, large hump on the bonnet to clear the deep Bristol engine, distinctive 'eyebrows' at the tops of the front wheel and large tail fins. Although Lucas had developed this body design through wind-tunnel tests, there seems little doubt that the basic style had been inspired by Frank Costin's body for the Lotus Mk 8, which had been developed *without* wind-tunnel testing.

In all eight cars were delivered in 1955 but it must be remembered that Listers could be supplied as complete cars (which incurred purchase tax), in component form or as a bare chassis without engine, gearbox or body. The deliveries were as follows:

BHL3 (registered VPP9): sold to solicitor Ormsby Issard-Davies for Alan Moore to drive; Lucas aerodynamic body. This car was later fitted with chassis BHL1.

BHL4 (registered 4 CNO): sold to Bill Black for Jack Sears to drive; Lucas aerodynamic body.

BHL5 (registered HCH 736): John Green for David Hampshire to drive; Lucas aerodynamic body.

BHL6 (registered SNX 590); Ken Eaton; one-off body; not raced extensively and later passed to that great Aston Martin enthusiast Kenneth Yeates. Chassis identification believed correct.

BHL7 (registered NVE 732): Noel Cunningham-Reid of the Six-Mile Stable; Lucas aerodynamic body. Chassis identification possibly correct.

BHL8: Supplied to Murkett Bros. Ltd. of Huntingdon, who were Jaguar and Rover dealers; one-off body; raced with Rover engine and offered for sale in 1958 with Jaguar 2.4-litre engine. Chassis identification possibly correct.

Scott-Brown with the Lister-Bristol at Silverstone in May 1955. He retired because of a blown gasket. Note that the car no longer has pointed headlamp covers, the hump in the bonnet has a small mesh-covered intake and one side-light cover is missing (T. C. March)

Lister's season started with the British Empire Trophy at Oulton Park and after the indignities and humiliation of 1954 it proved very satisfactory. In his heat Scott-Brown finished second to Parnell's experimental 2.5-litre Aston Martin DB3S and won the handicap final at 73.53 mph from McAlpine (Connaught) and Parnell. Sears was fifth in the heat and sixth in the final. Success after success, with very few failures, followed with wins for Scott-Brown in the 2000 cc race at the Easter Goodwood meeting, the 2750 cc race at Ibsley at the end of April, a retirement because of a blown gasket at the May Silverstone meeting (Moore was third in the 2000 class), two wins at Snetterton on Whit Saturday (including beating Peter Collins' ex-works Aston Martin in the Unlimited race), a win over Salvadori's ex-works Aston in the Unlimited race at the Crystal Palace on Whit Monday and a win in the 2000 cc class and second to Salvadori's Aston in the Eastern Counties '100' race at the end of June. Some comment on these successes is necessary. There was now less opposition in the 2000 cc class because Salvadori was now racing a particularly ill-handling brute in the shape of a Cooper-Maserati and Tony Crook had temporarily retired from racing. Archie had beaten Salvadori at the Crystal Palace only after the latter had spun on wet tar and lost his lead.

In July Scott-Brown won from Salvadori with the Cooper-Maserati at Brands Hatch, he retired because of a broken throttle on the start line of the Sports Car race at the British Grand Prix meeting at Aintree (David Hampshire won the 2-litre class for Lister) and more successes followed over the August Bank Holiday weekend. In the Unlimited Sports Car race at the Crystal Palace on the Saturday Archie had to settle for second place behind Salvadori with a works Aston Martin DB3S, but he won the Unlimited Sports Car race at Brands Hatch on the Monday. At the International Charterhall meeting he won the 2700 cc race with Cunningham-Reid third, and in the Unlimited *Newcastle Journal* Trophy he was third behind Titterington (Ecurie Ecosse Jaguar D-type) and Rosier (Ferrari Monza), but beat Sanderson's Ecurie Ecosse D-type into fourth place.

The following weekend Archie made a rare

The 1956 Lister-Maserati was sleek, low and very quick, but plagued by engine problems. Scott-Brown is seen in the British Empire Trophy at Oulton Park (T. C. March)

mistake at the International Snetterton meeting. He was leading the 2750 cc race when he missed a gear at the hairpin, the Lister went out of control and Archie ducked beneath the dash as the car rolled. In the Goodwood Nine Hours race Lister honour was upheld by private owners, and the 2000 cc class was won by David Hampshire/Peter Scott-Russell, who finished ninth overall. At the Le Mans start Scott-Russell had bashed the front of the Lister against another car and the night hours were covered on one headlamp. Another retirement in the *Daily Herald* International Trophy at Oulton Park followed for Scott-Brown, who accelerated the Lister into the back of Salvadori's Aston while Roy was trying to find a gear that would actually engage! At the International, Aintree the crankshaft of the works Lister broke and victory in the 2000 cc class went to Cunningham-Reid. Salvadori had acquired the ex-Green Lister by the Castle Combe meeting at the beginning of October (Gilby were considering running a Lister in 1956) and finished third in the 2000 cc Sports Car race behind Bueb (Cooper-Climax) and Chapman (Lotus-Climax).

It had been a magnificent season for Lister, and when the works Lister-Bristol was advertised for sale at £1850, the copy read—and with justification—'. . . Apart from five retirements due to mechanical trouble or accidents this car has not lost a race this season to any car of up to 2 litres. It has, in fact, not only proved itself to be the fastest 2-litre sports car in the country by a long way, but apart from the works Jaguars and Aston Martins one of the fastest sports cars irrespective of capacity.' In fact the car was not sold, but was dismantled, and soon its famous registration would be seen on an even faster and equally successful Lister.

Lister-Maserati

For 1956 Lister produced a much revised works car with new sleek bodywork and Maserati A6GCS engine based on the original chassis BHL1 registered MER 303. Brian Lister and Don Moore believed that the added power and punch of the Maserati engine could ensure the team's continuing success in the 2-litre class. Perhaps if they had liaised more closely with Sid Greene of Gilby Engineering and Roy Salvadori they would have changed their minds; for although Gilby found the A6GCS very reliable (which Lister did not), they had been unhappy with the narrow power band and torque characteristics of the engine, and when they installed the engine in a Cooper chassis, they simply produced an ill-handling brute. The Lister chassis was inherently a better-handling design, and although they suffered less problems in that department, by Lister standards 1956 proved a complete disaster.

The chassis design of the 1956 car was largely unchanged, but there were now Girling 10 in. disc brakes, mounted inboard at the rear. The most significant change was the abandonment of the Lucas body style by a new sleek and very low design, nicknamed the 'flat iron' and based on a model of the MG record-breaking car EX 179. Because of the low, flat design, the rounded front and rear wheelarches were much higher than the main body area, there was a small headrest, the slim, tapering nose meant a very small frontal area and weight was slashed by using aluminium interior panelling as a stressed structure in the nose to carry the radiator, the front body panels and the cooling ducts for the front brakes and radiator. Cars for customers were built to the same design, save that there was a very large hump in the nose to clear the Bristol engine. The 1956 cars were raced by Noel Cunningham-Reid (this was a new car retaining the 1955 registration NVE 732), Austen Nurse (whose car had the registration from the ex-Green car, HCH 736) and Ormsby Issard-Davies—but with competition cars such as these the dividing line between a rebuilt car and a new one is fine indeed.

In the British Empire Trophy Scott-Brown finished second in his heat to Parnell's 2.5-litre Aston Martin, but made a pit stop in the final because of overheating and finished well down the field in thirteenth place. At the May Silverstone meeting Scott-Brown finished ninth, but won the 2000 cc class ahead of Lister-Bristols driven by

BELOW *In 1957 the Lister-Maserati was sold to Ormsby Issard-Davies and driven by bearded Alan Moore, seen here in the 1957 British Empire Trophy at Oulton Park (T. C. March)*

RIGHT *In the 1957 British Empire Trophy, Gilbert Baird with the ex-Austen Nurse 1956 Lister-Bristol leads Horridge whose Lister was fitted with non-standard bodywork (T. C. March)*

Moore and Nurse. He set fastest lap in a handicap race at Snetterton on Whit Saturday, but retired with piston failure at Goodwood on the Monday. At Aintree in June Scott-Brown finished fourth overall behind Salvadori (Aston Martin), Titterington and Bueb (both with Jaguar D-types) and won the 2-litre class from other Listers driven by Cunningham-Reid and Moore. Scott-Brown drove a stirring but short-lived race at the British Grand Prix meeting before the Lister expired with a repetition of piston failure in the Sports Car race. It was in this race that Austen Nurse crashed his Lister very heavily, allegedly as a result of the failure of a non-Lister part in the steering. Nurse was soon at the wheel of another Lister-Bristol, a half-completed 1956 project which he acquired from John Green. The car wrecked at Silverstone was to form the basis of a Lister-Jaguar completed late in 1957 by Tom Kyffin's Equipe Devone. At Oulton Park for the *Daily Herald* International Trophy, run on a streaming, wet track, Scott-Brown drove a magnificent race and the Lister-Maserati held together so that he finished fifth overall behind a quartet of works Aston Martins and won the 2000 cc class easily. By this stage Lister had really lost interest in the Maserati-powered car and their energies were directed in other directions.

Postscript

At this time Lister development aimed in two directions. The team's Formula 2 1500 cc single-seater appeared in time to run in the 1956 Gold Cup race at Oulton Park, but the entry was scratched and the car was scrapped without running under its own power—Brian Lister was quite satisfied that it would never make the grade. A year later Lister produced a much improved Formula 2 car, but, again, it was never raced by the works, was sold and run in a few events by its private owner.

The main thrust of the team, however, was still in sports car racing, and in 1957 Lister produced their first Jaguar-powered car, based on the original Lister-Bristol chassis, MVE 303. During 1957 Lister's former glory was revived and Archie Scott-Brown and the new car enjoyed a phenomenal run of success. During the year Archie and Roy Salvadori at the wheel of works Aston Martin DBR1 3-litre and DBR2 3.7-litre cars resumed their titanic duels—with Archie coming across the line first, except at the September Silverstone meeting, where Salvadori with the DBR2 won for the first and only time.

By 1958 Lister were supplying Lister-Jaguars to other teams, including Briggs Cunningham, Ecurie Ecosse and Équipe Nationale Belge, and Archie continued his run of success in British events. He had, however, come up against a very serious opponent at the wheel of a Lister, Kansan Masten Gregory, who drove the Ecurie Ecosse dark blue car. Gregory beat Archie at the May Silverstone meeting and they met again at Spa in Belgium later in May. The race was run in the wet and Gregory was leading, right on the limit, arms crossed and fighting the car all the way, with Scott-Brown right behind him. At La Source Archie lost control, glanced against the memorial to Dick Seaman, who had been killed at Spa in 1939, scraped the Clubhouse wall, hit a road sign that broke the right-hand track rod and the Lister rolled over down the hillside falling away from the road. The car caught fire and Scott-Brown suffered burns to which he succumbed the following afternoon. On the day of the Spa race Archie's great friend and rival Roy Salvadori was competing in the Monaco Grand Prix. Roy was quite convinced that 'Wilkie' Wilkinson of Ecurie Ecosse, with so much experience of Jaguar engines, was able to squeeze just that much more power out of the Scottish team's car and Archie was trying too hard to stay with Gregory.

When Archie died, the spirit of Lister died. The cars competed for the rest of 1958, and for 1959 they introduced a much revised car with chassis and body designed by Frank Costin. But already Lister was really a name of the past. In short-distance British events the Listers had to fight hard to stay with the latest Lotus 15s and Cooper Monacos and in long-distance endurance racing, limited so far as World Championship events were concerned to 3000 cc since the start of 1958, the Lister's 3-litre Jaguar engines were hopelessly unreliable. During 1959 the team suffered another blow. Works Lister driver Ivor Bueb was killed at the wheel of a Formula 2 car at Clermont-Ferrand in late July 1959. Brian Lister was already planning to withdraw from racing at the end of the year, but with the news of Bueb's death, the decision took effect immediately.

Lola

Eric Broadley's rise to fame as a constructor of competition cars mirrored that of Colin Chapman. Special-building was followed by a line of immensely successful sports/racing cars and then Broadley moved on to single-seaters. At that point Broadley's career moved in a very different direction. After building a very small number of prototype GT cars, Broadley became an employee of Ford Advanced Vehicles and went through an unhappy phase of involvement in the Ford GT40 project before becoming once more an independent constructor. Broadley has only three times in his long career been involved in the construction of Formula 1 cars, the spaceframe Climax V-8 powered cars raced by the Bowmaker team in 1962 (and subsequently raced by Reg Parnell's private team), the 1967 Honda chassis and now the new Ford-powered cars entered from the beginning of 1986 by the Beatrice team.

The first Lola, built to comply with the 750 Motor Club's 1172 Formula for Ford side-valve powered cars, appeared in mid-1956 and was raced that year without conspicuous success by Eric and his cousin Graham Broadley. By 1957 the Lola was fully sorted and, with Eric doing most of the driving, it won the 750 Motor Club's Champion Cup, Eric drove it to victory in the Ford Championship of Ireland at Kirkistown and was second in the scratch 2000 cc unsupercharged class of the Leinster Trophy on the Wicklow circuit. At the end of the year work was put in hand on a new Climax-powered sports/racing car and the first Lola was sold to Alan Wershat who modified it and raced it with great success as the Lolita.

Mk I sports racing cars

It is worth having a quick look at the situation in the 1100 cc class of sports car racing in 1958. Formula Junior had, as yet, made no impression in the UK and the 1100 cc class of sports car racing was still that used by up and coming drivers to make their mark. The class was still dominated by cars powered by the Coventry-Climax FWA engine and Lotus tended to regard the class as their private bailiwick. It was dominated by the Lotus Elevens with the Elvas and the occasional Tojeiro as poor also-rans. The emergence of the Lola transformed the scene.

When all constructors were using the same power unit, the key to success was very low weight and superior roadholding. The Lola was exceptionally light, but it also possessed remarkably superior roadholding. Most of the components of the new car were constructed in a lock-up garage in Bromley, but the front bodywork was built by Maurice Gomm at Byfleet. The basis of the Lola was a multi-tubular space-frame weighing only 60 lb without fittings. At the front suspension was by tubular wishbones, with a very wide base and facing forwards, and coil spring/damper units. The independent rear suspension consisted of lower wishbones, trailing arms and coil spring/damper units. Transmission from the Climax engine was through a single dry-plate clutch, a 4-speed gearbox (using a BMC casing with special close ratio gears) to a BMC hypoid bevel final drive with Lola Elektron casing. The body was neat, sleek and low.

The new Lola, registered 600 DKJ, was not finished until the middle of the 1958 season and first ran at the Crystal Palace that month. It had not been driven at all until the day before the race, the unlimited capacity sports car event, and Eric Broadley, under the mistaken impression that the Climax engine required running in as with an ordinary engine, drove a very sedate race. Later in the month he raced the Lola at Snetterton and finished second in the 1100 cc sports car race to Keith Greene's Lotus. The August Bank Holiday Brands Hatch meeting was next on the programme and proved a mixture of immense promise and ignomy. John Bolster wrote in *Autosport*:

'Heat 2 [of the 1100 cc sports car race] brought the sensation of the day, which was provided by Eric Broadley's Lola. The little Coventry-Climax-engined car was visibly quicker through the corners than anything else, and in practice it had been the first sports car ever to lap the Hatch in under a minute [This was of course the old, short Brands Hatch circuit]. Broadley

First overseas outing for the Lola-Climax was in the 1959 Nürburgring 1000 Km race in which it was driven by Ashdown and Broadley. The car retired when Broadley slid into a ditch (Edward Eves)

immediately piled up a huge lead to win by 28 secs. from John Brown's Elva, and equalled the class lap record of 60 secs. in the process . . . .

'In the Final, Brown's Elva shunted Lola on the starting grid, which may have disconcerted Broadley. At all events he spun at the beginning of Bottom Straight, during which he motored sideways across the bows of several horrified competitors without disaster, and received the black flag for his pains . . . .'

Later in the day Broadley finished fourth in the 1500 cc race after starting from the back of the grid and set fastest lap. Shortly afterwards he crashed and damaged the car badly at Goodwood after going off the road to avoid another competitor and there was a frantic rush to rebuild the car in time for the Tourist Trophy held on the same circuit two weeks later. In this race Broadley was partnered by Peter Gammon. Two wheels had been damaged in the Goodwood shunt and there had been no chance to replace them with the result that the Lola started at Goodwood without a spare wheel. Inevitably a tyre punctured, nine minutes were lost while a new tube was fitted and the Lola finished at the tail of the field, but with the consolation of setting fastest 1100 cc lap at 87.45 mph.

It was only at this point that Broadley gave up his job as a building site manager and then only because his employers had taken a less than sympathetic view of his week's 'sick leave' prior to the Tourist Trophy. Lola Cars Ltd was formed and work started on production cars in Maurice Gomm's workshops at Byfleet. Two new cars were

Peter Ashdown with his works Lola finished third overall, won the 1100 cc class and set a new class record in the Sports Car race at the British Grand Prix meeting at Silverstone in July 1960 (T. C. March)

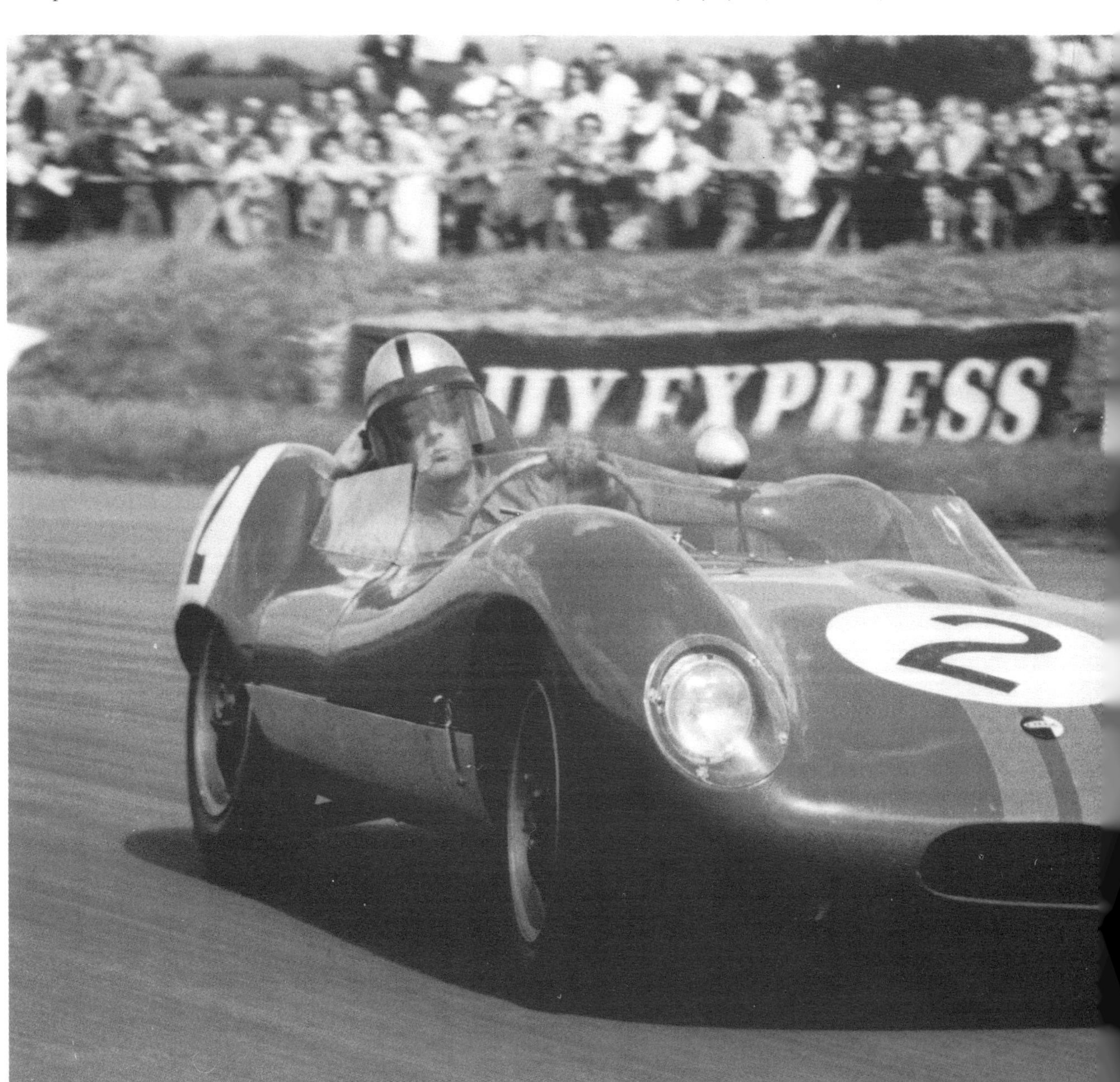

sold to Peter Ashdown and Michael Taylor, while Peter Gammon acquired the prototype. A third car for Broadley himself was completed in May. The two Peters, Ashdown and Gammon, raced as a works team under the name Lola Équipe. After spinning off at Chapel Curve at the May Silverstone meeting and skidding into a ditch at the Nürburgring 1000 Km race, Broadley concentrated most of his efforts on design and construction, although still acting as test driver.

Throughout 1959 the Lola drivers enjoyed a fantastic run of success, dominating the 1100 cc class and proving more than a match for the ill-handling Len Terry-designed Lotus 17. Lolas took first three places in the 1100 cc sports car races at the Easter Goodwood meeting and at Aintree in April and first two places in the 1100 cc class at the May Silverstone meeting. In July Ashdown, despite engine problems, finished fourth and won his class in the Sports Car race at Rouen and he won the 1500 cc sports car race at Clermont-Ferrand from Jean Behra's Porsche. Gammon and Ashdown again took the first two places in the 1100 cc sports car race at the Crystal Palace in August and at the International Brands Hatch meeting at the end of the month. In the Tourist Trophy at Goodwood Ashdown/Ross finished sixth overall, won the 1100 cc class, another Lola finished third in the class and Lola took the team prize. A few weeks later Ross drove a Lola to voctory in the Queen Catherine Cup at Watkins Glen.

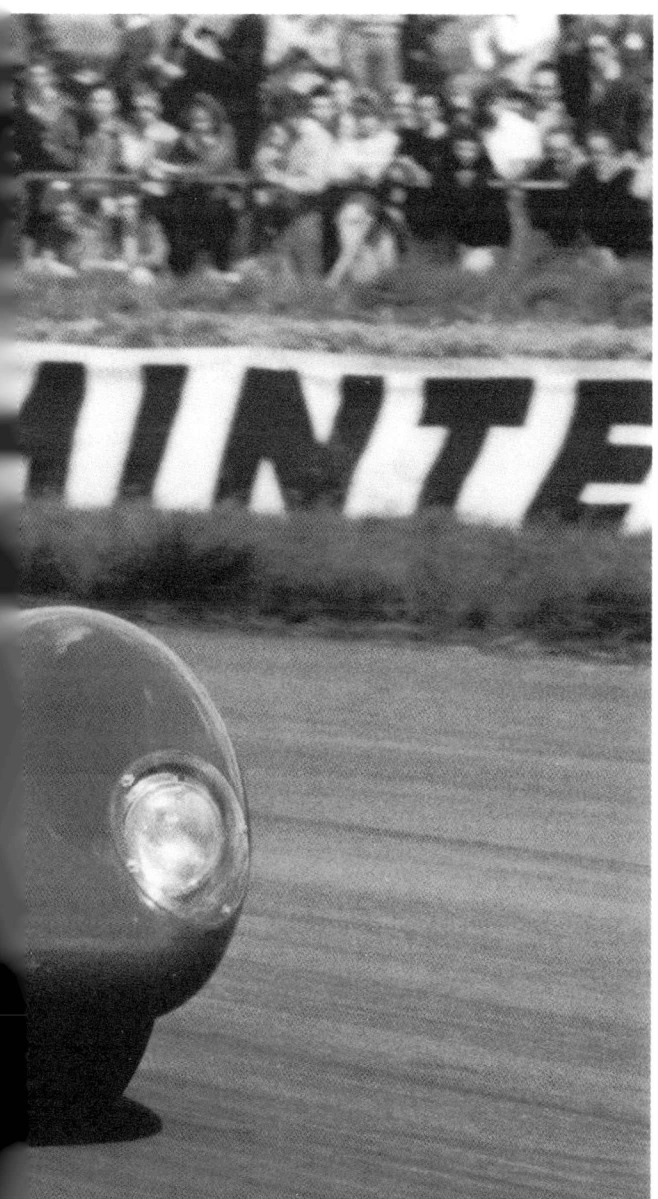

Shortly after the Tourist Trophy the class-winning car was loaned to John Bolster to test for *Autosport* and his test is reproduced overleaf. For Broadley and Lola it had been an incredibly successful year and for 1960 modifications to the design were few. The main change was the introduction of fibreglass bodywork by Specialised Mouldings and as a result of the split with Maurice Gomm production was transferred to Bromley. At the beginning of 1960 Broadley also introduced his first Formula Junior single-seater, a front-engined design of which a total of 29 were built. One of these cars was fitted with a Coventry-Climax 1460 cc engine by Peter Gammon and driven by him in Formula 2 events.

The first of the 1960 sports/racing cars was supplied to Voegele to run in the Sebring 12 Hours race and with Ashdown and Roth as co-drivers won the 1100 cc class—despite 40 minutes spent in the pits sorting out a problem with the bonnet. In British events Lolas were driven, amongst others, by Bill de Selincourt, Chris Steele, Chris Meeke, Alan Rees and the Hon. Edward Greenall and the make maintained its stranglehold in the 1100 cc class. Voegele/Ashdown, de Selincourt/Lawrence and Hitches/Hicks took the first three places in the 1100 cc class of the Nürburgring 1000 Km race. Voegele/Ashdown drove a Lola at Le Mans, but retired on the Sunday morning because of a holed piston.

The Lola sports/racing car remained in production until 1962 (the year in which the mid-engined Lotus 23 assumed domination of the Small-capacity Sports Car classes) and a total of 35 were built. There was one further car built in 1967 for Mike Fraser. This car, with enlarged 1149 cc Climax engine, ran in 21 races during the year (and was placed in all except two) and won the Guards Championship. In 1961 Broadley built the first rear-engined Lola Formula Junior cars (between 1961 and 1963 a total 30 of slightly different types were constructed) and in 1963 came the first of a new and immensely competitive GT Prototype design.

FINE THANKS! John Bolster grins happily in the cockpit while Eric Broadley looks just as pleased. The venue is Snetterton.

JOHN BOLSTER TESTS THE

FABULOUS LOLA

The All-conquering 1,100 c.c. Sports Racing Car

No success story has ever been quite so sudden and complete as that of Eric Broadley and his Lolas. It is literally true that the arrival of this little bombshell has completely rejuvenated the 1,100 c.c. sports class, which was rapidly losing the interest of the public. It is equally true to say that Lola victories are now taken for granted, and it would almost be headline news if one were beaten. Thus, no better choice could be made for a road test subject in this important issue of AUTOSPORT.

The basis of the Lola is a multi-tubular frame which weighs just under 60 lb. bare. It is suspended independently all round on what is generally termed the wishbone system. In front, the tubular wishbones have a very wide base and face forward at an appreciable angle, by virtue of the rear bearings on the frame being more widely spaced than the front ones. The stub axles articulate on nylon ball joints at the top and trunnions at the bottom. The steering has an Elektron case, which contains a Lola rack and a Morris Minor pinion.

The independent rear suspension is by helical springs and Armstrong telescopic dampers, and the suspension arms work on rubber bushes. These features are shared with the front suspension, but here the resemblance ends. Immense trouble has been taken to avoid rear wheel steering, and the Elektron housings for the Timken taper roller hub races are located in all planes. Long trailing arms of substantial section look after the fore and aft location, and the large diameter tubular half shafts, with their Hardy Spicer universal points, act as the upper wishbones. The bottom wishbones have wide bases, while in front of them, and working on the same centres, a pair of extra radius arms still further inhibit steering by the rear wheels.

The Elektron bolt-on wheels carry 5.00 x 15 ins. rear tyres, while the front size is 4.50 x 15 ins. The Lockheed brakes with Alfin drums have wider shoes in front. Right in the nose of the car, a Gallay radiator with a copper core keeps the engine cool. A fuel tank is mounted to the left of the scuttle, and an extra one can be fitted on the right for long-distance races. A tap allows either tank to be selected.

A Coventry-Climax engine in Stage 3 tune probably develops 90 b.h.p. with two twin-choke Weber carburetters. This well-known light alloy single overhead camshaft unit drives through a $7\frac{1}{4}$ ins. Borg and Beck clutch with a racing centre plate. The gearbox casing is from the small B.M.C. box, containing special Lola close-ratio gears. The chassis-mounted hypoid is also a B.M.C. product in a Lola Elektron case. Various ratios are available for different courses.

The Lola which I used for my test was the actual one which won the 1,100 c.c. class in the T.T., and indeed it had not been touched since that epic. I stole it out of the paint shop, where it was due to receive another coat of B.R.G., so the appearance was not as immaculate as usual, but all the performance was there.

On taking the wheel, I found that the lateral location provided by the bucket seat was very good, to the extent that I had positively to force my posterior into position; however, I was comfortable once I had settled into place. The engine started at once, the clutch gripped very positively, and I was away.

The special close-ratio gears make a purposeful scream as one accelerates. Wheelspin can be induced, but it is easy to make a good getaway and the engine does not tend to "fluff". The acceleration is obviously very fine indeed, and continues right up the range. One hundred m.p.h. cames up on any straight, and it is only above this considerable velocity that the Lola ceases to feel like a $3\frac{1}{2}$-litre car.

I am sure that the superiority of the Lola in circuit racing comes from its sheer cornering power. The steering is extremely quick and very direct, but one gets used to this at once. On fast curves, the handling characteristic tends towards understeering. An extremely good feature is the stability over bumps, there being no tendency whatever to hop. It is, above all, the way in which the

THERE IS a good driving position and all the necessary instruments are in the right place. The car even has door pockets!

THE SLEEK LINES of the Lola are well shown in this photograph, as is Bolster's comfortable driving position. The car was due for a respray when Bolster "stole" it from the works!

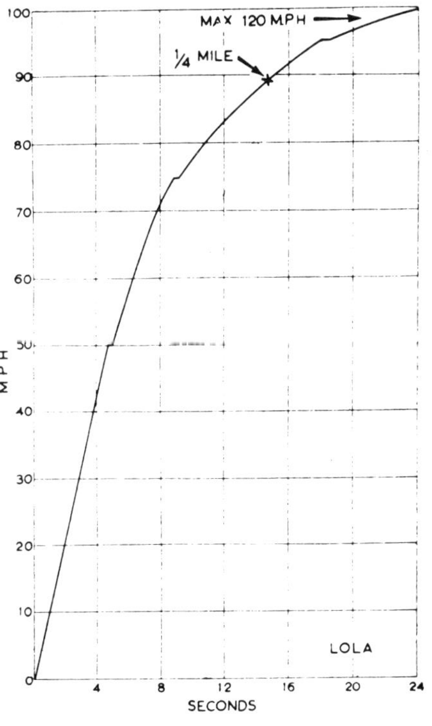

ACCELERATION GRAPH

SPECIFICATION DATA

Car Tested: Lola sports-racing two-seater. Price in kit form, £1,540.

Engine: Four cylinders, 72.4 mm. x 66.6 mm. (1,097 c.c.). Direct valve operation from single overhead camshaft driven by gears and chain. Head and block of light alloy. Compression ratio, 10.5 to 1. Approx. 90 b.h.p. at 7,000 r.p.m. Two twin-choke Weber carburetters. Lucas coil and distributor.

Transmission: Borg and Beck 7½ ins. single dry plate clutch with racing centre plate. Four-speed gearbox with central lever, ratios 4.55, 5.60, 7.55, and 10.92 to 1. Open propeller shaft. Chassis-mounted hypoid unit. Hardy Spicer articulated half shafts without slip joints.

Chassis: Multi-tubular space frame. Independent front suspension by wishbones, helical springs, and telescopic dampers. Rack and pinion steering. Independent rear suspension by wishbones, trailing arms, helical springs and telescopic dampers. Lockheed brakes in 10 ins. Alfin drums, width 1¾ ins. rear, 2¼ ins. front. Bolt-on Elektron wheels, fitted 4.50 x 15 ins. front and 5.00 x 15 ins. rear tyres.

Equipment: 12-volt lighting and starting. Rev. counter. Ammeter. Oil pressure and temperature and water temperature gauges.

Dimensions: Wheelbase, 7 ft. 1 in. Track, 4 ft. Overall length, 11 ft. 9 ins. Width, 4 ft. 11 ins. Weight, 7½ cwt.

Performance: Maximum speed, 120 m.p.h. (approx.). Speeds in gears: 3rd 95 m.p.h., 2nd 75 m.p.h., 1st 50 m.p.h. Standing quarter-mile, 14.6 secs. Acceleration: 0-30 m.p.h., 2.8 secs.; 0-50 m.p.h., 4.6 secs.; 0-60 m.p.h., 6.4 secs.; 0-80 m.p.h., 10.6 secs.

Fuel Consumption: In races, 19-20 m.p.g.

rear wheels stay glued to the road that makes the Lola such a fantastic car on corners.

On wet roads it is fairly easy to break the rear end away by a burst of throttle on an appropriate gear, but that high-geared steering remains master of the situation. Naturally, a car of this calibre demands some finesse in handling, but once the knack has been acquired one has absolute confidence in one's ability to control the little machine. The authentic drifting attitude may easily be attained by the appropriate use of the loud pedal.

The brakes are extremely powerful. A slight tendency to pull to the right was no doubt a legacy of many hours of racing in the T.T. The Lola is so small and light that the brakes do not have a very arduous task to perform.

For various reasons, a journey to my usual fast test stretch was impracticable, and the performance figures were not obtained under ideal conditions. The ground was damp, and it actually rained quite hard during some of the tests. The performance figures do not therefore represent the ultimate of which the Lola is capable. Even so, they do give a very fair idea of the potency of this little car. They also show that for sheer traction on slippery roads you can't beat an independent rear end.

I was very impressed by the sturdy construction of the Lola. The reliability of these cars has been exemplary in races, and certainly the machine did everything that I asked of it during my tests. It is small but has none of the flimsiness that has characterized some 1,100 c.c. sports cars. The body is practical, even having such things as door pockets, and a very impressive feature is the good steering lock—a rare virtue among sports-racers. It would appear to need virtually no modification to pass the new and more severe international regulations. It is intended to evolve a sleeker nose shape in the interests of better aerodynamics.

Having watched Lolas winning races, one is naturally all the more interested to drive one. Without doubt it is sheer roadholding, which permits extremely fast cornering, that is the secret, backed up by excellent acceleration in the range where it is most useful. A really sound design in which all the basic requirements are met, coupled with a very high standard of construction, adds up to an ideal sports-racing car that is immensely enjoyable to drive. It made one elderly ex-racing driver feel years younger! The manufacturers are Lola Cars, Ltd., Napier Road, Bromley, Kent.

FRONT. The tubular wishbones have a very wide base and face forward by an appreciable angle. The chassis frame weighs just under 60 lbs. bare!

REAR. Inboard brakes are a feature here. Suspension is by helical springs and Armstrong telescopic dampers and the suspension arms work on rubber bushes.

Mk 6 GT cars

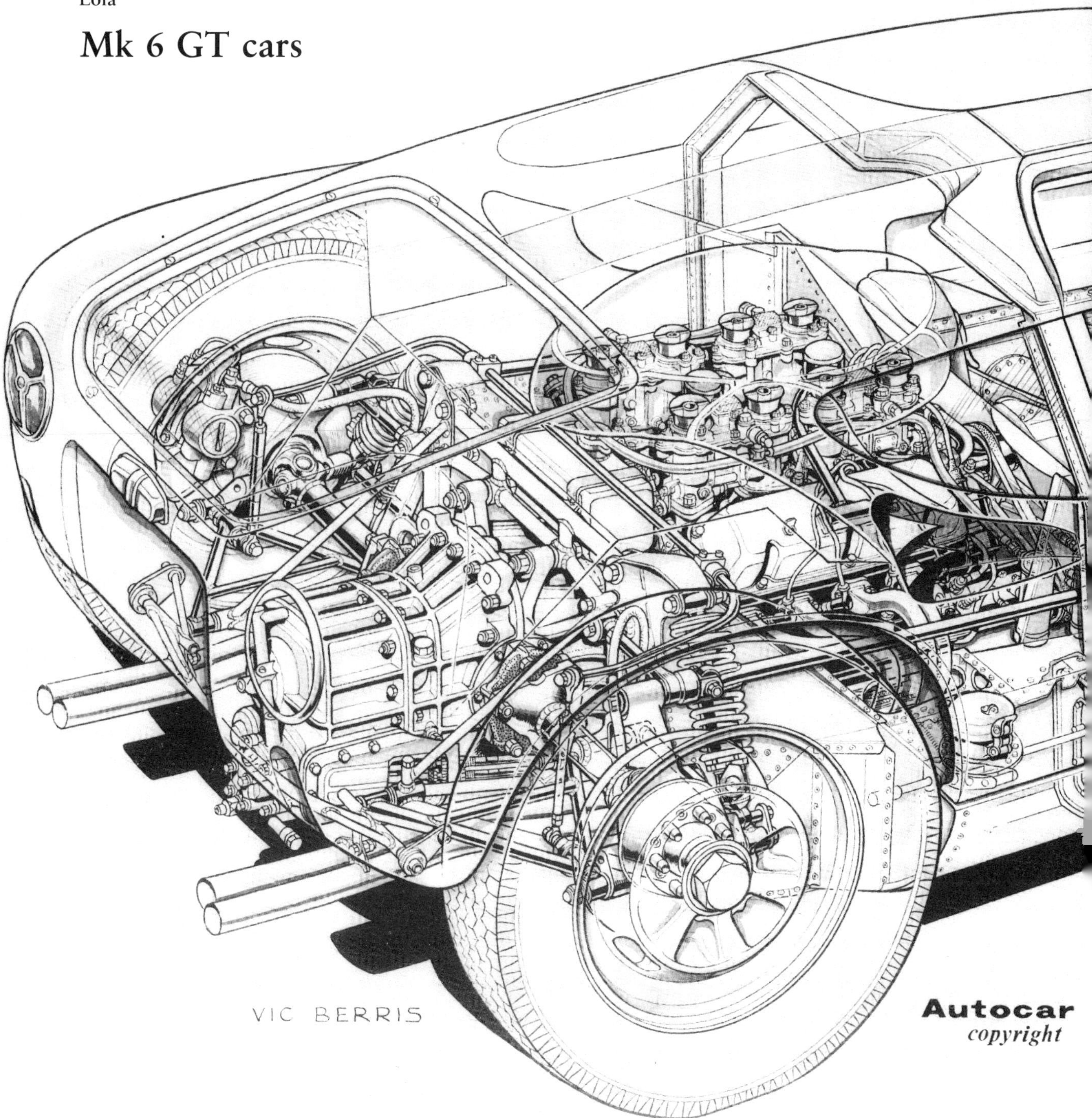

When Lola revealed the new Mk 6 GT car at the Racing Car Show early in 1963, it represented a radical divergence from previous Broadley design practice. From the introduction of the first Climax-powered sports/racing car in 1958, there had been a steady development progression through space-frame sports and Formula Junior cars. The GT was in a different league, of monocoque construction, advanced in concept and apparently destined for a leading role in International Prototype racing.

The basis of the GT was a monocoque central chassis section forming a stiff, light, wide and uncluttered passenger compartment. This central section consisted of twin box-member sills also acting as the fuel tanks with outer faces formed by duralumin sheet and inner faces formed by sheet steel bent to a U-section; these side-members were linked by a steel floor plan with boxed bracing members on which the seats and the housing for the central remote control gearchange were mounted.

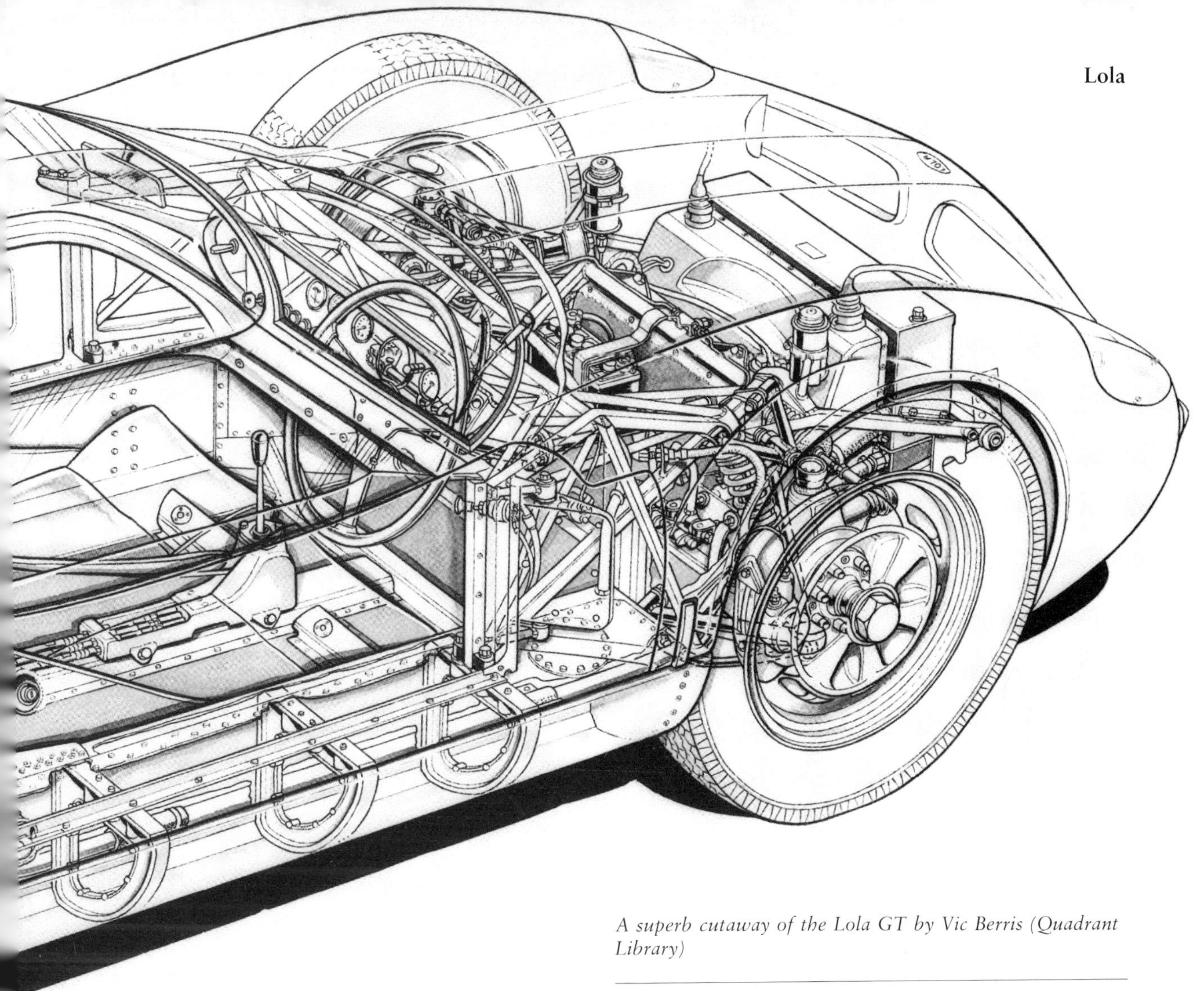

A superb cutaway of the Lola GT by Vic Berris (Quadrant Library)

Within the side 'booms' were four cast magnesium formers with bosses to take the attachments for the door frame and roof structure. Towards the rear the side booms tapered inwards to carry the engine. The engine was the 4727 cc V-8 Ford (initially 4.2-litre) driving through a Colotti 4-speed gearbox. The gearbox projected through the centre of the main rear cross-member which mounted the rear suspension.

At the front and attached to the scuttle was a mainly square-section tubular structure which carried the front suspension, together with the cross-flow radiator and spare wheel. Front suspension was by double wishbones and inclined coil spring/damper units, together with an anti-roll bar. To carry the rear suspension there was a fabricated extension to the main side booms and the suspension was formed by lower wishbones, upper transverse links, and long forward-facing radius arms with inclined coil spring/damper units. Girling disc brakes were fitted front and rear and there were 15 in. light alloy knock-on wheels. The wheelbase was 7 ft 8.25 in. and front and rear track 4 ft 3.5 in. The body was a very neat fibreglass coupé. Apart from Saab rack-and-pinion steering, there were many proprietary components incorporated for detail fittings, including Triumph Herald fastening catches to secure the front and rear bodywork which hinged upwards and Ford Cortina Mk 1 rear lights! The weight was a mere 16 cwt, resulting in a power to weight ratio of 325 bhp per ton and, thanks to excellent aerodynamics, a maximum speed approaching 180 mph—faster than contemporary 1500 cc Formula 1 cars.

Race debut for the Lola GT came in the Unlimited Sports Car race at the May Silverstone meeting, in which it was a reserve entry. At this stage in its development the Lola was fitted with a 4.2-litre engine and single downdraught carburettor. Originally it had been intended that John Surtees should drive, but this was neatly vetoed by Ferrari to whom Surtees was contracted and so South African Tony Maggs deputized. Starting from the back of the grid Maggs did everything that

ABOVE *At Le Mans in 1963 this Lola GT driven by Attwood and Hobbs ran well until Hobbs crashed at Tertre Rouge because of gearbox problems (Quadrant Library)*

RIGHT *Brian Redman with the Red Rose Team's Lola T70 in the 1966 Tourist Trophy at Oulton Park. He finished third in the first heat, but retired in the second heat because of transmission problems (T. C. March)*

was asked of him, driving a neat, steady race to finish fifth in the over 2000 cc class. Shortly afterwards the Lola was entered in the Nürburgring 1000 Km race for Maggs/Olthoff, but it was delayed by a rear wheel working loose and damaging the driving pins and finally eliminated by engine trouble.

At Le Mans two cars had been entered, but only one, a brand new car with full 4.7-litre engine, driven by Attwood/Hobbs started the race. The Lola ran steadily until delayed by a slipping dynamo belt, but gradually picked up places so that it was in 12th position by midnight. However, by this hour the Lola was already in the pits again because of a broken gear-selector bolt and stayed there for two hours before rejoining the race. At 5.30 am Hobbs was unable to engage third gear on the approach to Tertre Rouge, lost control, the Lola bounced off the banks and was completely wrecked. A third chassis was built to replace the crashed car. In time for the August Bank Holiday meeting at Brands Hatch a Lola had been supplied to the John Mecom team to be driven by Augie Pabst, but he retired after only two laps because of loss of oil pressure. Later in the year this car was re-engined with a 6-litre Chevrolet unit and Pabst drove this to victory in the Nassau Tourist Trophy.

It was evident that such an ambitious car could not be developed and raced without financial backing that vastly exceeded Lola's own resources and the sponsorship provided by oil companies and other suppliers at the time. The solution came when Broadley was invited to join Ford Advanced Vehicles and the Lola GT formed the basis of the Ford GT40. By 1965 Broadley was back in business on his own at Slough, a sad, wiser man, disillusioned by the division of authority and lack of freedom within the Ford organization. There followed a range of Lola sports cars and single-seaters that achieved greater success than any of Broadley's previous designs.

T70

Incorporating many features of the Ford GT40, Broadley's T70 Group 7 sports/racing car was one of the most successful of its breed. It was based on a monocoque chassis fabricated from sheet steel and alloy, incorporating 25-gallon fuel tanks. At the front suspension was by double wishbones (with very wide-based lower wishbones), coil spring/damper units and anti-roll bar, with rear suspension by reversed lower wishbones, single top links, twin radius rods, coil spring/damper units and anti-roll bar. Rack-and-pinion steering was fitted, there were Girling disc brakes (12.5 in at the front and 12 in. at the rear) and 15 in. cast magnesium wheels (8 in. rims at the front and 10 in. at the rear). The body was a simple, but very aerodynamic fibreglass structure, built by Specialised Mouldings, with quickly detachable front and rear sections attached by Dzus fasteners. The engine was either a Chevrolet (usually a 5.9-litre developed by Traco to produce around 450 bhp) or a Ford V-8 (4.7-litre with a power output varying between 360 bhp and 390 bhp).

From the moment of its introduction the T70 proved immensely successful and sold in substantial numbers. John Surtees with his very potent red Chevrolet-powered car finished second in the

Perhaps the most successful of all T70s was the Sid Taylor car driven by Denis Hulme. Hulme is seen here on his way to victory in the 1966 Tourist Trophy (T. C. March)

Sports Car race at the end of March at Silverstone (the race was shortened because of torrential rain), Hobbs and Dibley were third and fourth at the Easter Goodwood meeting, Hobbs with a Ford-powered car finished second in the Tourist Trophy now held at Oulton Park and Dibley was second at the May Silverstone meeting. It must be remembered that these races were fiercely contested with strong entries from both Lotus with the 30 and McLaren. Hobbs and Attwood finished second and third at Mallory Park on Whit Sunday and Surtees scored a brilliant victory in the Guards Trophy at Brands Hatch at the end of August. Later in the year Surtees contested the North American series of races and after winning the Player's Quebec race, suffered an horrific practice crash with the Lola at Mosport Park in practice for the Canadian Grand Prix when a rear hub carrier broke. Surtees suffered terrible injuries and it was a near-miracle that he was fit to race again by the start of the 1966 season.

In all Lola built 15 T70s in 1965 and in 1966 produced the improved Mk 2 version with all-alloy centre monocoque (it was the prototype of this model that Surtees had driven to victory in the Guards Trophy the previous year). The Chevrolet engine in 6-litre form was now standard wear. In addition to Team Surtees' entries, driven by either David Hobbs or Surtees, the Sid Taylor-entered car driven by Denis Hulme received works support. In the early part of the year this car proved unbeatable and Hulme won the Archie Scott-Brown Memorial Trophy at Snetterton, the Tourist Trophy at Oulton Park, at Silverstone and Mallory Park in May and the Martini Trophy at Silverstone in July. At the Guards Trophy at Brands Hatch in July the

winner was Hugh Dibley with a T70 entered by Racing Partnerships (Jersey). Surtees came to the fore with wins at Croft and Brands Hatch in August and he also won the Player's Quebec race, the Los Angeles Times Grand Prix and the Stardust Grand Prix in the Can-Am series. Two other races in the Can-Am series, together with the Nassau Trophy were also won by Lola T70s in 1966. Production of the T70 Mk 2 amounted to 32 cars.

Group 7 racing came to an end in Britain after 1966 and the only market was now for competitors in the Can-Am series. In 1967 Lola built a mere four T70 Mk 3 cars for racing in this series.

T70 Mk 3 GT

For 1967 Broadley developed a GT version of the T70 and it was intended that in due course this should be homologated as a Group 4 sports car and would be competing alongside the Ferrari 275LM and the Ford GT40. In the meanwhile it had to run as a prototype and was offered with the Chevrolet 6-litre engine mated to the Hewland LG500 gearbox/final drive unit. In addition John Surtees and Lola had got together to form Lola Racing to campaign endurance races with cars powered by the Aston Martin V-8 engine.

From the moment that the project was announced many knowledgeable onlookers had reservations about the use of the Aston engine. This 5064 cc (98 × 83 mm) V-8 design with light alloy cylinder block and twin overhead camshafts per bank of cylinders was a bulky, heavy unit (it weighed 525 lb). As adapted for competition work, it featured dry sump lubrication and, initially four twin-choke Weber carburettors in the vee of the engine (by Le Mans in June Lucas fuel injection had been adopted). Unless the Aston Martin engine could produce 100 bhp/litre with complete reliability, then it had nothing more to offer than a well-developed Chevrolet and unlikely to prove

ABOVE *John Surtees with the Lola-Aston Martin at the 1967 Le Mans Test Weekend at which he set third fastest time (David Phipps)*

RIGHT *Another view of the Lola-Aston Martin, at the Esses, at the 1967 Test Weekend. This view shows clearly the distinctive 'arrow-head' paint finish*

anything of a match for the 7-litre Fords or 4-litre Ferrari P4.

Early in the year the Aston engine was tested in a T70 sports/racing chassis, but rumours were circulating that two engines had blown up during testing and Surtees was said to be regretting that the team was not using Chevrolet engines. The Le Mans Test Weekend in April provided some encouragement for the team. Fastest was Bandini with the P4 Ferrari in 3 min 25.5 sec., Mike Parkes was second fastest for Ferrari in 3 min 25.5 sec., Surtees was third fastest with the Lola-Aston Martin distinguished by its dark green and white stripe with arrowhead in 3 min 31.9 sec. and the fastest of the 7-litre Fords driven by Mark Donohue could not better fourth fastest time in 3 min. 32.6 sec.

Two of the new Mk 3 coupés with Chevrolet engines ran in the Spa 1000 Km race. One crashed in practice and non-started, but the other car driven by Paul Hawkins and Jackie Epstein finished fourth behind the winning Mirage—but only one works Ferrari was entered (and was delayed by gear-change problems) and there were no Fords. The Lola-Aston Martin made its debut in the hands of Surtees/Hobbs in the Nürburgring 1000 Km race, Surtees set second fastest lap in practice and after a delayed start caused by magneto problems went really well in the race moving up to seventh place before the rear suspension broke. The real debacle came at Le Mans where two cars were driven by Surtees/Hobbs and Irwin/de Klerk. The race had barely started, before both entries were out with engine problems. It was an appalling display by Aston Martin, happily not repeated in recent years with the Aston Martin-powered Nimrod and EMKA projects, and the Team Lola cars were

immediately re-engined with Chevrolet units. During the remainder of the year there were strong Lola-Chevrolet entries at Reims (where they were fastest in practice and initially led the race) and in the BOAC race at Brands Hatch and other, less important races, but the only successes gained were a win by Gardner with Epstein's car at the Norisring and by Paul Hawkins in the Cape Three Hours race in South Africa at the end of the year.

At the end of 1967 the CSI, the governing body, changed the rules at short notice and with effect from the start of the 1968 season Prototypes were limited to 3 litres and Competition Sports Cars (of which not less than 50 had to be built to achieve homologation) to 5 litres. The Lola scraped in as a Competition Sports Car by taking into account the total of sports/racing and GT cars built. By 1970 these changes to the rules had spawned both the Porsche 917 and Ferrari 512S and against such opposition the 5-litre Lola-Chevrolets had no real chance of success. In addition the Lolas never achieved the reliability necessary to win endurance races.

In 1968 a quasi-works Lola was fielded by Sid Taylor, but ran almost exclusively in British events. In International events cars were run by Jo Bonnier and Ulf Norinder, but achieved nothing much in the way of success. At Sebring a Mk 3 driven by Patrick/Jordan led until eliminated by piston failure and in the BOAC '500' race at Brands Hatch Bonnier/Axellson finished sixth—the only finish by a Lola in the first six of a Championship race in 1968. In British Group 4 events it was a very different story and Lola dominated these short races; Brian Redman won at Oulton Park in April with the Sid Taylor car, with the same car Denis Hulme won at the May Silverstone meeting, the Martini race at Silverstone and the Tourist Trophy at Oulton Park and Frank Gardner drove Taylor's car to victory at Mallory Park, Brands Hatch and Croft. In addition Mike de Udy with his own car won at Oulton Park in August. Overseas minor victories were gained at Anderstorp (Bonnier), Vila Real (de Udy) and Innsbruck (Chris Craft).

At the 1969 Racing Car Show Lola introduced the improved Mk 3B version of the T70 with detail changes to improve the handling, other minor modifications that made the cars easier to work on, lighter bodywork and conventional front-hinged instead of gull-wing doors. With 5-litre Traco-developed engine the T70 Mk 3B had a price tag of £7450 and 1969 was the last year the model was in production.

One of the latest cars was acquired by Roger Penske (and even that maestro of careful preparation and development could not achieve reliability), while others were raced by Paul Hawkins, Joakin Bonnier, Ulf Norinder, Team Elite (driver Trevor Taylor), Scuderia Filipinetti and Sid Taylor.

At the start of the 1969 season the Penske-

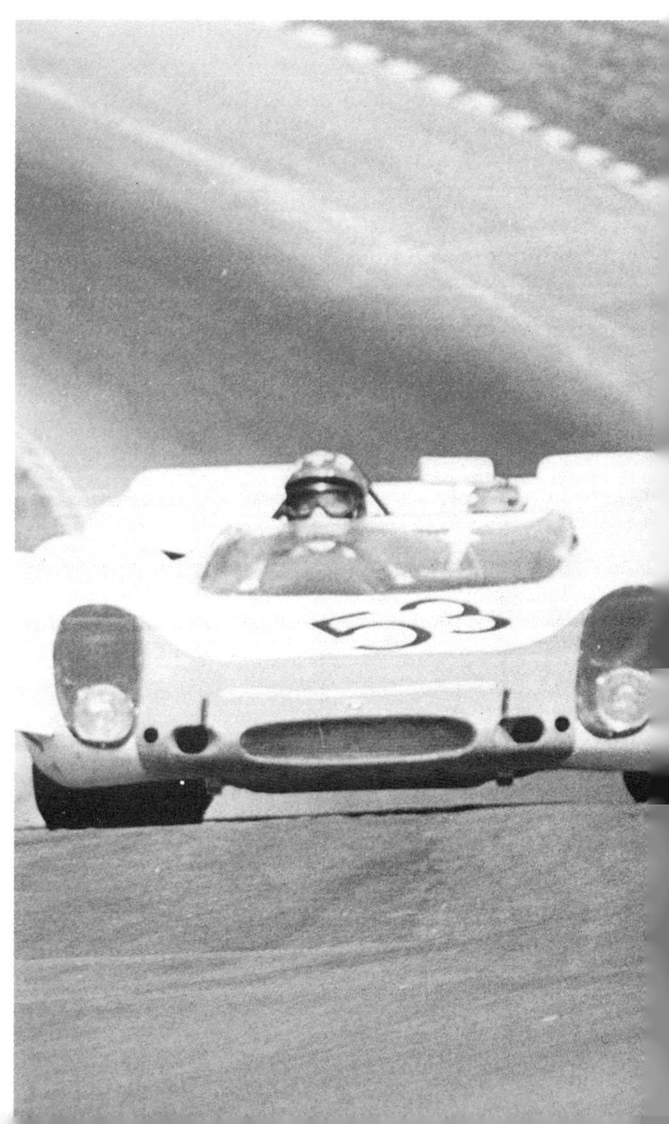

entered car driven by Mark Donohue and Chuck Parsons scored a remarkable victory in the Daytona 24 Hours race, the first in the Championship series. It was a remarkable victory in that the normally very reliable 3-litre Porsche 908s had been plagued by cracked exhausts and mechanical problems. Even the Lola had spent over an hour in the pits because of exhaust problems, it rejoined the race over 40 laps in arrcars and its winning average was only 99.27 mph compared with the 106.70 mph average of the winning Porsche 907 the previous year. At Sebring the T70 of Leslie/Montschenbacher finished sixth and Gardner/de Adamich took fifth place at Monza. One of the finest Lola drives of the year was Herbert Müller's performance with the Scuderia Filipinetti entry in the arduous Targa Florio; for this race the car had been specially strengthened and after a delayed start Müller held third place at the end of the first 44.7-mile lap, but a tyre punctured Müller lost a lot of time getting the car back to the pits and his co-driver Bonnier retired at the end of the third lap. Bonnier/Müller were the most successful Lola drivers in 1969 and later took fifth place in the Spa 1000 Km race and second place in the Austrian 1000 Km event in August.

In British races the T70s still enjoyed considerable success with wins by Hulme at Silverstone and Thruxton, Hawkins at Snetterton, Redman at Thruxton, Chris Craft in the Martini Trophy at Silverstone and at Croft and Trevor Taylor in the Tourist Trophy at Oulton Park. The Tourist Trophy was marred by an horrific accident that cost the life of popular Australian Paul Hawkins; Hawkins went off the road at Island Bend, hit a tree, rolled and caught fire and there was simply no

LEFT *In 1968 Denis Hulme won the Tourist Trophy for the third time. In 1968 he was at the wheel of Sid Taylor's Lola T70 Mk 3 (Guy Griffiths)*

BELOW *The Hawkins/Williams T70 Mk 3B moves over in the 1969 BOAC 500 race to let through the winning works Porsche 908 of Siffert/Redman (Nigel Snowdon)*

Bonnier (Mk 3B entered by Scuderia Filipinetti) leads Hawkins (Mk 3B) in the 1969 Tourist Trophy at Oulton Park. This was the race in which Paul Hawkins crashed with fatal results (Guy Griffiths)

chance for the marshalls to rescue him from the inferno. Overseas a number of minor successes had been gained, including a win by Hawkins at Dijon, Bonnier at Montlhéry, Redman at Karlskoga and Gardner at Innsbruck. At the end of the year Lolas won four of the five races in the Springbok series in Southern Africa.

By 1970 the T70 was no longer a serious contender in endurance racing, although a number of entrants persevered. Minor successes included a win by Attwood (with David Piper's car) from Teddy Pilette (Team VDS entry) at Montlhéry in May, by Attwood at Dijon and by Pilette at Montlhéry in June and by Gosselin (VDS entry) at Vila Real. Lola had become increasingly involved in building 2-litre cars for the European Championship and developed a 3-litre version which Bonnier's team raced in 1971. Sadly Bonnier lost his life when he crashed one of these cars at Le Mans.

The story of the T70 GT Mk 3 is very much a story of what might have been. It handled well, it had immense potential, but its career in endurance racing was marred by lack of reliability and the fact that all entries were made by small teams running on tight budgets without the resources to undertake a major development programme.

In 1985 Lola, now based at Huntingdon, remains very much a successful racing car manufacturer with a long and distinguished history that embraces a long line of successful single-seater victories at Indianapolis and a prominent role in Formula 3000.

Lotus

There is now no more famous name in motor racing than Lotus; a name that ranks with the all-time greats, Alfa Romeo, Bugatti and Ferrari; a name and greatness forged in less than 30 years from the appearance of the first Lotus 'special' in 1947. Engineering undergraduate Colin Chapman's first Lotus was a trials car based on the chassis of a 1930 Austin 7 saloon and fitted with a plywood and alloy body. Chapman ran the Mk 1 Lotus in two trials in 1948 and the same year graduated from university. Soon work started on a second car, the Mk 2, also intended for trials work. The basis was again an Austin 7 chassis, but this time to be powered by a Ford 1172 cc engine. Work was interrupted when Chapman joined the Royal Air Force, but the car was eventually finished in 1949 with a Ford 8 hp engine. After a couple of trials Chapman abandoned this first power unit and substituted a Ford 10 hp. Influenced to a great extent by his growing interest in motor sport, Chapman's spell with the RAF lasted just about a year, he took up a job with a firm of constructional engineers in London and in 1950 Chapman and the Lotus Mk 2 tackled a full competition season. Not content with merely entering trials Chapman ran the Lotus, now with mildly modified engine, in a number of speed trials and race meetings. Perhaps his greatest success was a win in the Eight Clubs meeting at Silverstone in June; he won a 16-lap scratch race after a furious duel with Gahagan's Bugatti Type 37 and Guy Griffiths' photograph of the duelling pair is now one of the classics of motor racing photography.

Later in 1959 Chapman sold the Mk 2 to trials specialist Mike Lawson and shortly afterwards also sold the original Mk 1 car. The next Lotus was to be a car to comply with the 750 Motor Club's 750 Formula for Austin 7 based cars and it was to prove so successful that the Club was forced to change the rules. The new Lotus, the Mk 3, was built in co-operation with brothers Michael and Nigel Allen. The much modified Austin 7 chassis was fitted with a neat, compact aluminium body with full-length undershield, a Ford 8 front axle split to provide swing-axle independent front suspension, together with a remote-control Austin 'Nippy' gearbox. What was so different about the Lotus was the engine which, apart from all the usual modifications seen in 750 Formula racing, had the normal two-port Austin 7 block 'de-siamezed'; this was achieved by opening up the inlet ports and building up special manifolds from welded sheet steel with a vertical steel strip in the centre of the manifold extending into the ports. A Stromberg twin-choke downdraught carburettor was used and the result was the same as if the Austin cylinder head had a twin carburettor induction system. The performance of the Mk 3 was incredible for an Austin 7-powered car, it enjoyed a fantastic run of success in 1951 and the outcome was that the 750 Motor Club introduced a ban on dividing the siamezed inlet ports.

A second 750 Formula car, typed the Mk 3B, was completed and sold to Adam Currie and also in 1952 a second trials car, typed the Mk 4, was built for Mike Lawson. At the beginning of the year the Lotus Engineering Company had started trading and occupied small premises in Tottenham Lane,

The classic photograph of Colin Chapman (Lotus Mk 2) battling hard with Dudley Gahagan (Bugatti Type 37) at the Eight Clubs meeting at Silverstone in 1950 (Guy Griffiths)

ABOVE *Adam Currie cornering hard at Silverstone in 1952 with his Lotus Mk 3B. Note the enormous 'power bulge' on the left-hand side of the bonnet (Guy Griffiths)*

ABOVE RIGHT *The prototype Lotus Mk 6 made its debut at the MG Car Club meeting at Silverstone in July 1952. Here it is seen with Michael Allen at the wheel (Guy Griffiths)*

Hornsey, part of property owned by Chapman's father. Chapman had been planning to build another 750 Formula car, based on the Mk 3, but to be capable of 100 mph, with much improved suspension and brakes and fully equipped for road use. Instead Chapman, still working in his spare time while Michael Allen worked for the business full-time, started work on what was to be first production Lotus, the Mk 6.

Even progress on the Mk 6 was delayed while Lotus built a special for the Clairmonte brothers and to be known (originally) as the Mk 7. This car, intended to be powered by a 2-litre ERA engine, was to be built to comply with the then current 2000 cc Formula 2. The Clairmonte brothers ran into major problems when the ERA engine was wrecked and elected to take delivery of the bare chassis and body unit. This multi-tubular chassis with front suspension by double wishbones and inboard coil spring/damper units and a de Dion axle at the rear was eventually completed for Club racing as a sports car powered by a 2-litre Lea-Francis engine. Its stark two-seater body painted black, this car known simply as the Clairmonte Special was a formidable contender in Club racing in 1953–4.

The basis of the Mk 6 was a multi-tubular chassis, weighing 55 lb without fittings and 90 lb with all mounting brackets and stressed panels. For

the front suspension Chapman retained swing axles located by radius rods and with inclined coil spring/damper units. At the rear there was a Ford rigid rear axle located by a Panhard rod and torque tube and suspended on coil spring/damper units. The body was the work of Williams and Pritchard of nearby Edmonton who were also responsible for all the stressed parts incorporated in the chassis. The power unit of the first car was the 1508 cc Ford Consul with the stroke shortened to bring it just within the 1500 cc category and with twin SU carburettors. Transmission was by a Ford 3-speed gearbox with Buckler close-ratio gears.

This prototype Mk 6, registered XML 6, made its debut at the MG Car Club meeting at Silverstone on 5th July, 1952 and scored two second places. The car was raced in a number of other events, but following the August Boreham meeting was wrecked in a road accident through no fault of Nigel Allen who was at the wheel. Chapman and Allen were forced to withdraw from racing for the remainder of the year and at the end of 1952 Allen withdrew from the business. Chapman reformed the firm as Lotus Engineering Co. Ltd and laid down the components to build eight production Mk 6 cars.

Amongst the first customers were P. A. Desoutter (who raced his car with Ford engine in 1172 Formula events organized by the 750 Motor Club), Fred Hill (he fitted his car with a 746 cc supercharged MG engine and raced it as the 'Empire Special') and Peter Gammon (who did not race his car until 1954). Another early example was purchased by Nigel Allen and another car was built by Mike Costin; Costin soon became a member of the Lotus organization and this Mk 6, registered 1161 H, was raced by both Chapman and Costin.

Chapman drove 1161 H with 1099 cc side-valve

The most successful Mk 6 was the MG-powered car raced by Peter Gammon in 1954. The engine was transferred from the MG which Gammon raced in 1953. Here Gammon is seen at the BARC meeting at Goodwood at the end of March 1954 (LAT)

engine in the 1500 cc sports car race at the Crystal Palace in September 1953 and greatly impressed by holding his own with some of the more potent British 1500 cc sports/racing cars. After this meeting John Bolster tested 1161 H for *Autosport* and wrote:

'At the Crystal Palace on 19th September, we beheld an astonishing sight. During a sports car race, in which some of the "hottest" 1½-litre machines in the country were engaged, a vehicle propelled by a *side-valve* Ford 10 engine, linered down to 1100 cc, proved itself capable of fighting it out with the best. This was what a contemporary described as, "the preposterously fast Lotus", and it was the talk of the paddock afterwards.'

Bolster described the Mk 6 in detail, praised its performance, roadholding and construction and concluded by saying,

'As Mr. Chapman has no intention at present of invading the Rolls-Royce and Bristol market, he has given a little less attention than those two manufacturers to sound deadening and exhaust silencing. In consequence, particularly at peak revs. with the hood up, one can definitely hear the machinery at work, to put it mildly. Let us remember, though, that I took the car exactly as it was raced at Crystal Palace, apart from the replacement of the hood and screen, and for touring purposes one could easily fit larger silencers.

'I feel that the Lotus is the best attempt yet to provide the enthusiast with a competition car at a price he can afford to pay. In essentials, it is just as sound an engineering job as the most expensive sports car, and the economy is only brought about by the clever adaption of mass-produced components. Its excellent handling qualities ensure not only that the driver has safe and enjoyable motoring, but that he will automatically receive the right sort of training, with nothing to unlearn if he graduates to big-time racing. It is a fine little road car, too, and lots of fun to drive.'

By 1954 the Mk 6 was in full production and cars were being raced extensively. Both Peter Gammon and Mike Anthony raced their cars with 1496 cc MG XPAG engines and Gammon with his car, UPE9, in particular, enjoyed a phenomenal run of success. He won almost innumerable races at Club level, defeated Chapman with the Mk 8 on more than one occasion, took third place in the British Empire Trophy at Oulton Park and in the 1500 cc Sports Car race at Silverstone in July finished second to Chapman, beating Herrmann's works Porsche. Other interesting variants were Bill Perkins' Mk 6 with 2-litre BMW engine, Fred Marriott's car with FWA Climax engine and John Harris' similar car with de Dion rear axle. The Mk 6 dominated 1172 Formula racing for two years, as late as 1956 John Lawry won the 1200 cc class of the *Autosport* Production Sports Car Championship. When production ceased at the end of 1955 around

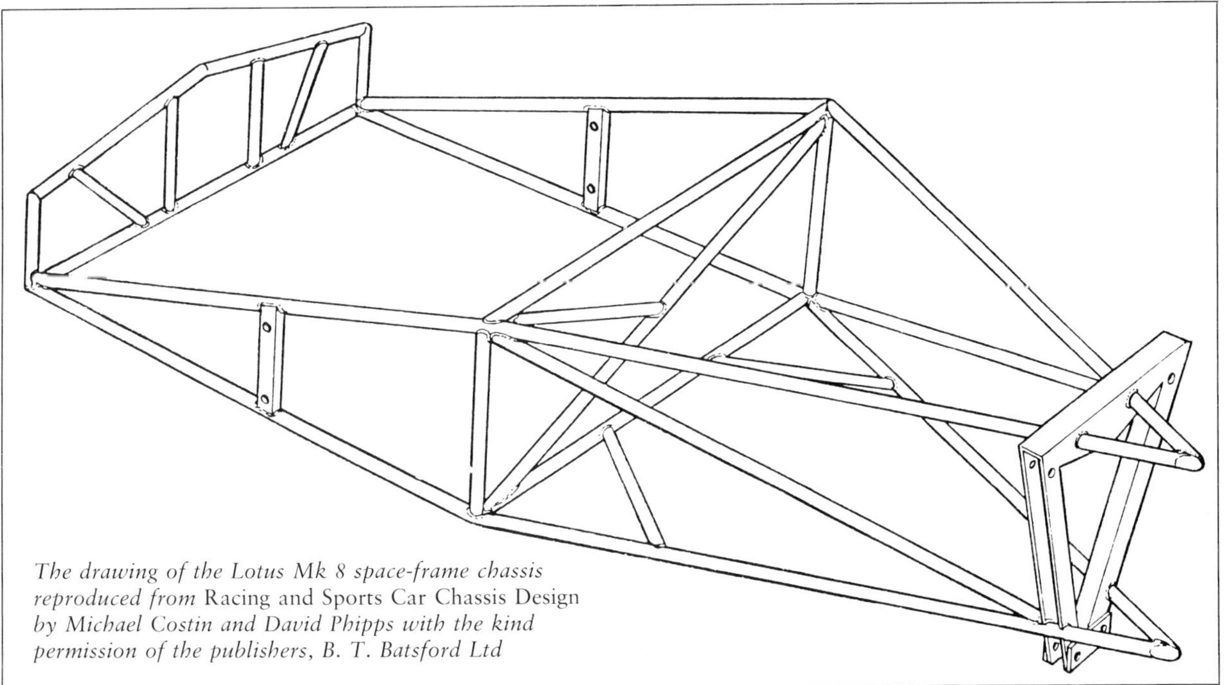

The drawing of the Lotus Mk 8 space-frame chassis reproduced from Racing and Sports Car Chassis Design *by Michael Costin and David Phipps with the kind permission of the publishers, B. T. Batsford Ltd*

one hundred cars had been built and it was eventually replaced by the Seven that appeared at the end of 1957.

Lotus Mk 8

Throughout the 1950s Lotus development represented a steady progression and Chapman's sports/racing cars became increasingly more sophisticated and increasingly more successful so that they achieved near-domination in the 1100 cc and 1500 cc classes in British events (but not, apart from Le Mans, in continental endurance racing). It was, however, with the Mk 8 that Chapman first made a real impression on the International motor racing scene.

By 1953 there were a number of makes competing in the 1500 cc class, almost all powered by the MG XPAG engine in a variety of forms and all relatively conventional in terms of chassis and body design. With no readily available engine but the MG, Chapman sought to and succeeded in building a car that was lighter, far more aerodynamic and cornered far better than any of its rivals.

Using the experience gained with the Mk 6, Chapman evolved a very light, exceptionally stiff space-frame constructed in $1\frac{1}{4}$ in. 20-gauge steel tubing (the complete chassis frame weighed only 35 lb) and some purists have argued that this was the first true space-frame. The design was analytically described in *Racing and Sports Car Chassis Design* by Michael Costin and David Phipps (B. T. Batsford, 1961):

'Structurally, the most nearly perfect sports car chassis yet made is that of the Lotus Mark 8. Very simple, extremely light and very stiff, this chassis—the only one of its type ever made—is still giving good service after six years of use, and this despite the fact that it is made up of 20 gauge and 18 gauge tube. As can be seen from the accompanying drawing, the primary structure is fully triangulated and therefore extremely stiff. It consists of two sections on either side of a central bulkhead, the forward section being triangular in plan view, the rear triangular in side elevation. Only nineteen members are used in its construction, and the total weight is 21 lb. All members are straight and there are no structural offsets.

'From a practical viewpoint, however, this chassis is open to a great deal of criticism. It was designed as a pure structure, with little thought for the loads to be fed into it, and thus it was necessary to add to the ideal basic structure a number of less satisfactory secondary structures through which these loads could be engineered. It has since been shown that it is far better to merge primary and secondary structures in the interests of a superior overall chassis. In addition, practical experience soon showed that even the ideal basic layout had serious limitations from the point of view of maintenance. As an instance of this, it was necessary to dismantle the engine to get it in and out of the chassis. Cylinder head, manifolds, oil pump, water pump, distributor, front mounting, starter and dynamo, all had to be removed before the engine would pass through the narrow opening in the top frame. Because of the disturbance involved this almost inevitably meant that the engine produced less power in the car than when it was built up on the test bench. In addition, the use of stressed bodywork interfered seriously with the servicing of many smaller components.

'By contrast with the simplicity of the primary structure, the secondary structure necessary to feed suspension and other loads into the chassis is extremely complicated. To deal with the front suspension loads involved by the use of a swing axle layout, it was decided to build a triangular frame of top-hat section sheet steel, with the base of the triangle passing across the top chassis members some 6 inches to the rear of the front upright member. The outer ends of this transverse member were designed to accommodate the top eyes of the suspension unit. Just inboard of these pick-ups are welded the two other members of the triangle, which converge to form pick-up points for the swing axle eyes at their apex near the undertray line.

'This triangular frame deals with the main front suspension loads. Suspension drag loads and brake torque reactions are taken out by radius arms located at a point approximately three-quarters of the way along the bottom chassis tubes; any consequent bending loads are taken out into the undertray by further tubes which run diagonally back towards the centre of the car, meeting the transverse bulkhead at the front of the undertray section.

'One of the aims of this design was to mount the engine in such a way that loads could be reacted directly through the front suspension—in fact to hang the engine on the front suspension. This led to the construction of an extremely complicated front engine mounting, which consists of a tubular pyramid of four $\frac{5}{8}$ in. thick wall steel tubes picking up at various points on the front of the engine and converging to meet at a steel bush which acts as a housing for a Silentbloc-type bush. This is supported with the axis of its mounting bolt in a fore-and-aft plane and passes through two vertical flanges of the top-hat section member on the centre line of the chassis. From the chassis viewpoint this is quite satisfactory, but special triangular brackets are necessary to avoid twisting of the steel sandwich plate at the various pick-ups around the front timing cover of the M.G. engine. The rear mounting is taken from the normal M.G. position on the gearbox and loads are taken out into the propeller shaft tunnel, which is of stressed skin construction and deseighned to take bending loads from the gearbox as well as driving and brake loads (in the form of torque loads resolved into bending) from the differential unit.

'As at the front, a secondary structure is necessary to take out rear suspension loads. Vertical loads are taken out at the apexes of the triangles which form the seat-back bulkhead and lateral loads are fed into the undertray. The differential unit, which also provides lateral location for the de Dion assembly, is located by four mountings, one above and one below on the centre line and one on each side. Loads from the latter are taken out into the side walls of the propeller shaft tunnel by means of steel brackets. In practice this layout has given considerable trouble, as the passage of loads from extremely stiff brackets into 20 gauge aluminium leads to straining and eventual failure. Trouble has also been experienced with the complicated mountings for the transverse coil springs, which incorporate piston-type shock absorbers as suspension linkages. Fore-and-aft suspension loads are taken out by parallel, horizontal arms into a vertical side frame member, located at the junction of the main side frame member and a secondary tube which comes forward to meet it from the seat-back bulkhead. This member also helps to overcome a possible weakness in the shallow section of the chassis side frame immediately in front of the seats.

'The Lotus Mark 8 was the first sports car to feature fully aerodynamic bodywork, designed by Frank Costin and supported on the chassis by light alloy sheet bulkheads. Only the front section of the bodywork is removable, the remainder being riveted to the sheet alloy which supports it. The front body mounting consists of a tubular and sheet steel structure coming forwards from the front vertical member of the chassis and also incorporating the radiator mountings.'

This is a long and detailed description of the Mk 8 chassis, but not only did this design form the basis of the whole line of Lotus sports/racing cars, but Mike Costin was at the time responsible for Lotus development. One or two points require comment. The reference to 'the only one of its type ever made' refers to the prototype Mk 8, registered SAR 5, which was sold by Team Lotus and raced in 1955 by Austen Nurse and in 1956 by Roy Bloxham. All production Mk 8s had modified chassis which featured much more easily removable body panels that improved accessibility at the cost of some loss in rigidity.

The 1467 cc engine built up from MG and Morris components and fitted with a Laystall-Lucas light alloy cylinder head and twin $1\frac{3}{4}$ in. SU carburettors was said to develop 85 hp at 6200 rpm. It drove through a 4-speed MG gearbox. Fuel capacity was 22 gallons, with a 12-gallon tank in the tail and side tanks with a capacity of 10 gallons. Lockheed drum brakes were used front and rear and those at the rear were mounted inboard. The bodywork designed by Frank Costin was the result of a great deal of aerodynamic research. There were twin tail-fins, fairings over the rear wheels, a very low nose-line and a full-length undertray with ducts for the rear brakes. No headlamps were mounted in the wings; instead they folded away into the engine bay and to erect them it was necessary to remove the engine cover, which was secured by Dzus fasteners. Once erected, they were of course higher than headlamps fitted to very low competition cars. There was a perspex driver's

Colin Chapman and the Mk 8 in the Sports Car race at Silverstone in May 1954. He won the 1500 cc class of this rain-soaked race (LAT)

screen and a metal tonneau over the passenger seat. The body was constructed by Williams & Pritchard, who were responsible for most Lotus bodies of the 1950s.

Chapman entered the Mk 8 in the British Empire Trophy at Oulton Park on 10 April, 1954; the Lotus was still unpainted, it was crashed on the way to the circuit, extensively rebuilt and allowed to practice in a special session. Chapman started from the back of the grid, but soon retired in the 1500 cc heat because of a blown cylinder head gasket. It was a dismal start to what was to prove a magnificent season for Chapman and the Lotus.

The following Monday week was the Easter Goodwood meeting and the Lotus ran in an Easter handicap only to drop out of the running because of engine trouble. A month later Chapman ran in the Sports Car race at Silverstone, finishing fifteenth overall and first in the 1500 cc class—but it must be admitted that there was not much in the way of opposition apart from Coombs' Connaught, and the Connaughts were the only real opposition to the Mk 8 in 1954. A week later the car was entered in the 71-mile Eifelrennen at the Nürburgring. At this time Chapman was still in full-time employment in central London, so he drove the car to work on the Friday, parked it in St. James's Square, was joined by Mike Costin on the Friday evening and set off to catch a cross-Channel ferry. The Lotus arrived at the circuit at Saturday lunchtime. Because of Chapman's inexperience as a racing driver, the organizers would not accept his entry and he arranged for the car to be driven by Erwin Bauer. Bauer drove a good race to finish fourth behind the Borgwards of Bechem and Hartmann and Giardini's works Osca. Immediately after the race on the Sunday, Chapman and Costin headed back to the coast, crossed overnight and the Lotus was back in St. James's Square in time for the start of work on Monday morning. Whatever criticisms there were of Chapman in his later days, his early enthusiasm and dedication brought rewards that were well earned.

At the inaugural meeting on the Aintree circuit on 29 May, Chapman crashed the Mk 8 in heavy rain, but although the bodywork was badly damaged, Chapman and his enthusiastic helpers had the car ready to race again by the Whitsun Goodwood meeting on the Monday week. He finished sixth overall and won the 1500 cc class in the 21-lap Johnson Challenge Trophy race. In June at the Crystal Palace Chapman shot through to take the lead in the Sports Car race, overtaking Alan Brown (Cooper-Bristol), Roy Salvadori (Maserati A6GCS) and Tony Brooks (Frazer Nash), pulled out a good advantage and set a new sports car lap record of 70.88 mph before a half-shaft broke.

By the Brands Hatch meeting on 4 July, Chapman, Peter Gammon and Mike Anthony (the latter two with Mk 6 cars) were running as 'Team Lotus' and Chapman had to settle for second place to Gammon in two 1500 cc Sports Car races.

During the course of the day Chapman twice broke the sports car lap record, finally leaving it at 70.86 mph. By the British Grand Prix at Silverstone the first Mk 8 had been supplied to a private buyer, John Coombs, whose car was fitted with a very powerful 1484 cc Connaught engine. In the 1500 cc sports car race at Silverstone there was very strong opposition in the shape of a works Porsche 550 driven by Hans Herrmann, who was fastest in practice. In the race Herrmann was slow off the mark, Gammon took the lead with the Mk 6, Chapman went in front on lap 4 and at the end of this 17-lap race the order was Chapman (who had averaged 81.72 mph), Gammon (who set joint fastest lap with Herrmann at 84.30 mph), Herrmann and Coombs. Anthony finished in ninth place, so that Team Lotus took the team prize. It was a popular victory, but it must be remembered that the 550 Porsche was designed for endurance events.

A week later Chapman was in action again on the now forgotten Fairwood aerodrome circuit near Swansea, winning the 1500 cc sports car race, finishing second to Scott-Brown's Lister-Bristol in the 2500 cc event and retiring with a rod through the crankcase in the Unlimited event. This caused enormous problems, because Chapman was due to compete at the Nürburgring the following weekend, August Bank Holiday, as well as run in two British events. By dint of frantic effort the car was ready for its channel crossing on the Wednesday night and duly appeared for the sports car race on the morning of the German Grand Prix. Two other Mk 8s were entered, both newly delivered to private owners Dan Margulies (co-driving with Bauer) and Nigel Allen. Allen blew up his engine during practice, but it was repaired in time for the race on the Sunday. All three Mk 8s retired, in Chapman's case because of a broken de Dion tube. Chapman drove straight back to the coast, was delayed on the way when a suspension link broke and caught the night ferry to tackle, with a surfeit of enthusiasm, the clearly impossible—running at two British meetings on the same day. At Brands Hatch Chapman finished fourth in the first heat of the National Sports Car Championship with a rough-running engine caused by a blown cylinder head gasket. This was repaired and he then drove

Two months later Chapman and the Mk 8 were in action again at Silverstone, winning the 1500 cc race at the Grand Prix meeting. It was one of Chapman's best races (T. C. March)

to the Crystal Palace, arriving just in time for the 2000 cc sports car race. The Lotus retired on the second lap and Chapman returned to Brands Hatch to borrow Nigel Allen's Mk 8 to drive in the final of the Sports Car race, but again retired with engine problems. It seems that both Chapman's car and Allen's suffered the same problem, the carburettors were set up to run at the Nürburgring altitude of around 2000 feet and without further sorting would not run properly at the much lower British altitudes.

Despite the fiasco of the August Bank Holiday weekend the Lotus had made its mark as the potentially, if not always, fastest British 1500 cc car. Business pressures forced Chapman to cut back on his racing and it was not until the end of the year that he and Mike Costin gave up their employment to concentrate on Lotus full-time. Other Mk 8s were sold to Dickie Steed (who was the first to install a Coventry-Climax FWA engine in a Lotus), Brian Naylor and Cunane. A small number were also sold in the United States. In August Chapman finished third in a Sports Car race at Castle Combe behind Salvadori (Maserati) and Scott-Brown (Lister-Bristol) and co-driving with Costin he crashed in the Tourist Trophy on the Dundrod circuit. A victory followed in the 1500 cc Anerley Trophy at the Crystal Palace, he was sixth and first 1500 cc driver to finish in the 2000 cc sports car race at Goodwood, and was beaten into second place in his class at Aintree by McAlpine (Connaught). At the final Snetterton meeting of the year Chapman spun in front of Scott-Brown's Lister-Bristol and both cars were badly crumpled.

In November John Bolster road-tested the works Mk 8, SAR 5, for *Autosport* and recorded a maximum speed of 121.5 mph, 0–60 mph acceleration of 8 secs. and 0–100 mph in 23.8 secs. Overall fuel consumption was reckoned to be around 30 mpg. Bolster used the car for both long and short journeys and tried it round Brands Hatch. He concluded his test by commenting, '. . . I shall remember its incredible steadiness at maximum speed, and the ease with which it can be taken round appreciable curves at over 100 mph. . . .'

Lotus Mk 9

There was no doubt that in 1954 Chapman had evolved a fine recipe for success with the Mk 8 and the 1955 car was a direct development of this, with modifications that were in the main of a detail nature. The chassis was of lower weight and more compact mainly due to the use of smaller-section tubing. The rear de Dion layout was modified to incorporate stronger hubs and articulated half-shafts. The body had been subtly restyled so that it was shorter with higher tail fins, the nose was reshaped to improve air flow to the radiator and front brakes, and there were hinge-down doors on both driver's and passenger side. Accessibility was much improved and the whole of the upper half of the front bodywork could be removed, giving access to the engine, front suspension and the rear of the instrument panel. A rear panel could be removed to give access to the rear axle and inboard-mounted rear brakes. The perspex screen was lower, but wrapped more fully round the driver and was attached to the driver's door and the metal tonneau cover. A 6-gallon fuel tank was mounted in the tail of the car, but for long-distance racing auxiliary tanks of various sizes could be installed on the passenger side of the body.

The first two cars delivered to the United States to compete in the Sebring 12 Hours race in March were fitted with Coventry-Climax engines and the 1954-type 9 in. brakes. They were in effect the prototype Mk 9s. The standard 1955 production Mk 9 (and the works cars in their early form) used 11 in. × 2¼ in. brakes with Elektron drums with deep radial fins extending to the edge of the drum and with steel liners. Later in the year Girling 9 in. disc brakes were adopted on the works cars, still inboard at the rear.

In effect three different versions of the Mk 9 were made. At the beginning of the season there were two works cars, registered 9 FHX (MG-powered) and XPE 6 (powered by the Coventry-Climax FWA 1100 cc single-cam engine) and the Climax version was that supplied to private purchasers. On the works cars MG J2 'crash' gearboxes were used because they were lighter than the TC gearboxes, with synchromesh on the upper ratios fitted to production cars. Because of purchase tax and lack of workshop space Lotus preferred to sell cars to private purchasers in component form, but the price tag for a complete car was £1150 plus purchase tax. After the 1955 Le Mans race Lotus offered the Climax-powered car as the 'Le Mans'. In addition purchasers were offered the 'Club' with Ford 1172 cc engine, gearbox and back axle and drum brakes with modified brake linkage.

At Sebring the two cars were entered by Frank Miller (with George Rabe as co-driver) and Norman Scott (with Samuelson as co-driver). Both cars ran well, leading the 1100 cc class, but Samuelson, blinded by the sinking sun, went off and holed the sump and the Miller/Rabe car was disqualified for receiving a push-start after a pit stop.

Throughout 1955 Lotus struggled to satisfy a large number of orders for both the Mk 6 and the Mk 9 (around 40 of the latter were built) as well as run a works team. The first works car, with MG engine, appeared at the British Empire Trophy at Oulton Park in April and it soon became evident that Lotus would not have an easy time in either the 1100 cc or the 1500 cc class. In the smaller category the team would be up against the Cooper-Climax (which was yet to race) and in the 1500 cc class the streamlined works Connaught of Kenneth McAlpine and the Peter Bell-owned Connaught driven by Les Leston provided formidable opposition. The Mk 9 appeared in Oulton Park in primer and Chapman missed practice and started from the back of the grid in his heat; he came through to hold fourth place, but retired because of engine overheating.

This run of misfortune continued. At the Easter Goodwood meeting Chapman retired after only two laps because of engine trouble; at Ibsley Chapman got on to the grass and wrecked the undertray on a lump of concrete (but set fastest lap

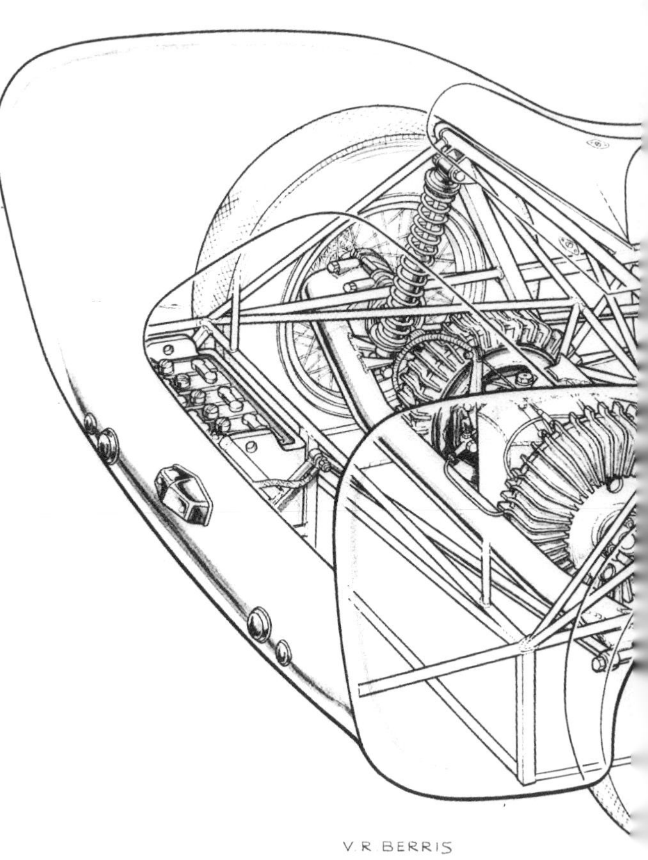

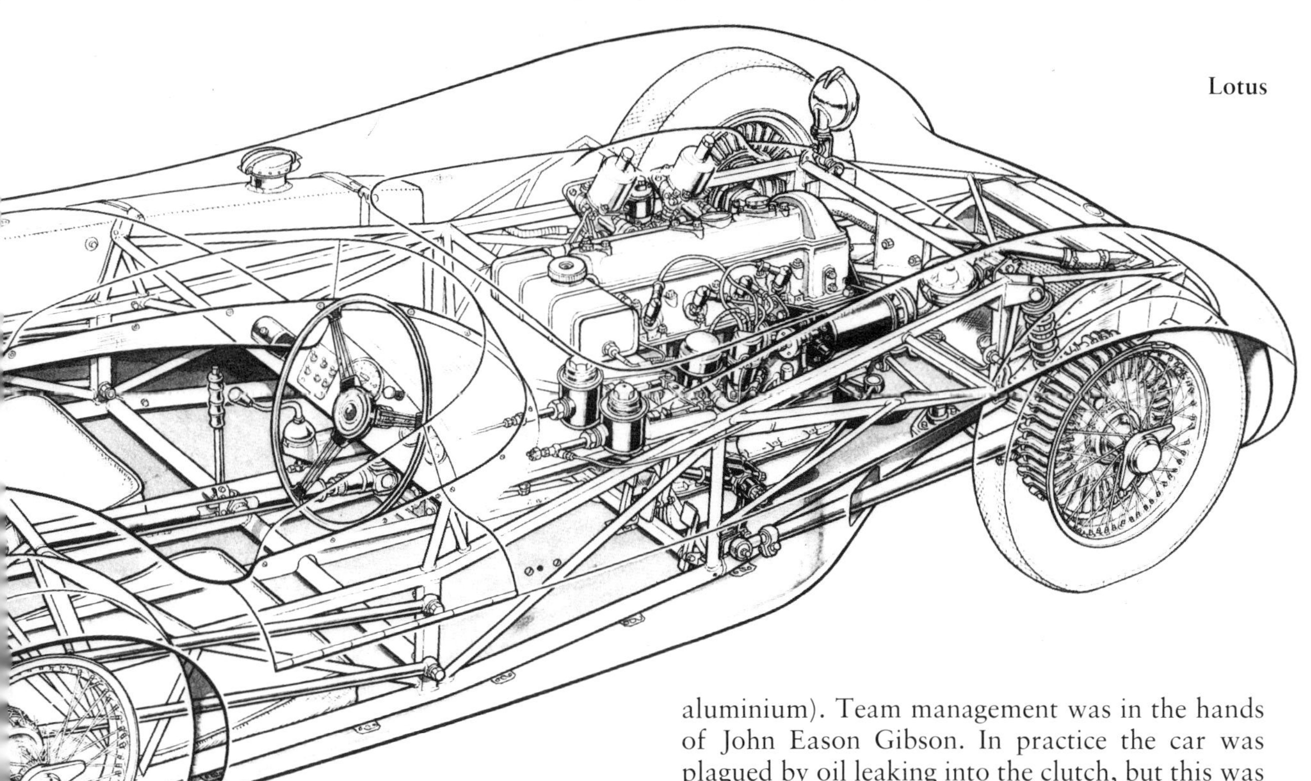

ABOVE *A fine cutaway drawing of the Mk 9 by Vic Berris (Quadrant Library)*

LEFT *Ron Flockhart at the wheel of the works Lotus Mk 9 at Le Mans in 1955. The car was disqualified*

at around 83 mph); at the May Silverstone meeting the Lotus-MG broke its crankshaft. Over the Whitsun weekend Lotus fortunes greatly improved for Chapman. On the Saturday he won the 1500 cc sports car race at Snetterton from Sopwith's Cooper-Climax, setting fastest lap at 84.23 mph, on the Sunday Peter Jopp (who was still waiting to drive the works Climax-powered car) won at Brands Hatch and on the Monday Chapman won at Goodwood from Parnell with Sopwith's Cooper-Connaught.

At Le Mans the Climax-powered works car made its debut in the hands of Chapman and Ron Flockhart, who had been asked to drive because of his very considerable experience. Peter Jopp drove the car in practice to gain experience. The car, XPE 6, had been very carefully prepared, had conventional headlamps under perspex covers and was somewhat more substantial than the usual Mk 9 (for example it was panelled in heavier 22-gauge aluminium). Team management was in the hands of John Eason Gibson. In practice the car was plagued by oil leaking into the clutch, but this was sorted out before the race. From the start Chapman led the 1100 cc class, lost time (and the class lead) because of a slipping clutch and six hours after the start slid off the road into the sand at Arnage. Although he reversed out and rejoined the race, the Lotus was disqualified because Chapman had not waited for a signal from the marshals before rejoining the track. It seemed that the organizers were reacting strongly to the horrors of the accident involving Levegh's Mercedes three and a half hours earlier.

In July Lotus completed the construction of a new assembly shop that eased the flow of production Lotus cars for private purchasers. For Team Lotus it was very much business as usual and after Le Mans the continuing programme of running in British races resumed. The Brands Hatch meeting on 10 July proved less than successful for the team; in the 1100 cc race, Chapman at the wheel of the Climax-powered car could manage only a remarkable dead-heat for second place with Bueb's Cooper behind the winning works Cooper of Russell and Jopp, with the MG-powered car an unsatisfactory fourth in the 1500 cc race behind three 1100 cc Coopers. However, winning form was soon resumed. At the British Grand Prix at Aintree Chapman drove a magnificent race with the MG-powered car to finish ninth overall, win the 1500 cc class and defeat all the 2-litre entries (Scott-Brown retired the Lister-Bristol right at the start). On August Bank Holiday Saturday (actually 30 July) Chapman scored a win in the 1500 cc sports car race at the Crystal Palace, a win in his heat of the 1500 cc Air

Kruise Trophy at Brands Hatch on the Monday, but only third place in the final after the MG engine began to run rough. At Snetterton a couple of weeks later Chapman retired the MG-powered car because of a broken half-shaft, but Coombs, whose 1955 Connaught-powered car lacked tail fins, won the 1500 cc class of the small-capacity sports car race, but was beaten by Salvadori with Sopwith's 1100 cc Cooper-Climax.

There followed a series of important British sports car races. At the Goodwood Nine Hours race Team Lotus entered the MG-powered car for Chapman/Jopp and the Climax-powered car for Flockhart/Cliff Allison. It was not to prove a good race for Lotus. On only the first lap Tony Gaze spun his Aston Martin DB3S and collided with the 1100 cc car, wrecking the nearside front suspension. After lengthy work in the pits, the Mk 9 Climax rejoined the race only to retire because of a slipping clutch. In the early part of the race the MG-powered car led the 1500 cc class (which included the Moss/von Hanstein Porsche), but retired in the seventh hour when the flywheel parted company with the rest of the engine.

The following weekend the team contested the *Daily Herald* International Trophy at Oulton Park, a race that attracted a very strong and interesting entry. It did not prove a good race for Team Lotus. Allison crashed heavily with the 1100 cc car, while Chapman was never out of trouble with the 1500 cc car, stopping at the pits for the replacement of a fractured steering arm and retiring because of oil in the clutch. A week later Chapman won the 1500 cc sports car race at Aintree with the MG-powered car from the Connaughts of Brooks and Leston. At the Tourist Trophy on the Dundrod circuit in Northern Ireland, a round in the Sports Car World Championship, Team Lotus entered the 1500 cc car to be driven by Peter Jopp/Mike Anthony and the 1100 cc car by Colin Chapman/Cliff Allison. Early in the race Chapman held fourteenth place, leading all the cars up to 2000 cc, but all this advantage was lost when an oil pipe broke and Chapman/Allison finished eleventh overall and second in the 1100 cc class behind the Bueb/MacDowel Cooper-Climax. Peter Jopp was involved in the multi-car accident that brought use of the Dundrod circuit to an end, but fortunately escaped unhurt.

There remained only a number of less important British events on the Team Lotus programme for 1955. The following weekend Chapman with the Climax-powered car won a 1250 cc race at the Members' Goodwood meeting from the private Lotus entries of Steed and Page. At Snetterton he retired in the 1500 cc race because of a broken throttle and at Castle Combe finished second to Bueb's Cooper-Climax in both the 2000 cc Sports Car race and an Invitation race. Two more races remained, both at Brands Hatch, in October, when Chapman succeeded in beating Bueb and at the first of the famous Boxing Day meetings, when Chapman again won from Bueb.

Lotus Engineering Ltd. had enrolled as members of the Society of Motor Manufacturers and Traders, but initially as makers of accessories! This should have entitled the company to a stand in the gallery only at the Earls Court Show, but by special concession a small stand was made available in the main ground floor exhibition area. A very specially prepared and finished Mk 9 without body panels was exhibited; subsequently this car was fitted with a very handsome open body by Ghia and exhibited at the Geneva Motor Show in 1956.

In the autumn of 1955 the works Climax-powered Mk 9 was loaned to *The Autocar* and *Motor Sport* and Peter Garnier and William Boddy, for these journals, drove it for long distances on the road and reported in glowing terms. John Bolster of *Autosport* was even luckier and was allowed to test both Climax- and MG-powered works cars. He achieved quite staggering performance figures (those for the Climax-powered car in parentheses): maximum speed: 128.6 mph (127.7 mph); 0–60 mph: 8.6 sec (7.8 sec); 0–100 mph: 22.4 sec (23.6 sec); standing quarter-mile: 15.4 sec (15.8 sec). For both models the fuel consumption was said to be 30 mpg on the road and 20 mpg under racing conditions.

Bolster wrote:

> 'Compared with last year's car, the body is greatly improved; the vibration of the panels at high engine revolutions has been noticeably reduced. The general sensation is that one is sitting in a solidly constructed vehicle, and there seems no reason why the body should not stand up well to a hectic competition career .... The racing successes of the Lotus need no underlining from me. However, I now have a fuller understanding of how they have been achieved. Particularly in the case of the Climax-engined car, one finds a machine which is so well balanced that all the power can be used nearly all the time; and on the rare occasions when this is not so, those Girling discs give straight-line braking as powerful as it is dependable.'

After the great promise shown by the Mk 8 in 1954, perhaps more consistent success could have been expected in 1955 and some of Team Lotus's outings were, to say the least, disappointing. By 1956, however, and the introduction of a further improved car, Lotus began to get both 1100 and 1500 cc categories completely sewn up.

Lotus Mk 10

Largely as the result of persuasion by Mike Anthony, Chapman produced an interesting variant of the 1955 Lotus, known as the Mk 10, powered by a Bristol engine and using a Bristol gearbox. Despite the very considerable depth of the Bristol engine, the bonnet was only 2.5 in. higher than on the standard Mk 9. The transmission line was lowered and a Salisbury hypoid final drive with a choice of three ratios was used. This was the first Lotus to be fitted with disc brakes and Dunlop discs were used front and rear. All-up weight was 11 cwt. Less engine and gearbox Lotus quoted a price of £925. Mk 10 cars were delivered to Mike Anthony (PCD 13), Peter Scott-Russell (JBW 648) and Cliff Davis (NOY 1). Other cars were sold to Dr. Vaughan Havard (RCR 520, but used very little because of the owner's ill-health), Mike Young (his car was powered by a Connaught 2-litre engine) and George Nixon (Turner 1500 cc engine). It is now a matter of legend that a Mk 10 was ordered by James Dean, but he was killed before it could be delivered. This car was to have been fitted with an Offenhauser engine. It was anticipated that the Lotus-Bristol would be unchallenged in the 2-litre class, but the Mk 10s proved no match for Scott-Brown's works Lister-Bristol and indeed had difficulty in coping with other Listers that were not so well driven. With the benefit of hindsight it would seem that the Lotus lacked the balance of the Lister and at most races its handling looked decidedly inferior.

Mike Anthony first appeared with his car in the 2000 cc sports car race at Goodwood on Easter Monday and, as with all Anthony's cars, it was immaculately turned out, but at this early stage in its career still unpainted. There was a tussle for the lead between Scott-Brown (Lister) and Brooks (Frazer Nash), but Anthony was never in touch with the leaders and finished third. This was to be the pattern for the rest of the year. Anthony took a second to Scott-Brown at Ibsley, won at Goodwood on Whit Monday and finished second at Brands Hatch on August Bank Holiday Monday; Scott-Russell took a class second at Snetterton in August and in the Goodwood Nine Hours race Davis/Bicknell finished twelfth overall and second in their class. Scott-Russell won the 2000 cc class in

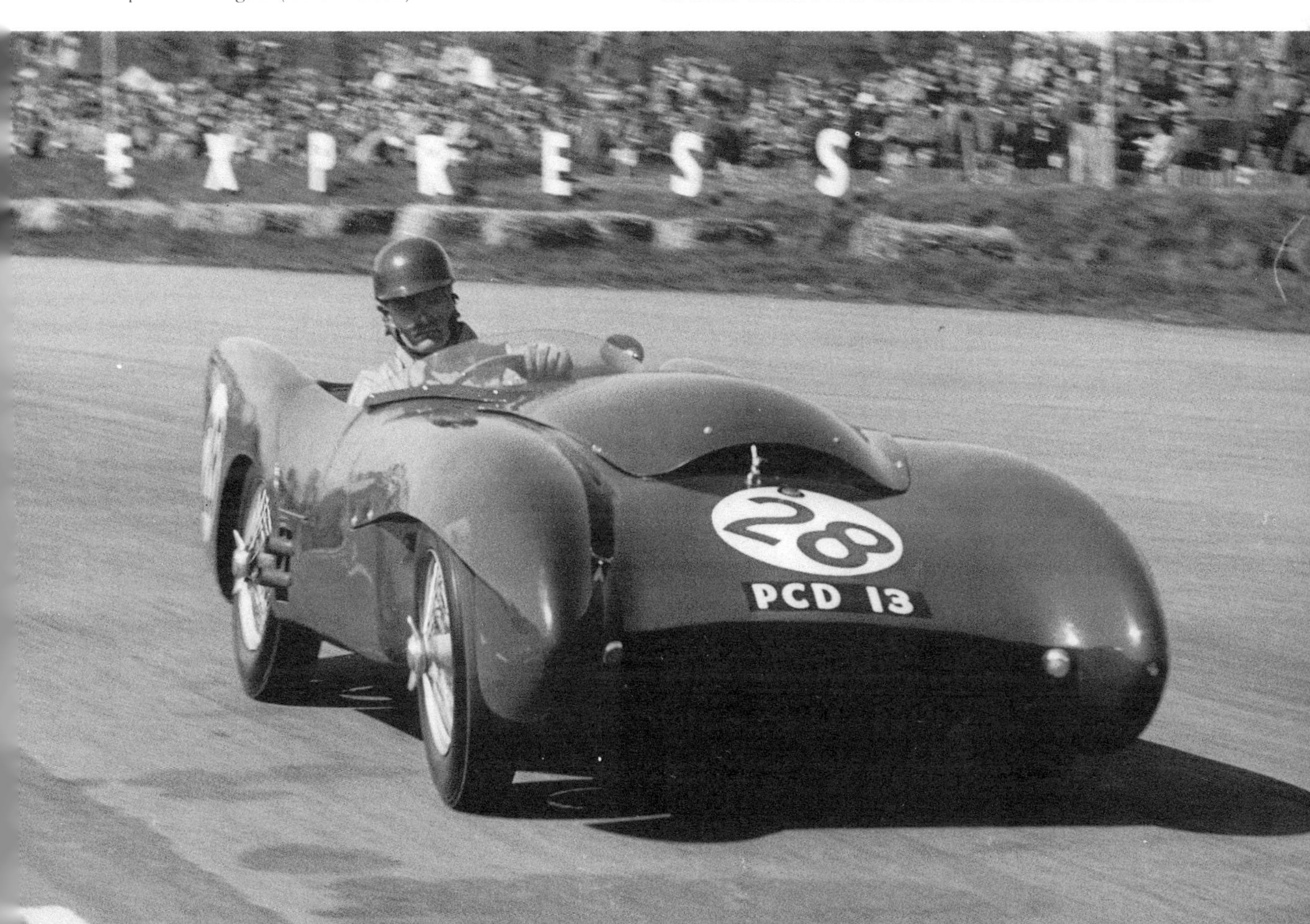

Mike Anthony with his Bristol-powered Mk 10 in the Sports Car race at Silverstone in May 1955. The Mk 10 was characterized by the deeply curved bonnet panel to clear the deep Bristol engine (T. C. March)

the *Daily Herald* International Trophy at Oulton Park, but the only other finisher in the class was Anthony, whose car had blown the head gasket, was constantly stopping to top up the water and covered barely half race-distance. At Aintree the following weekend Scott-Russell finished second to Cunningham-Reid (Lister-Bristol) in the 2000 cc class. Finally, at the Boxing Day Brands Hatch meeting C. M. Lund won the Unlimited Sports Car race with Anthony's Mk 10 from Scott-Brown at the wheel of a Jaguar C-type.

In 1956 Anthony sold his Mk 10 to Dimitri Kasterine, who raced it with mixed fortunes in the black and white colours of the Six Miles Stable and moved to another and rather special Bristol-powered car which will be described shortly. Peter Scott-Russell was still racing his Lotus in 1956, but it caught fire and was burnt out at Silverstone in May after going off the track (he spent several years rebuilding it) and Cliff Davis was still racing his Mk 10 in 1957.

Lotus Eleven

1956

The year 1956 marked a significant turning point in Lotus fortunes. With the introduction of the much improved Eleven, the appearance of a 1500 cc version of the Coventry-Climax engine and, as the year progressed, the concentration of the rival Cooper team more and more on the new single-seater Formula 2 category, Lotus achieved almost overwhelming domination of British 1100 cc and 1500 cc sports car racing, and significant success in major continental events.

Chapman had decided to drop the 'Mark' in reference to Lotus models and so the new car was known simply as the 'Eleven' or '11'. As Chapman intended, it made it simpler to describe the different models in later years when high numbers had been reached. The new car followed the design principles of the Mk 9 closely, but had been improved in almost every respect. The space-frame chassis was constructed in 1 in. and ¾ in. 18- or 20-gauge tubing. Suspension followed previous Chapman design practice, but with a number of modifications. At the front the swing axles had a lower pivot and this reduced the pronounced understeer of the Mk 9. There was a new and lighter de Dion axle at the rear through which the articulated half-shafts passed and this axle was located by twin radius arms either side. New rack-and-pinion steering was fitted, Girling disc brakes were used front and rear, there was a lighter and completely ducted radiator and the fuel tank had been moved from the tail; in standard form a 9.5-gallon tank was mounted on the left-hand side of the body, but for long-distance racing an additional 11-gallon tank could be installed on the right-hand side.

Generally the Eleven was smaller and more compact than its immediate predecessor and it was distinguished by completely new bodywork. Although the scuttle was the same height as on the Mk 9, both bonnet and tail swept down more steeply, and the distinctive tail fins had been replaced by higher rear wings with just the suggestion of fins; most cars were also fitted with a very prominent driver's headrest. Conventional headlamps were now mounted behind perspex covers. Accessibility was better than ever, as both front and rear sections of the body pivoted on the ends of the frame and could be removed if required. Bottom-hinged doors were fitted both sides and the interior of the Eleven was properly trimmed, with Dunlopillo padding for the seats and map pockets in the doors.

Originally announced in Climax-powered and Ford-powered versions, the Eleven was consolidated during the year as three individual models with distinct specifications:

Le Mans

The serious competition model with Coventry-Climax FWA engine inclined 10 degrees to the left in the chassis, thereby permitting a carburation arrangement with horizontal induction tracts; gearbox using Austin A30 casing with special Lotus close-ratio gears (later the MGA gearbox was substituted); Girling 9.5 in. disc brakes mounted outboard at the front and inboard at the rear. The majority of these cars were fitted with the Coventry-Climax FWA 1098 cc engine, but works cars and private owners favoured by Climax were supplied with the new FWB 1460 cc engine developing 142 bhp at 6750 rpm.

There were so many of these cars raced during 1956 that it is not practical to list more than the most prominent drivers: Ivor Bueb (car fitted with FWB engine, entered by Bueb's Ecurie Demi-Litre Team and usually driven by Mike Hawthorn), Keith Hall (YTN 444), Tommy Sopwith's Équipe Endeavour (TMY 400 fitted with FWB engine), David Piper and Bob Hicks (RNM 222 and VPG 34—these cars were taken on a long and successful tour of minor continental races), Innes Ireland (5 BPH) and Alan Stacey (YKX 55).

Lotus offered the 'Le Mans 75' at £1337 and 'Le Mans 85' with Stage 2 FWA engine at £1387 and the installation of the FWB engine added about £250 to the price.

Club

The Climax engine and Lotus gearbox were retained, but there was a live rear axle located by parallel trailing arms and drum brakes (9 in. at the front and 8 in. at the rear) and the Club was available with full-width screen, wipers and a hood. The price was £1083.

Sports

Primarily intended for road use, this version was similar to the Club, but was fitted with the Ford 1172 cc side-valve engine and Ford gearbox. The price was £872. This model enjoyed considerable success and Graham Hill drove one in the 1956 *Autosport* Production Sports Car Championship. The following year Ian Walker acquired this 'Club', fitted it with a Willment inlet over exhaust cylinder head and drove it to victory overall in the *Autosport* Championship.

The first of the new Elevens were shipped out to the United States to run at Sebring and Chapman flew out to co-drive the FWB-powered car entered by Briggs Cunningham. This was crashed in practice by Len Bastrup, so Chapman co-drove a 1100 cc car with Shepherd, only to be eliminated by a burnt-out starter motor.

After the 12 Hours race Chapman flew back to look after the Lotus entries at the Easter Goodwood meeting. Here newcomer to Team Lotus, Reg Bicknell, drove a 1460 cc Eleven (RCR 400), slowed by handling problems, to fourth place in the 1500cc sports car race. Like all members of Team Lotus at this time Bicknell paid his own way. By the British Empire Trophy at Oulton Park Chapman was at the wheel of another new Eleven with FWB power (9 EHX) and Ecurie Demi-Litre had taken delivery of their Eleven, which was driven by Hawthorn. There was strong opposition from the Cooper team, who had entered cars for Salvadori, and Moss. Chapman won the heat from Salvadori and Hawthorn, but in the final he spun away his lead and the finishing order was Moss, Chapman, Salvadori and Hawthorn. In the 2000 cc race at Aintree later in April, Chapman took over Allison's Team Lotus entry to win the 1100 cc class, while Hawthorn won the race outright with the Ecurie Demi-Litre entry.

There were two very significant factors about this class of racing in 1956. The 1100 cc and 1500 cc sports car were proving so competitive and numerous that they were rapidly ousting 500 cc Formula 3, which had been the popular 'starter's' Formula for so many years. Furthermore it was possible for a well-driven, well-prepared car such as Hawthorn's Ecurie Demi-Litre entry or, a little later, the Coombs entries driven by Salvadori to beat the works cars.

At Brands Hatch at the end of April Graham Hill drove a Team Lotus entry (DEC 494) to win the 1100 cc race and finish second to Bicknell in the 1500 cc event. Chapman was beaten into second place by Salvadori (works Cooper) at the May Silverstone meeting, but it was only a minor setback and Elevens, both Team Lotus and private entries, were winning races weekend after weekend. One of the most exciting was at Goodwood on Whit Monday, when Chapman and Hawthorn had the most incredibly close dice in the 1500 cc sports car race, both spinning at Madgwick, colliding and rejoining the race—Chapman won by a good margin after Hawthorn stopped at the pits for his car to be checked. They met up again in the Whitsun Trophy, a combined Unlimited Sports and Formule Libre race in which Hawthorn drove a fantastic race to finish second, splitting the Ecurie Ecosse D-type Jaguars and setting a new 1500 cc lap record of 89.26 mph—only a fifth of a second slower than Titterington's new class lap record with the D-type. Chapman was out of this race with a stripped second gear before he reached the first corner.

In June, Bicknell travelled with his 1500 cc car to Porto to compete in the 92-mile City Cup in which he finished third behind Salvadori (works Cooper) and Nogueira (Porsche). Bicknell was a good Club driver, but not really 'International' material and at this time Chapman was proving himself a truly able driver and the only member of Team Lotus able to exploit the full potential of the Eleven. It was a loss to motor racing when Chapman retired early in 1957 to concentrate on the engineering side of the business and team and management, but by this time Team Lotus had a full team of really able drivers.

Ecurie Demi-Litre entered a couple of continental events, but without success. Their Eleven, to be driven by Hawthorn/Hamilton, non-started because of gearbox trouble in the Supercortemaggiore Grand Prix at Monza and in the 1500 cc Reims 12 Hours race driven by Bueb/Mackay Fraser led until first and second gears went. Team Lotus was out in force in the Coupe Delamare Debouteville, the $1\frac{1}{4}$-hours race preceding the

Colin Chapman and the works FWB-powered Eleven on their way to second place in the first Formula 2 race at Silverstone in July 1956 (Louis Klementaski)

Rouen Sports Car Grand Prix, and scored a clean sweep, although there was not much in the way of serious opposition. Chapman was the overall winner at 87.93 mph, Allison finished second and won the 1100 cc class and Harry Schell with the 1500 cc Sopwith car finished third after having led initially. Lotus might not yet be a significant force in International racing, but it was a strong pointer to the future.

Although Lotus were working on their own 1500 cc Formula 2 car for the new Formula that was to come into force in 1957, the cars were not ready by the first preview race held at Silverstone on the day of the British Grand Prix—the only proper single-seater in the race was Salvadori's Cooper. The new Cooper won and Chapman, whose Lotus was faster than the Cooper along the straights (not really surprising), took a good second place.

Following the 1955 Le Mans disaster, the 1956 24 Hours race was postponed until the end of July to allow circuit improvements to be carried out. Team Lotus entered a strong entry of three cars, a 1500 cc to be driven by Chapman/Mackay Fraser and 1100 cc cars for Bicknell/Jopp and Cliff Allison/Keith Hall. The cars were very carefully prepared, looked superb and to comply with the new Le Mans regulations had the chassis frames widened at the centre to permit full-width open cockpits; full-width screens were compulsory, but on the Elevens these wrapped right round with the side portions attached to the drop-down doors. Additional lights were mounted behind perspex covers either side of the nose. It was a difficult race, with heavy rain during the night hours, but all three cars survived until the Sunday morning. Allison/Hall were forced to retire after their car had been badly damaged in a collision with a large dog, the Chapman/Fraser 1500 succumbed to big end failure, but the other 1100 of Bicknell/Jopp survived to take seventh place overall and first in the 1100 cc class at an average of 89.97 mph. It was a magnificent performance by a car that had been built for short-circuit events, but some indication of the power deficiency of the Elevens can be judged from the fact that the 1500 was timed on the Mulsanne straight at 128.20 mph, compared with the 138.09 mph of the fastest of the works Porsche 550 entries that dominated the 1500 cc class.

For the remainder of the year Lotus sports cars continued to achieve success in British events. Mike Hawthorn had a very lucky escape in the *Sporting Life* Trophy at Oulton Park in August when, cornering too fast, he lost control of the Ecurie Demi-Litre Eleven, hit the bank and the car flipped and disintegrated, with parts striking Salvadori's Cooper. In September the sports Lotus Elevens were trounced, not unexpectedly, by the single-seater Coopers in the Formula 2 Gold Cup race at Oulton Park and Chapman and Flockhart (entered by Coombs) had to settle for third and fourth places. Towards the end of the year Herbert Mackay Fraser drove a 1500 into fifth place in the Shell Grand Prix at Imola and won the 1100 cc

Sports Car race on the Castelfusano circuit near Rome. After the Imola race Lotus had gone record-breaking at Monza and with Fraser at the wheel of an 1100 cc car had taken a string of class records, including 100 miles at 137.5 mph.

There were some interesting variants of the Eleven raced in 1956. Mike Anthony raced a car which he built up himself with a Bristol engine laid on its side. It was not a success, but it was immaculately prepared and made a fine show on the specially lengthened Standard Vanguard transporter which Anthony built (deliberately aping the high-speed transporter used by Mercedes in 1955). Brian Naylor transferred the engine from his Maserati 150S and drove his new Lotus-Maserati to a win in the Leinster Trophy, while Alex McMillan fitted his Lotus with a Fiat-based 1100 cc Stanguellini engine claimed to develop 95 bhp at 7300 rpm and Fiat gearbox.

1957

In late 1956 Lotus announced the team's new Formula 2 car, which had immense promise but proved far less successful than the rival Cooper. From this point on there was a marked cross-fertilization of design innovation between Lotus single-seaters and sports/racing cars and with the passing of the years Lotus concentrated more and more on single-seaters at the expense of sports car development.

For the 1957 season Lotus introduced the Series 2 Eleven, which featured the double wishbone and coil spring front suspension of the Formula 2 cars and a strengthened de Dion rear axle to cope with the power of the 1475 cc twin-cam FPF Climax engine that became available in 1957. Elevens were now offered in four versions, the Le Mans 150 (twin-cam FPF engine), Le Mans 85 (Stage 2 Climax 1100), Club 75 (Climax 1100 engine, drum brakes and live rear axle) and Sports 45 (with Ford 1172 engine, drum brakes and live rear axle).

In February 1957 there appeared the following announcement in *Autosport* based on a press statement from Lotus:

'The three Lotus Formula 2 cars, which will concentrate on Formula 2 championship events at home and abroad will be driven by Colin Chapman, Cliff Allison and H. Mackay Fraser. [In fact Chapman retired from racing and did not compete in Formula 2.] For sports car events, three private owners, Keith Hall, Peter Ashdown and Alan Stacey, will be entering their own 1100 cc cars for all suitable events, under the auspices of Team Lotus and with full works backing.

'For certain major International sports car events, such as Sebring, Le Mans and Reims, teams of special cars will be built and the drivers will be selected from the six already mentioned.

'Finally, Lotus Engineering wish to make it clear that no other organization racing under a name similar to Team Lotus (such as Ecurie Lotus, Equipe Lotus or Scuderia Lotus) has any connection with the works.'

The last paragraph was inserted in the statement because of Chapman's concern about the many private owners racing Elevens, for whom it could be only too easy to pass themselves off as associates of the works. Lotus plans roughly followed the statement, but in fact there were not three Formula 2 cars ready at the start of the season and Keith Hall took Chapman's place in the Formula 2 team. Graham Hill also drove for Team Lotus on occasions.

Nineteen fifty-seven started well for Lotus with an 1100 cc class win in the Sebring 12 Hours race by Chapman/Sheppard/Dungan, who finished eleventh overall. The British Empire Trophy at Oulton was held as three class races and the smaller-capacity races were completely Lotus-dominated with the first three places in both events. In the 2000 cc race Chapman led until he spun off and fought his way back to finish second to Flockhart with a Coombs-entered Eleven. This domination continued at Goodwood on Easter Monday, where Elevens took the first seven places in the 1500 cc race. In the Belgian Sports Car Grand Prix at Spa Naylor won the 2-litre class with his latest Lotus-Maserati and Mackay Fraser won the 1500 cc class. It was the same story in British National races throughout the year.

Le Mans was to prove the greatest triumph in Lotus sports car history. A total of five specially prepared cars was entered and their performance can be summarized as follows:

1500 cc car to be driven by Mackay Fraser/Jay Chamberlain. Suffered dropped valve in practice (a common shortcoming with early twin-cam Climax engines) and non-started.

1100 cc car (DEC 494) to be driven by Peter Ashdown/Alan Stacey, but taken over for the race by Fraser/Chamberlain. Finished ninth overall, won the 1100 cc class and classified second in the Index of Performance.

1100 cc car (UDV 609) privately entered by John Green for John Dalton/Bob Walshaw. Finished thirteenth overall and second in the 1100 cc class.

1100 cc car (YAR 527) privately entered by André Hechard and Roger Masson. Finished sixteenth overall and fourth in the 1100 cc class.

5 BPB
39

750 cc car (XAR 11) (powered by 744 cc Climax FWC engine) driven by Cliff Allison/Keith Hall. Finished fourteenth overall, won the 750 cc class and the Index of Performance.

The success of the 750 cc car with a one-off Climax engine was particularly satisfying, as it broke the domination of the French DB team in the Index of Performance. For this race a number of body changes had been made to the Elevens to best exploit the Le Mans regulations, which specified a full-width screen, two proper seats and flexible tonneau. The windscreen curved backwards at the top in a line with the rear body, which was raised to the height of the tail fins; over the passenger seat a flexible tonneau linked the top of the screen and the top of the rear body.

It is also worth remembering that at Le Mans in 1957 private Jaguar D-types finished first, second, fourth and sixth.

Immediately after Le Mans the Lotus team travelled to Rouen to compete in the Coupe Delamere Debouteville, where they met up with the Coombs team who had entered their 1500 with Ron Flockhart at the wheel. Flockhart won the race and the 1500 cc class with Chamberlain second with the works car, while Chapman with DEC 494 finished second in the 1100 cc class to de Tomaso's Osca after a pit stop for water and Allison won the 750 class. Another quite magnificent performance.

Tragedy followed the following weekend at Reims. Chamberlain crashed one of the 1100 cc cars heavily in practice for the 12 Hours race and Chapman, inevitably preoccupied with making arrangements for his medical treatment, failed to present the cars for compulsory fuel-draining and Team Lotus was disqualified. In the Formula 2 race Mackay Fraser drove a stripped sports car and was killed when he lost control and crashed at the very fast Garenne curve.

Other continental successes later during the year were both gained by Allison; a victory in the 1500 cc race at Roskilde in Denmark and another victory in the 1500 cc race at Spa after de Tomaso's Osca blew up two laps from the finish. Just before the Earls Court Show Lotus went record-breaking again at Monza with one car and supercharged engines of 750 cc and 1100 cc. Piston failure before the record attempts resulted in abandonment and a quick return to Britain.

ABOVE LEFT *This 750 cc Lotus Eleven driven by Cliff Allison and Keith Hall won the 750 cc class and the Index of Performance at Le Mans in 1957. Passing is the Jaguar D-type of Duncan Hamilton (LAT)*

BELOW LEFT *With this Coombs-entered twin-cam Climax-powered Eleven, Ron Flockhart won the 1500 cc Sports Car race at the* Daily Express *Silverstone meeting in September 1957 (T. C. March)*

BELOW *Alan Stacey drove this Series 2 Lotus 11-Climax into second place in the 1100 cc heat of the 1958 British Empire Trophy at Oulton Park (T. C. March)*

1958

Throughout 1958 the Eleven Series 2 remained in production and dominated the 1100 cc class of racing. With the exception of one race, however, the cars were no longer fielded by Team Lotus, which was too busily engaged with the new 15 sports/racing car and Formula 1 and 2 racing. The

exception was Le Mans. Two 750 cc cars were entered, a Team Lotus entry for Stacey/Dickson and Masson/Hechard. Both cars were fitted with new Climax FWMA 745 cc engines, live rear axles (to reduce transmission power loss), drum rear brakes and magnesium-alloy wheels. The new FWMA engine of the works car broke in practice, so the 1957 744 cc unit was substituted. Elevens in 1100 cc form were entered for Ireland/Taylor (works entry) and Frost/Hicks (private entry). The race proved a complete débâcle for Team Lotus and the sole finisher was the works 750 in twentieth and last place.

Lotus 15

1958

Briefly the 15 may be described as an improved Eleven with many of the features of the Lotus single-seaters. The chassis was a multi-tubular space-frame of improved but basically typical Lotus design constructed from 1 in. and $\frac{3}{4}$ in. round and square tubes with the prop-shaft tunnel and floor forming stressed integral parts of the frame. Complete with mounting brackets the chassis weighed 65 lb. Likewise the body, one of the sleekest evolved by Frank Costin, was derived from the style of the Eleven, but with lower frontal area (possible because the engine was angled to the right in the frame), exceptionally aerodynamic wind-screen blending smoothly with the cockpit and streamlined headrest (but arranged so that the driver looked above rather than through it). In the tail were three tanks for oil and fuel, the battery and the spare wheel, which fitted under the headrest. In accordance with now usual practice, the front and rear sections of the body were hinged and quickly removable.

The most significant changes were concealed beneath the shapely panelling. As mentioned, the Climax FPF engine was canted to the right, 60 degrees from the vertical, and although this ensured a very low bonnet line, it necessitated the construction of special manifolding for the twin Weber carburettors. The gearbox/ZF final drive unit was that used in the Formula 2 cars and Lotus were hoping that the lubrication problems that had plagued this unit in 1957 had been cured.

The gearchange was centrally mounted and was of the so-called 'positive-stop' type with all five forward gears in line, neutral between first and second and reverse selected by a separate linkage with the knob behind the passenger seat to prevent it being accidentally engaged. Once first had been selected, gear-changing was simply a matter of forward for up through the box and back for downward changes. In practice many drivers considered the gear-change to be neither positive nor stop and were concerned about the risk of engaging a wrong gear on downward changes and locking the rear wheels. Coombs introduced a very simple safety catch that prevented first being selected once the car was on the move. Another problem was that because of the long linkage to the gearbox in unit with the final drive, the change could be very woolly and imprecise.

At the front, suspension was by the double wishbone and coil spring layout seen on both the Formula 2 cars and the Eleven Series 2, while the Formula 2 'strut' suspension had been adopted at the rear. The Chapman strut suspension was based on the drive-shaft (which located the wheel laterally), a forward-facing radius arm and the strut member (the coil spring/damper unit), which converged into an aluminium casing just behind the wheel. The radius arm was attached to a lug containing two small bearings and projecting from the front of the casing; the suspension unit was attached in a circular housing at the top of the casing and, set at an angle, ran to a lug on a rear chassis member; the drive-shaft, with universal joints at each end was inclined upwards by 3 degrees at the wheel and so the rear wheels had a slight negative camber. It was a very simple, very effective suspension layout that gave near-enough identical handling with light or heavy fuel load and it was lighter than a de Dion arrangement.

For sale to private customers the power unit was the 1.5-litre Climax FPF, but the works cars used 2-litre engines. Centre-lock wire wheels were the standard fitting, but the works cars used the now very familiar 'wobbly-web' Lotus magnesium-alloy wheels and these could be supplied on customer cars. Girling disc brakes were mounted front and rear (inboard at the rear).

The 15 driven by Graham Hill made its debut in the Unlimited Sports Car race at Goodwood on Easter Monday, but retired near the end of the race because of gearbox trouble. Hill was quoted as saying, 'It was like stirring a box full of nothing.' The following weekend two 2-litre works cars were driven by Hill and Allison in the British Empire Trophy at Oulton Park and Roy Salvadori drove Pierre Berchem's 15, the prototype car fitted with a 1.5-litre engine. In their heat Allison and Salvadori finished first and second and it looked as though there would be a mighty battle in the final between the 15s and the works Aston Martins (Hill failed to

Graham Hill with the new Lotus 15 in the 1958 British Empire Trophy at Oulton Park. He finished sixth in his heat after a pit stop and just failed to qualify for the final. The 15s were very quick, but far from reliable (T. C. March)

qualify for the final because of a pit stop caused by a loose plug). In fact the Lotus challenge soon evaporated, Allison retired because of loss of oil pressure and Salvadori was eliminated by a problem with a rear hub.

More problems followed at Aintree. On the warming up lap the distributor on Hill's car disintegrated. It was changed on the grid, and in his haste to get away he damaged a gear-selector and was left struggling to find a gear; Allison's car stalled its engine and was rammed by Hamilton's Jaguar. At the May Silverstone meeting Team Lotus fortunes improved. Hill won the 1500 cc Sports Car race and set a new class lap record of 97.56 mph, but Allison retired the 2-litre car in the Unlimited Sports Car race.

At Le Mans two 15s were entered by Team Lotus, but on the basis of their performance so far in 1958 it was evident that their prospects of lasting the distance were slim indeed. Both entries featured a revised engine arrangement and this was now canted a mere 17 degrees to the left from the vertical and resulted in a bonnet bulge that disrupted the smooth air flow of the Costin design. Lotus had found that the original engine arrangement had simply not worked satisfactorily and had caused many problems, not the least of which was a power loss. Other features of the Le Mans cars (including the Elevens entered in this race) were higher tails, which were said to be more aerodynamic, and inflatable tonneau covers running from the top of the windscreen to the tail. The 2-litre 15, driven by Allison and Hill, was immensely fast in practice, but up with the leaders in the race for a mere three laps before it succumbed to gasket failure. The second 15, a 1.5-litre car driven by Chamberlain/Lovely, lasted rather longer, but suffered a persistent misfire and was eventually eliminated when Chamberlain spun into the bank near the Dunlop Bridge to avoid a slower car and was rammed by Picard's Ferrari.

Back on home territory Salvadori brought Combs's 2-litre 15 across the line in second place behind Moss's Lister-Jaguar in the Sports Car race at the British Grand Prix meeting at Silverstone and Allison was third with a works car, winning the 1500 cc class. In September Salvadori scored another fine victory with the Coombs car, winning the Gold Cup Sports Car race at Oulton

ABOVE *At the British Grand Prix meeting at Silverstone in July Cliff Allison drove this Team Lotus 15 into second place in the Sports Car race (T. C. March)*

RIGHT *Lotus Engineering advertisement for the 15 in the February 1959 issue of* Sports Car and Lotus Owner. *The car shown is John Coombs' with Roy Salvadori at the wheel—but for 1959 Coombs and Salvadori switched to the new Cooper Monaco*

Park almost unchallenged and setting a new sports car lap record of 86.28 mph. In contrast the works cars had failed miserably in the Tourist Trophy at Goodwood earlier in the month. The successes of Coombs' car added weight to the view that the 15 was basically a very sound and competitive design, the race-winning performance of which needed to be complemented by high standards of preparation. In contrast the works were simply trying to do too much, racing both sports cars and single-seaters without the resources or the time for proper development and preparation.

In August 1958 Lotus had introduced a Series Two 15, primarily intended for export with the 1.5-litre Climax engine mounted 17 degrees to the left from the vertical (as on the Le Mans cars); a BMC B-series 4-speed gearbox was mounted in unit with the engine and with the normal H-pattern gearchange and a final drive with BMC gears in a Lotus chassis-mounted casing.

1959

For 1959 Lotus introduced a Series Three version of the 15, again intended as a customer car, as it was not originally the intention to field entries in sports car events. There was some stiffening of the chassis frame, but the main changes were to the suspension. At the front the upper wishbones had been 'reversed' so that they now passed behind the wheel centres, which made space for a larger radiator and oil cooler. The front track was 1 in. narrower. The 2-litre Climax FPF engine angled 17 degrees to the left was the standard installation and this was used in conjunction with the BMC 4-speed gearbox. An improved version of the 5-speed gearbox was also available. Lotus Engineering were anxious to promote sales of the 15 (now quite likely to lose out to the Cooper Monaco) and one of their advertisements is reproduced. It is ironic that the car shown is Coombs' with Salvadori at the wheel, as Coombs switched to the Cooper Monaco for 1959 and his Monaco dominated British events in 1959!

In fact, despite Lotus's original intention, Graham Hill regularly drove a Team Lotus-entered 15 in British events, but achieved little success. At the Easter Goodwood meeting the distributor drive sheared on the warming-up lap, he finished third at Oulton Park (behind two Cooper Monacos),

At Aintree in July 1959 Graham Hill drove this Series 3 15 to victory in the Sports Car race (T. C. March)

second at Aintree (to Salvadori's Cooper Monaco) and retired with transmission failure at Silverstone in May while leading the race. At Le Mans Team Lotus entered a 2.5-litre 15 for Graham Hill/Derek Jolly, and although it worked its way through to seventh place at the end of the second hour, it started to jump out of fourth gear and this resulted in Jolly over-revving the engine. The other 15 entered, a 2-litre driven by Ireland/Stacey, was delayed by a broken wishbone and eventually retired with a blown engine. Both 15s at Le Mans were Series Three cars with 5-speed gearboxes. In July, Hill, with a 2.5-litre car, won a minor race at Mallory Park and a fine victory followed in the Sports Car race at the British Grand Prix at Aintree (but Salvadori was not entered!) Another victory for Hill followed at Brands Hatch on August Bank Holiday Monday and he won again at the Brands Hatch International Meeting later in the month. In the United States Lotus distributor Jay Chamberlain had been racing a 2-litre 15 with considerable success.

By 1960 the 15 was still available, but very much a back number, as Lotus efforts were firmly centred on the new 18 Formula One and Junior cars and the Elite, which was achieving great success in the GT category. Private Lotus 15s were raced by Tommy Dickson, David Piper and Michael Taylor, but achieved little success in the face of Coombs' latest Cooper Monaco. Early in the year Dickson won at Oulton Park with Taylor in second place, finished third at the Easter Goodwood meeting behind the Monacos of Salvadori and Blumer and finished second to Salvadori at Silverstone in May—but then graduated to driving the Ecurie Ecosse Cooper Monaco. At Aintree in April, Piper drove a very spirited race, chasing Salvadori hard until a spanner left under the bonnet by a mechanic

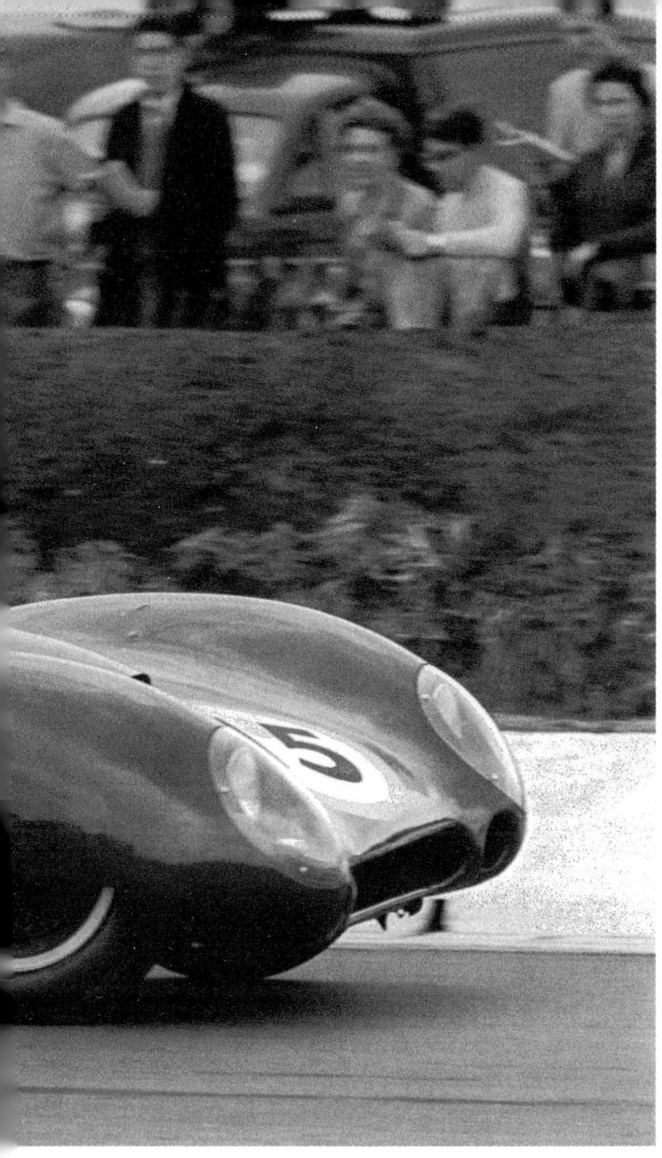

jammed the accelerator wide open and he went off the road. By 1961 the racing days of the 15 were over until 1962, when test pilot 'Dizzy' Addicot rejuvenated a 15, fitted a Buick 3.5-litre engine and raced it in British events with great élan—and considerable success.

Lotus 17

For 1959 Chapman produced what was intended as a logical replacement of the Eleven and to carry on the long run success enjoyed in the 1100 cc class. The new 17 was smaller, lower and lighter than its predecessor, but it was not a great success. Len Terry was primarily responsible for the design of the 17, which featured a space-frame very much in accordance with the usual Lotus practice and was constructed from $\frac{5}{8}$ in. and $\frac{3}{4}$ in. square and round 20-gauge tubing with the floor and prop-shaft tunnel acting as stressed members. For the first time Lotus used strut-type front suspension, with lower wishbones and almost vertical coil spring/damper units. At the rear the suspension was again of the strut type as used on the 15. The body was a composite of aluminium and fibreglass, very sleek and shapely. Cast magnesium wheels were fitted and there were Girling 9.5 in. disc brakes, mounted inboard at the rear. The 17 was offered with a choice of 1100 cc or 750 cc Climax engines inclined 10 degrees to the left, but the latter had appeal only for entries at Le Mans

The 17 proved unreliable, underdeveloped and no match for the 1100 cc Lolas that were securing a stranglehold in the class. The 17 missed the Easter Goodwood meeting, but ran three weeks later at Aintree, where Stacey came through from the back

BELOW *The Lotus 17 was not a successful design. This is the Gilby Engineering car driven by Keith Greene in the 1959 Tourist Trophy at Goodwood (G. Goddard)*

of the grid to take the lead but retired because of gearbox trouble. This proved to be the pattern for the season and the team was out of luck again at Le Mans. Here two 17s were entered, both privately owned, but running in the name of Team Lotus and powered by 745 cc engines. Inevitably both cars ran quickly, but failed to last long; Alan Stacey/Keith Greene and Michael Taylor/Jonathan Sieff were both eliminated by overheating problems. By the end of the year Lotus had given up the struggle and ceded the 1100 cc class to Lola.

Lotus 19

In 1960, Lotus raced the new 18 mid-engined Formula 1 car that scored victories at Goodwood on Easter Monday, in the BRDC Trophy at Silverstone, the Monaco Grand Prix (which Moss won with the Rob Walker-entered Lotus) and the United States Grand Prix (again Moss with the Walker car). In August 1960, Lotus introduced the new 19 sports/racing car that followed the design of the 18 very closely.

As usual there was a multi-tubular space-frame, constructed from 1 in. and ¾ in. 18- and 16-gauge tubing and built up in three sections: a forward section that carried the mountings for the front suspension with ahead of it a lighter frame carrying the water and oil radiators and the oil tanks; to the rear of this was a sheet and tubular steel scuttle frame, and this scuttle was linked to the rear section by the centre cockpit area; to the rear of the cockpit there was the third section, consisting of the engine bulkhead and the tubular rear engine bay. Front suspension was by double wishbones and coil spring/damper units and at the rear a system of lower wishbones, the unsplined drive-shafts providing transverse location, parallel radius arms and coil spring/damper units. The engine was the 2.5-litre Coventry-Climax FPF and there was a 5-speed Lotus gearbox. The body was in fibreglass with a quickly detachable nose section and one-piece engine cover.

After Moss had tested the car at Silverstone—because of its superficial similarity to the Cooper Monaco it soon became known jokingly as the Lotus Monte Carlo—it was taken to Sweden and Moss drove it to victory in a 56-mile race at Karlskoga. Lotus built only 12 of these cars—partly because of the shortage of 2.5-litre engines—and

BELOW *Tony Maggs at the wheel of a UDT-Laystall Lotus 19 at Goodwood in 1962 (David Phipps)*

RIGHT *Another view of a UDT-Laystall 19, this time Innes Ireland in the Sports Car race at Oulton Park in September 1962. It was one of Innes' many wins with the 19 (BP)*

nine including the prototype were sold in the United States, whilst three were sold to the UDT-Laystall team and raced in British events in 1961 by Henry Taylor, Graham Hill and Cliff Allison. In Britain these cars were immensely successful and they scored a whole string of successes in the United States, including a win by Dan Gurney in the 1962 Daytona Continental Three Hours road race; with a few minutes to go to the chequered flag, the Climax engine broke its crankshaft and Gurney crossed the finishing line on the starter motor.

Lotus 23

Undoubtedly the 23 was the last successful sports/racing car to be built by Lotus and was a straightforward adaption of the Lotus 22 Formula Junior design. There was a similar multi-tubular space-frame, but rather wider, and similar suspension, at the front by double wishbones and coil spring/damper units and at the rear by a system similar to that of the 1961 Formula 1 car, lower

wishbones, top links, parallel radius arms and coil spring/damper units. The engine was normally the Formula Junior 1098 cc Cosworth-Ford and this was used in conjunction with a modified Volkswagen gearbox. The body was in fibreglass with detachable panels—low, sleek and very compact. It was a formula for sports/racing cars adopted by a number of other constructors, including Brabham and Merlyn, but the 23 was faster and handled better than its rivals and dominated its class of racing. It was also inexpensive—£1650 ex-works in component form.

The best performance of the 23 during the year was in the Nürburgring 1000 Km race, where a car was entered in the name of the Essex Racing Team but under the supervision of Mike Costin. This 23 was fitted with a 1498 cc twin overhead camshaft Lotus engine, based on the Ford 116E block soon to be fitted to the Ford Classic and developing around 140 bhp. The drivers were Lotus Formula 1 team members Jim Clark and Trevor Taylor and Clark started the race in damp and very slippery conditions. He was first away at the Le Mans start, at the end of lap 1 led the entire field, which included strong Ferrari and Porsche entries, by 27 seconds and by the end of lap 8 had extended his lead to over two minutes. As the circuit dried out, so the field closed up on Clark and on lap 12, overcome by fumes from a leaking exhaust, he failed to correct a slide at Kesselchen (some 12 kilometres from the pits) and put the Lotus in a ditch and out of the race.

At Le Mans there were two 23s entered, a works car with 997 cc twin-cam Lotus engine and a UDT-Laystall ebtry with 745 cc Climax engine. When the Lotus entries were presented for scrutineering, the scrutineers rejected them on the grounds that the front wheels had four-stud fixing and the rear wheels six-stud, so that the spare wheel could be used on only one axle. Immediately Chapman changed the rear wheels to four-stud fixing, but when the cars were presented for rescrutineering, the scrutineers refused even to look at them, alleging that the rear wheels had been designed for six-stud fixing and with four studs they must be dangerous.

ABOVE LEFT *Jim Clark at the wheel of the exceptionally quick twin-cam Ford-powered Lotus 23 in the 1962 Nürburgring 1000 Km race (LAT)*

LEFT *Paul Hawkins at the wheel of a Lotus 23 entered by Ian Walker racing seen in the Sports Car race at the Gold Cup meeting at Oulton Park in 1962 (T. C. March)*

All the efforts of the RAC and other advocates on behalf of Lotus were to no avail and the cars were excluded from the race. It seemed clear that the exclusion had been a deliberate move to protect the interests of the French René Bonnet and Panhard teams in the Index of Performance. Chapman vowed that he would never again enter Le Mans and he never did.

The 23s racing with 997 cc, 1097 cc and 1599 cc engines achieved substantial success in British races, and later in the year there appeared the 23B with strengthened chassis and the Lotus-Ford 1594 cc twin-cam engine. In the United States George Follmer raced a car with a Porsche engine and in Britain Robin Widdows's car had 1-litre BRM power. A total of 131 23s and 23Bs of all types were built.

Lotus 30 and 40

In 1964 Lotus joined the ranks of those contesting Group 7 sports car racing with the 30 powered by a Ford 4.7-litre V-8 engine and intended primarily for sale to private entrants. The basis of the 30 was a backbone-type chassis, broadly similar in shape to that used for the Lotus Elan, with a transverse box-section at the front to carry the suspension and with two diverging arms at the rear to mount the Ford engine. The main centre backbone member was a deep box-section girder panelled in 20-gauge steel sheet. Within this backbone there was a 13-gallon rubber fuel tank and additional 9-gallon tanks could be installed in the sills of the one-piece fibreglass body. The front suspension was by double wishbones and coil spring/damper units and at the rear there were upper wishbones, reversed lower wishbones, radius arms passing through slots in the arms of the backbone and coil spring/damper units. The Ford engine was modified by Lotus and with a specification that included four Weber carburettors power output was around 350 bhp. Transmission was by a ZF combined 5-speed all-synchromesh gearbox and final drive unit. The rear suspension and gearbox were supported by a box structure linked to the engine bay beams and if the gearbox ratios had to be changed, it was necessary first to dismantle the rear suspension. Twin radiators were mounted behind low-set intakes in the nose and there was a one-piece fibreglass body, which caused problems of access for mechanical work. The design of the 30 was largely down to Chapman himself and he is said to have ignored the many criticisms of the design made by Lotus Chief Designer Len Terry.

The first car was delivered to Ian Walker Racing, who ran a semi-works team, and Clark drove it to second place on its debut at Aintree. When this car was destroyed later in the year during practice at Brands Hatch with Tony Hegbourne at the wheel, Ian Walker, who had already suffered the loss of an Elan at the Nürburgring, withdrew from racing. Jim Clark drove a 30 in North America, finishing third at Riverside, and he had led the Tourist Trophy at Goodwood until eliminated by brake and suspension problems. Despite the problems encountered with the 30 and its lack of success, Lotus sold 21 of the first series of cars at the very modest price of £3495 in component form.

After the first three cars had been completed, subsequent cars were built with a stiffer chassis

LEFT *Jim Clark with the Lotus 30 in the last Tourist Trophy at Goodwood, the 1964 event; he led for most of the race, but dropped back after two pits stops and finished at the tail of the field (David Phipps)*

BELOW LEFT *Jim Clark drove this Lotus 30 Series 2 in the 1965 Tourist Trophy at Oulton Park, but was plagued by mechanical problems (T. C. March)*

BELOW *A view of the installation of the 4.7-litre Ford engine in the Lotus 30 chassis (T. C. March)*

with 18-gauge panelling. For 1965 Lotus introduced the improved Series 2 cars with a number of changes to the chassis and with a detachable centre-section to the bridge carrying the rear suspension so that it was no longer necessary to strip the suspension to get at the gearbox. A total of 12 of the Series 2 cars were built in 1965.

Early in 1965 Clark scored wins with the 30 at the Senior Service '200' race at Silverstone in March, a race run in torrential rain and stopped short of the scheduled distance, and at Goodwood on Easter Monday. Private cars were run by the JCB team and by Willment, but not much in the way of success was gained. By the Austrian sports car Grand Prix at Zeltweg in August, Lotus had produced a much revised car typed the 40 (and later described by Richie Ginther as 'the 30 with ten more mistakes added'). The 40 featured a larger 5.3-litre Ford V-8 engine used with the Hewland LG500 combined gearbox and final drive, the chassis was strengthened, there were suspension modifications and revised bodywork. The 40 was distinguished by two enormous exhausts emerging from the decking of the engine cover.

The 40 retired at Zeltweg, where it was driven by Mike Spence, and in the Guards Trophy at Brands Hatch, where the driver was Jimmy Clark. Two cars were sent to North America to be driven by Clark and Ginther, but the only success was a second place by Clark at Riverside.

At the end of the year Lotus abandoned the 40, the last sports/racing car to be built by the company. It had suffered design faults, but the main problems were that Lotus development facilities were spread too thinly to get the cars properly sorted (like other British constructors at the time Lotus was contesting too many different classes of racing) and the 30 and 40 were no match for either the McLaren-Oldsmobile or the Lola-Chevrolet.

McLaren

Bruce McLaren's independent racing career began when he and Teddy Mayer formed Bruce McLaren Motor Racing Ltd and ran two Coopers in New Zealand at the beginning of 1964. A couple of months later McLaren acquired the ex-Roger Penske Zerex Special and a 3.5-litre V-8 Oldsmobile engine modified by Traco. The McLaren team installed the engine in the Zerex chassis and raced the car as the Cooper-Oldsmobile, but within a matter of months they were running cars of their own design and built in the team's workshops at Feltham.

Perhaps the least attractive view of an unsuccessful car—Sadler's Lotus 30 at the Clubmen's Championship at Silverstone in October 1965 (the author)

Bruce McLaren with the second McLaren M1A with 4.5-litre Oldsmobile engine and automatic transmission in the paddock at the 1965 Tourist Trophy (T. C. March)

M1A

By September 1964 the first McLaren-Oldsmobile sports/racing car, to be typed the M1A, was being tested at Goodwood. This first McLaren, designed by Cooper draughtsman Owen Maddock on a freelance basis, featured a fairly simple multi-tubular space-frame constructed from round and square-section mild steel tubing with sheet alloy panels bonded in and riveted to stiffen the bulkhead areas and form a stressed undertray. The main frame members carried the oil and water pipes. The suspension was conventional; at the front there were narrow-based lower wishbones and wide-based upper wishbones incorporating anti-dive with coil spring/damper units; for the rear suspension Maddock used reversed lower wishbones, single top links, twin parallel radius rods and coil spring/damper units. Girling 11.5 in. disc brakes were used and originally Cooper cast spoked wheels were fitted—but McLaren's own four-spoke wheels designed by Maddock were soon substituted. The engine was the Oldsmobile V-8 enlarged to 4.5 litres and with Weber 48 IDA carburettors the power output was around 310 bhp. Transmission was by the Hewland HD combined gearbox and final drive unit. The aluminium body was designed by Tony Hilder and built by Robert Peel Coachworks at Kingston upon Thames. Originally the car was painted in the New Zealand national colours of black with a silver stripe, but McLaren soon switched to a brick red colour with twin stripes.

Race debut for the M1A came at the Canadian Grand Prix for sports cars in September 1964 and Bruce McLaren finished third after a long pit stop to sort out a broken throttle linkage. The M1A retired at both Riverside Raceway and Laguna Seca. In November 1964 McLaren entered into a deal whereby Elva, by then part of the Lambretta-

Trojan Group, should build production McLarens at the Elva factory at Rye, and in all they built 24 M1A cars with Oldsmobile 4.5- and Ford 4.7-litre engines.

In 1965 Bruce McLaren continued to race the prototype M1A and a second car with Ferguson automatic transmission was completed. The first race of the year was at Silverstone in March, but Bruce McLaren spun and finished well down the field. He was second at Goodwood on Easter Monday, and retired the car with automatic transmission at Oulton Park in April. At the May Silverstone meeting the McLaren team scored a fine victory after the retirement of Surtees' Lola and winner Bruce McLaren also set a lap record of 115.03 mph. A retirement followed in the Player's '200' race at Mosport, but Chris Amon won for the team at St. Jovite (Bruce McLaren was competing at Monaco). Later successes with the M1A encompassed another win at St. Jovite (McLaren), a win in the Martini Trophy at Silverstone (Amon) and second place for McLaren at Brands Hatch on August Bank Holiday Monday.

M1B

This was the 1965–66 production car with more bulbous and stylish body designed by artist Michael Turner. It was marketed in the United States as the McLaren-Elva Mk 2. The first of these cars was to be driven by McLaren at Mont Tremblant in September 1965, but the crankshaft broke in practice and he non-started. Subsequently he finished second in the Canadian Grand Prix at Mosport to Hall's Chaparral, Phil Hill retired the M1B in the North Western Grand Prix at Seattle because of a sticking throttle and McLaren finished third in the *Los Angeles Times* Grand Prix at Riverside. McLaren rounded off a successful year with a win in the Governor's Cup race in the Bahamas Speed Week.

By 1966 McLaren had two M1Bs ready to race and they made their early appearances of the year in British events. At Snetterton on Good Friday, Chris Amon finished second to Denis Hulme with Sid Taylor's Lola—the Lolas with Chevrolet engines of up to 6 litres were just too powerful for the McLarens to beat—and it was much the same story at Silverstone in May when Hulme again won with the Lola followed across the line by Amon (whose car was fitted with a 5-litre engine) and McLaren.

The McLaren team then travelled to Canada, where Bruce McLaren won the Labatt '50' at Mont Tremblant and the Player's '200' at Mosport. By July the McLaren team had substituted the 100 bhp more powerful 5.4-litre Chevrolet engine and McLaren won again at Mont Tremblant. At the British Grand Prix meeting at Brands Hatch, Amon went off after a nudging match with Dibley's Lola and rejoined to finish third. In the Guards Trophy at Brands Hatch the McLaren team was again beaten and Bruce McLaren had to settle for second place.

Severe opposition from the Lolas and the Chaparrals faced McLaren in the CanAm season and they were quite soundly beaten. At Mont Tremblant, McLaren and Amon finished second and third to Surtees' Lola, at Bridgehampton Amon and McLaren finished second and third to Gurney's Lola and at Mosport both McLaren entries were eliminated by minor accident damage. The Chaparrals of Phil Hill and Jim Hall took the first two places at Laguna Seca and Bruce McLaren finished third. Both McLarens retired at Riverside and in the final race of the series at Las Vegas Bruce McLaren took second place. Overall in the Championship Bruce McLaren finished third.

RIGHT *In 1966 McLaren abandoned the Oldsmobile engine in favour of the more powerful Chevrolet. Chris Amon with this M1B fitted with 5-litre Oldsmobile engine finished second to Hulme's Lola at Silverstone in May. It was one of the last races using the Oldsmobile unit (T. C. March)*

BELOW RIGHT *At the British Grand Prix meeting at Brands Hatch in July Amon's M1B-Chevrolet collided on the first lap with Attwood's Sid Taylor-entered Lola. Although the front of the McLaren was badly damaged and steering lock reduced, Amon rejoined the race and finished third (T. C. March)*

M6A

At the end of 1966, Group 7 sports car racing came to an end in Britain and the emphasis was now very much on North America, where the CanAm series was growing in importance. Designer Robin Herd and his assistant Gordon Coppuck designed a McLaren for this series, the M6A, with monocoque chassis constructed from bonded and riveted magnesium and aluminium sheet. At the front suspension was by lateral upper and lower links, trailing radius rods and coil spring/damper units, while at the rear there were lateral top links, lower wishbones, twin radius rods and coil spring/damper units. Fuel capacity was 54

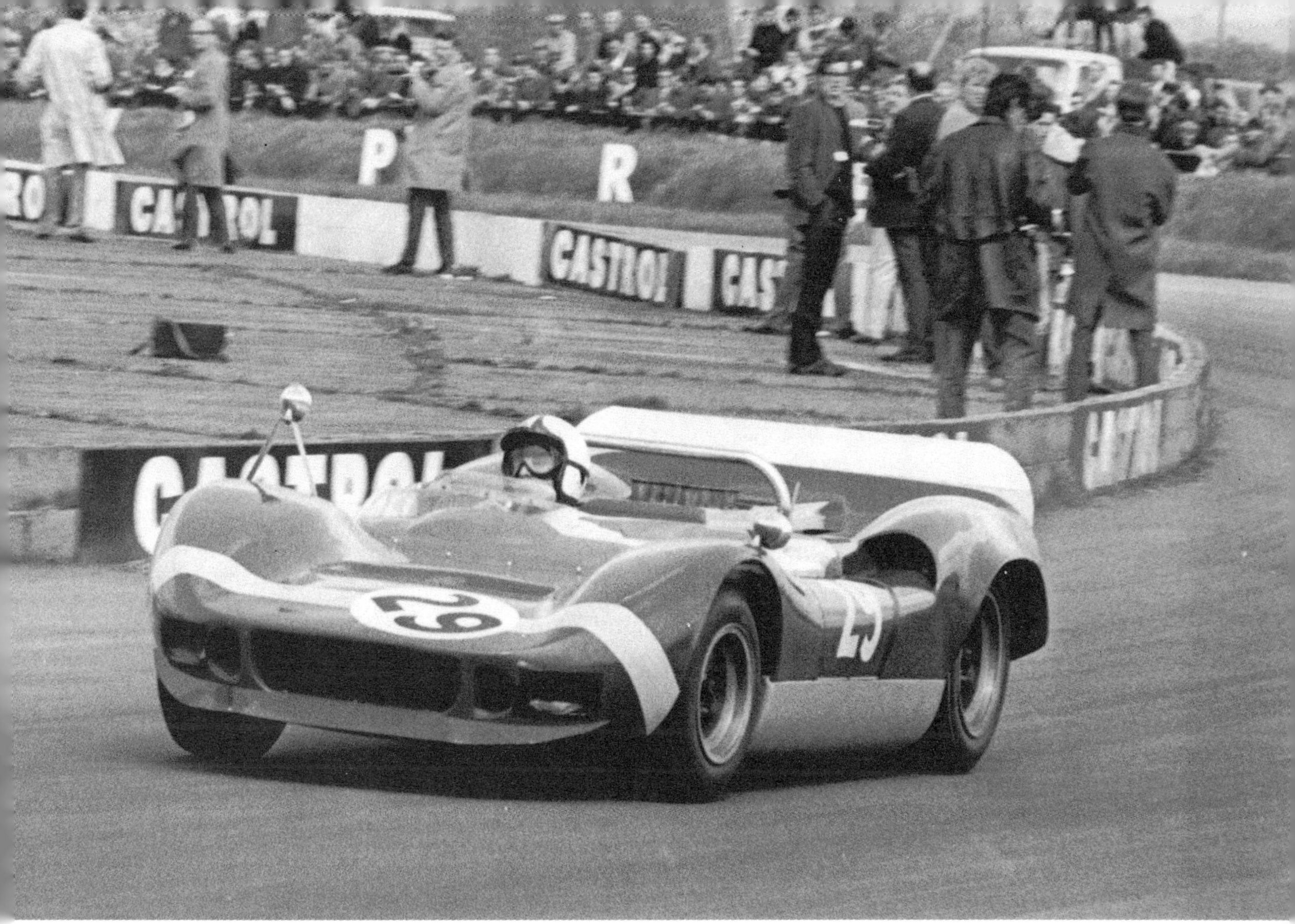

gallons, carried in three tanks, one each side in the monocoque sills and one in the scuttle. McLaren 15 in. cast magnesium wheels were fitted with 8.5 in. front rims and, for the time, exceptionally wide 13.5 in. rear rims, and there were Girling 12 in. disc brakes. One of the deficiencies of earlier McLarens had been the lack of power compared with their rivals, and to overcome this 5.8-litre Chevrolet engines were used. Extensively modified and with Lucas fuel injection, these engines developed over 500 bhp. The body was made in fibreglass panels by Specialised Mouldings Ltd. For the M6A the McLaren team first adopted the bright orange colours that were to distinguish the make until the Formula 1 cars were painted in Yardley colours in 1972.

After tests at Goodwood and Snetterton the McLarens were flown out to compete in the 1967 CanAm series. The last three years of sports car racing had been part of the learning curve for McLaren and with these latest and very competitive cars (with normal gearing they were capable of almost 180 mph in top gear) McLaren were to start an era of CanAm domination. The two M6As were driven in North America by Bruce McLaren and Denis Hulme, who was also to be a member of the McLaren Formula 1 team from 1968 onwards. There were six races in the series and the McLaren team won five, despite strong but not as well-organized opposition from Lolas driven by Surtees, Donohue and Gurney and Hall's Chaparral. In addition in these races, in which there were around 30 starters, it was usual for about half the field to consist of McLarens, the two works cars and the remainder private entries.

Hulme won the Road America race at Elkhart Lake, the Chevron Grand Prix at Bridgehampton and the Player's '200' at Mosport to make it a hat-trick. McLaren had retired at Elkhart Lake with engine trouble, but finished second at both Bridgehampton and Mosport. McLaren was the winner in the Monterey Grand Prix at Laguna Seca (Hulme blew his engine) and won at Riverside in the *Los Angeles Times* Grand Prix by a narrow margin from Hall (Chaparral). In the final round, the Stardust Grand Prix at Las Vegas, both McLarens retired and the race was won by Surtees (Lola) after Donohue's Lola had run out of petrol. McLaren and Hulme took the first two places in the CanAm Championship. Throughout the series the only problem had been blown engines and experience showed that these Chevrolet units had a very high oil consumption; because of this, cable-released 5-pint oil reserve tanks had been added by the Bridgehampton race and here the McLarens also appeared with ventilated disc brakes, Girling at the front and Kelsey-Hayes at the rear.

The very stylish M6GT coupé built by McLaren in 1969 (Nigel Snowdon)

M6B

This was the production version of the M6A built by Elva in 1968.

M6GT

These were very elegant coupés based on the M6B monocoque and were built in 1969. The first car was sold to David Prophet, who raced it and converted it back to open configuration. It has been suggested that four of these cars were built.

M8A

For the 1968 CanAm series the McLaren team produced the lower, wider, lighter M8A which incorporated the engine as a stressed part of the chassis structure. The Chevrolet engines, prepared in McLaren's California workshop, had a capacity of 6997 cc (107 × 95.5 mm) and a power output of 620 bhp; they were used with the Hewland LG600 combined gearbox and final drive. There was a total fuel capacity of 60 gallons—30 gallons each side—and larger ventilated disc brakes were fitted. The body by Specialised Mouldings was generally smoother in outline and there was a shallower rear wing. Design work on the M8A was by Swiss engineer Jo Marquart.

Opposition in the 1968 series came in the main from McLarens in private hands, including a 7-litre Ford-powered M6B for Peter Revson and Dan Gurney's much lightened M6B with Gurney-Weslake 5.3-litre Ford engine, and Hall's Chaparral. In the first race of the series at Elkhart Lake, Hulme won with dry tyres on a wet track, despite a broken rocker arm, from McLaren, and private McLarens took the next four places. At Bridgehampton both works McLarens blew their engines and the race was won by Donohue with Roger Penske's McLaren M6B. A fortnight later the works McLarens regained their winning form in the Klondike Trail '200' at Edmonton, where Hulme won from McLaren with Donohue in third place. The Monterey Grand Prix at Laguna Seca was ruined by torrential rain and the works McLarens were out of the picture; John Cannon won the race with a McLaren M1B and the works cars trailed home after spins and pit stops in second (Hulme) and sixth (McLaren) places. Bruce McLaren won at Riverside and Hulme was the victor in the final race of the series at Las Vegas. Hulme won the CanAm Championship, with Bruce McLaren in second place.

M8B

For 1969 the McLaren team was content to modify the 1968 cars and the most obvious changes were cut-backs in the front wheelarches of the bodywork and rear wings on struts acting on the rear hub carriers (aerodynamic devices of this kind had been banned in Formula 1, but were still acceptable in CanAm racing).

In all there were eleven races in the 1969 series and the McLaren team won every race. As in previous years, the principal opposition came from privately entered McLarens and the more the opposition diminished, the more obvious was McLaren's stranglehold on this class of racing. The only opponent of any real interest was Jim Hall's latest Chaparral driven by John Surtees. The cake was divided between the works McLaren drivers like this:

Hulme, 1st at Mont Tremblant, Edmonton, Lexington, Bridgehampton and Riverside; 2nd at Watkins Glen, Elkhart Lake, Michigan and Laguna Seca.
McLaren, 1st at Mosport, Watkins Glen, Elkhart Lake, Michigan, Laguna Seca and Texas; 2nd at Mont Tremblant, Lexington and Bridgehampton.

Bruce McLaren won the CanAm Championship and $158,750.

M8C

This was the 1970 production McLaren that differed in one important respect: the engine mounting was non-stressed so that customers could install their own choice of engine.

M8D

For 1970 the McLaren team developed the M8D based on a new chassis with 4 in. wider track and new bodywork with upswept tail fins bridged by a wing. This last change was made to comply with the much stricter rules as to aerodynamic devices that had been imposed on the organizing clubs by the Féderation Internationale de l'Automobile. The M8D was fitted with a 7.5-litre Chevrolet engine. Tragedy struck when Bruce McLaren was killed while testing one of these at Goodwood on 2 June. McLaren continued with their entries for the CanAm series with Denis Hulme (who had burnt his hands badly at Indianapolis) and Dan Gurney. When Gurney had to drop out of the team after two races because of a contractual conflict between

ABOVE *In the 1970 CanAm series McLaren entered the M8D and Denis Hulme won six out of the ten races in the series (Pete Lyons)*

ABOVE RIGHT *At Mosport, the first round of the 1971 CanAm series, Hulme (McLaren M8F) and Jackie Stewart (Lola T260) battle for the lead. Hulme won after Stewart had retired with the Lola (Pete Lyons)*

BELOW RIGHT *Peter Revson with his McLaren M8F in 1971 at Watkins Glen where he was the winner (Pete Lyons)*

Gulf (who sponsored McLaren in the CanAm series) and Castrol, who sponsored Gurney, Peter Gethin, who drove for McLaren in Formula 5000, took his place. There were ten races in the 1970 series, of which Gurney won the first two and Hulme won six of the remainder. Gethin was the winner at Elkhart Lake, finishing second on the road but being elevated to first place after Hulme had been disqualified for receiving a push-start after spinning off. At the Road Atlanta race at Georgia both works McLarens were eliminated by accidents and the race was won by Tony Dean with a Porsche 908.

M8E

This was the 1971 production car based on the M8D. A number of these cars were raced in the Group 7 Interseries races in Europe.

M8F

For the 1971 CanAm series, designer Gordon Coppuck evolved the M8F with strengthened monocoque, inboard rear brakes, aerodynamic fences running the full length of the body sides to form rear tail fins carrying the rear wing and with 8.1-litre Chevrolet engine claimed to develop 740 bhp. Peter Revson drove alongside Hulme in the CanAm series. There was not much in the way of opposition apart from the bevies of private McLarens and an exceptionally well-prepared Lola.

Of the ten races in the 1971 series, Hulme won three and Revson won five. Of the remaining two races, Stewart won with the Lola at Mont Tremlant after Hulme, feeling sick, eased his pace and fell back, while at Lexington both McLarens succumbed to universal joint failure and the race was won by Adamowicz with a privately entered ex-works M8B.

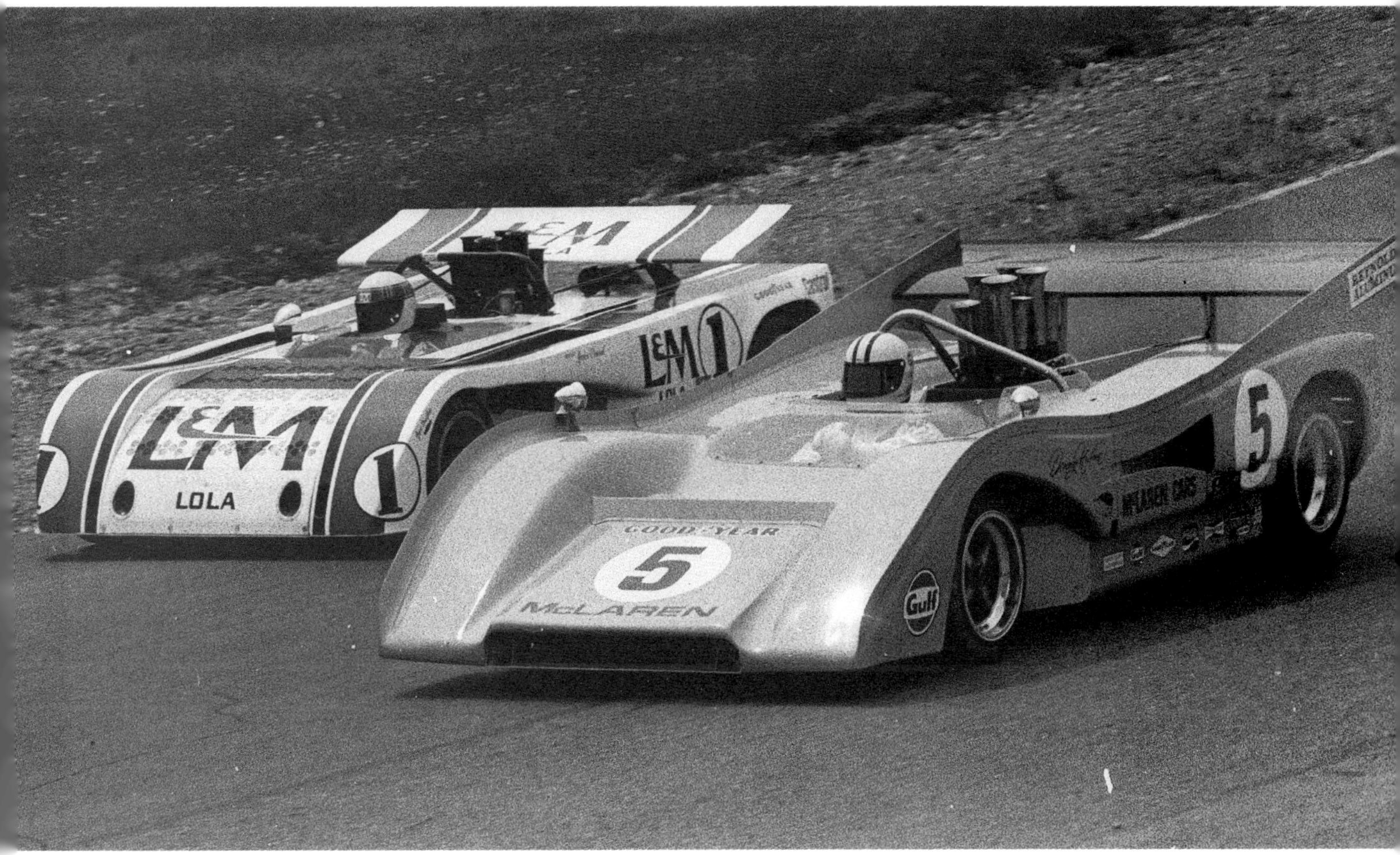
L&M
L&M 1
LOLA
1
5
GOOD YEAR
McLAREN
McLAREN CARS
Gulf

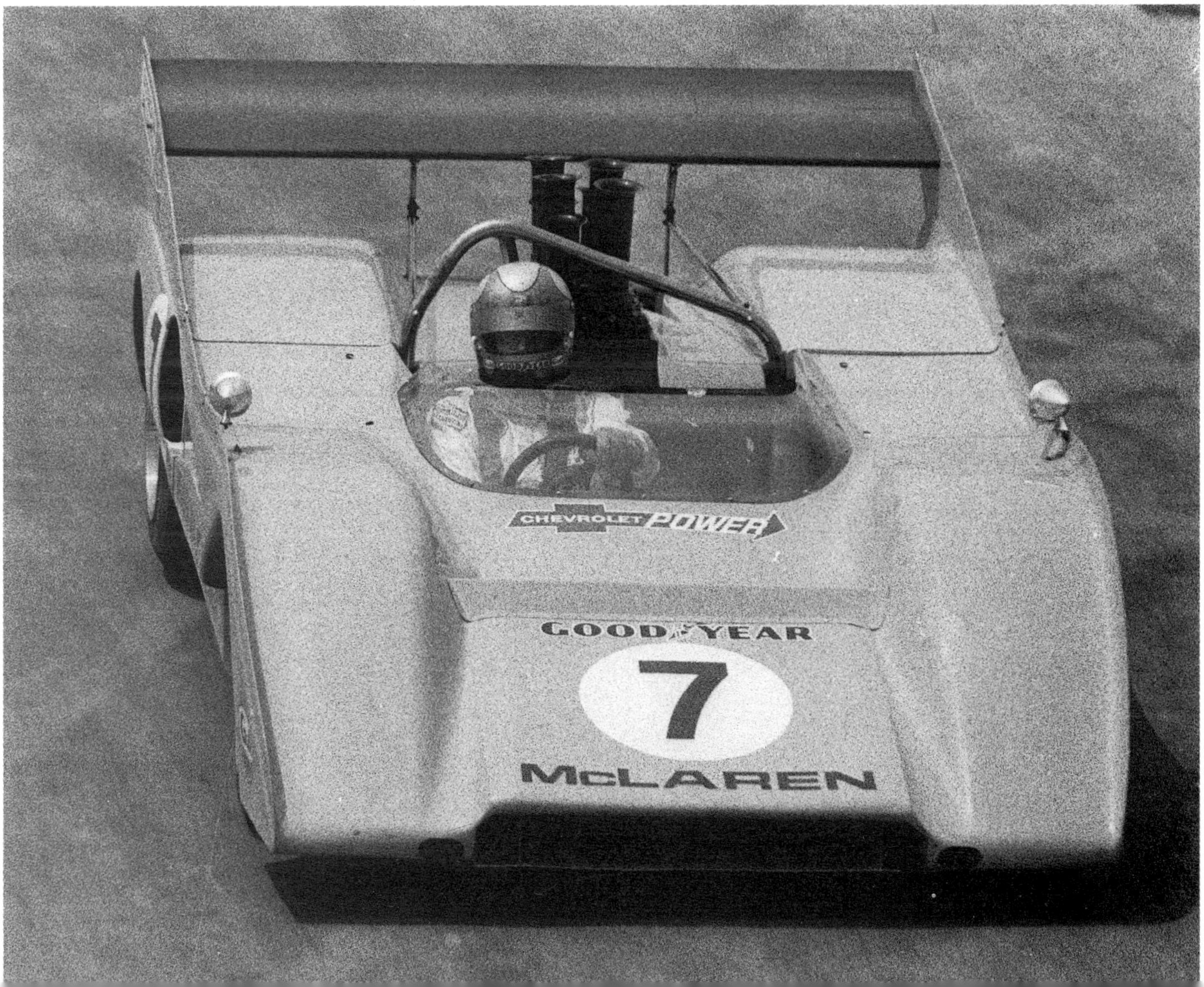
CHEVROLET POWER
GOOD YEAR
7
McLAREN

M12

This was the designation of the 1969 production McLaren.

M20

The last of the McLaren CanAm designs, with new monocoque of the so-called 'coke bottle' form with the widest point at the cockpit, main fuel tanks either side of the cockpit and additional tank at the rear giving a total capacity of 79 US gallons. The wheelbase was increased by 2 in. to 8 ft 4 in., there were side radiators just behind the cockpit and front-mounted wings as well as the rear wing bridging the tail fins. It had been the intention that Jackie Stewart should join Denis Hulme in the McLaren CanAm team, but he was forced to withdraw because of stomach ulcers and Peter Revson took his place. In 1972 the McLarens faced the most formidable opposition in the form of the turbocharged Porsche 917/10 run by Roger Penske and driven by Mark Donohue.

The series started well at Mosport Park, where Hulme won with Revson third, and the Porsche finished second after a pit stop. Both McLarens were eliminated in the Road Atlanta race, where Hulme crashed badly and Follmer won with a Porsche (Donohue was out of the race because of a bad crash in pre-race testing). At Watkins Glen, Hulme and Revson took the first two places, but thereafter it was downhill all the way and the works McLarens failed to win another race in the 1972 series. The Porsche won the next two races, Cevert won at Donnybrooke with an ex-works McLaren and the Porsche 917/10s won the three remaining races.

After 1972 McLaren withdrew from CanAm racing, which can be regarded as little more than a profitable sideline compared with their main activity of contesting Formula 1. Porsche dominated CanAm racing in 1973, withdrew from the fray and after a short period in which the Shadow team ruled supreme, the CanAm series withered away, losing its importance and International significance.

Merlyn

Colchester Racing Developments Ltd. of Little Bentley near Colchester in Essex had a history dating back to 1960, when Selwyn Hayward built a front-engined Formula Junior car to which he gave the name Merlyn. The car was well made, performed adequately and when it became apparent that there was a demand for a production version, Hayward in partnership with John Barrington-Lewis and Richard Neale set up Colchester Racing Developments as a small-scale racing car manufacturer. Four of the front-engined

The Mk 6 Merlyn raced by Peter Deal for two seasons

cars were built, but the appearance of the mid-engined Lotus 18 in Formula Junior had rendered all other designs obsolete and so Merlyn produced their own mid-engined Formula Junior car in 1961, and the following year 16 of these cars, typed the Mk 3, were built.

From this basic Formula Junior single-seater Hayward developed a sports/racing car known as the Mk 4. Hayward himself described the Mk 4 as 'nothing but a widened Formula Junior car.' There were no innovative features about the design, which was a multi-tubular space-frame with double wishbone and coil spring suspension at the front, and at the rear lower wishbones, top links, radius arms and coil spring/damper units. There were Merlyn cast magnesium wheels and Girling disc brakes were fitted front and rear. The body was a simple fibreglass structure, hinged front and rear for accessibility, with the fuel tank carried on the left-hand side. Most engines up to 1500 cc could be fitted (the usual engine was the 1100 cc Cosworth-Ford) and there was a Hewland combined gearbox and final drive unit. It was a car very much in the mould of the Lotus 23. The Merlyn Mk 4 served well a number of young drivers, including Piers Courage, Chris Irwin and Charles Lucas. Clive Lacey dominated the 1150 cc GT class in British races with one of these cars in 1965 and Richard Redgrave raced a Climax-powered example with success.

In all 26 Mk 4 cars were built in three versions. The majority were the standard 1962–63 Mk 4, but two or three were built for road use as the 4T with Ford Classic 1340 cc engines and steel wheels (in kit form the price was a mere £699). Included in the total is the improved Mk 4 that appeared in 1963 and featured lowered engine and gearbox, together with minor suspension modifications.

The next stage in development was the appearance of the Mk 6 sports/racing car in 1964, of which two slightly differing versions were manufactured in 1964–65. Hayward admitted that the Mk 6 was virtually identical to its predecessor, but there was a new body (primarily to boost sales), the chassis was stiffer as a result of improved triangulation, the gear-change was modified and there were nylon instead of rubber bushes in the suspension. The cars continued to perform well in British events and made the occasional overseas excursion. Inevitably, however, they were more at home in ten-lap races at Brands Hatch than in endurance races for which they were not designed. The Mk 6A was a further improved version with slightly modified rear suspension incorporating shorter wishbones and longer top links. One of these cars, with 1600 cc engine, driven by Tony Sargeant, won outright the two-part *Autosport* Championship final at Snetterton in September 1965—each heat of the race was over 176 miles and Sargeant finished second in the first and won the second heat. Sargeant also won his class of the Championship overall.

In 1964 Merlyn had built two Mk 8 sports/racing cars of more robust construction for export to the United States, where they were to be fitted with V-8 engines. At the end of 1968 the firm was planning the Mk 16 sports/racing car capable of taking engines up to 2000 cc and intended primarily for export. However, Merlyn was primarily a constructor of single-seater cars and that was where their efforts were concentrated in the late 1960s and early 1970s.

Mirage M2 and M3

Following John Wyer's acquisition of the Ford Advanced Vehicles organization at Slough, his new company, JW Automotive Engineering Ltd., had in 1967 raced modified Ford GT40 cars with engines enlarged to up to 5.7 litres as the Mirage with sponsorship from Gulf Oil and in that company's light blue and orange colours. In 1968 there were new rules that limited prototypes to 3 litres, while Competition Sports cars (of which at least 50 had been built) were permitted up to 5 litres. For two seasons Wyer had reverted to racing carefully prepared 4.7-litre Ford GT40s, still with Gulf sponsorship, and with these now outdated cars defeated the might of Porsche in several World Championship events, including the Le Mans 24 Hours race in both 1968 and 1969.

During 1967 Len Terry had been commissioned to design a new Mirage prototype (designated the M2/300 to distinguish it from the 1967 Ford-based cars) and this was extensively tested in 1968. The basis of Terry's design was an aluminium-alloy central monocoque with extensions running to the rear to carry the engine. The fuel was carried in the side pontoons of the monocoque and there was a total capacity of 26.5 gallons. Double wishbones and coil spring/dampers were used at the front and at the rear there were single top links, lower parallel links, twin radius arms and coil spring/damper units. As originally designed the front suspension incorporated 'anti-dive' geometry, but this was eliminated during development.

The biggest problem facing Terry and Wyer was the choice of power unit, as there was little

available in the way of potent 3-litre units. In 1967 the Ford-Cosworth was available to Lotus only and was not released to other customers until 1968. The team opted for a BRM 60-degree V-12 of 2999.5 cc (73.81 × 57.15 mm) with chain-driven twin overhead camshafts per bank of cylinders, two valves per cylinder, Lucas fuel injection and a power output of around 375 bhp. This engine had been designed by BRM with sports car racing in mind, but found its way into the 1967 McLaren that appeared late in the season and in Cooper and BRM's own cars in 1968. This engine was mated to

TOP *Debut for the Mirage M2 was in the 1969 BOAC 500 race at Brands Hatch. The drivers of the BRM-powered car were Ickx/Oliver, but they retired because of a broken half-shaft (Guy Griffiths)*

ABOVE *The Ford-powered Mirage driven by Ickx/Oliver in the 1969 Nürburgring 1000 Km race (LAT)*

RIGHT *The open Mirage of Ickx/Oliver following the Porsche 917 of Siffert/Ahrens in the 1969 Austrian 1000 Km race. They had a close fight in the early laps of the race—the 917 won and the Mirage retired*

the ZF 5DS-25 5-speed all-synchromesh gearbox. The body of the M2 was a very stylish but rather bulky coupé with twin radiators mounted either side just ahead of the rear wheels. Gulf sponsorship continued, and so the Mirages were painted light blue and orange.

Testing had started in the summer of 1968, but the team suffered a serious setback when Robin Widdows crashed badly with the first car in July at Snetterton. By 1969, when the Mirage was ready to race, it was already outdated, for it had been built to comply with the 1968 Prototype regulations specifying minimum windscreen height, ground clearance, cockpit weight and all-up weight and these restrictions were now much relaxed.

For the first two races of the year the team relied solely on the GT40s, but at the BOAC '500' race at Brands Hatch in April a Mirage was entered for Jacky Ickx/Jack Oliver. It was slow in practice, was running eighth at the end of the second hour and retired soon afterwards because of a broken drive-shaft. The Gulf Team missed the Monza 1000 Km race and the Targa Florio and next appeared at the Spa 1000 Km race, where two cars were entered. It was not a good race for the team, as the faster car driven by Ickx/Oliver was eliminated by fuel starvation problems and Hobbs/Hailwood trailed home in seventh place, six laps behind the winner.

By the next round of the Championship, the Nürburgring 1000 Km race, Wyer and his team had produced two revised versions of the Mirage. For Ickx/Oliver there was a car powered by the Cosworth Ford V-8 engine driving through a Hewland DG300 5-speed gearbox. The Ford engine was wider than the BRM and to get it into the chassis it was necessary to redesign the rear end of the car with the rear of the monocoque strengthened by riveted box-section members and a space-frame extension leading back to the rear suspension. The car driven by Hobbs/Hailwood was powered by the latest 48-valve BRM V-12 said to develop 450 bhp (perhaps in a flash reading on the dynamometer!) and loaned by the works. Oliver retired out on the circuit with collapsed rear suspension and Hailwood abandoned his car with loss of fuel pressure.

For Le Mans, Wyer relied on the GT40s and at Watkins Glen a further new version of the Mirage was entered. This was the M3/300, still retaining the Ford engine and Hewland gearbox, but with the combined roof and tail-section removed to produce a car of much lower weight and frontal area, but with a decidedly unattractive appearance. It was driven by Ickx/Oliver and ran much less reliably than its predecessors. At one stage Ickx held fifth place, but, on a wet track, the Mirage was handling atrociously and both drivers were greatly relieved when—after a change of coil spring/damper unit that had made no perceptible difference—the Ford engine lost its oil pressure and had to be retired. By the Austrian 1000 Km race the M3 had been fitted with a new exhaust system, lowered rear body section and lowered scuttle (to improve the driver's vision). Ickx led for the first three laps, took the lead again from Siffert's Porsche 917 on lap 24 and gained further ground when the thirsty German car stopped to refuel. As the race progressed, the Mirage pulled further and further into the lead, but it all came to nothing when a steering column bracket broke and the Mirage retired. Before the end of 1969 the Mirage scored one victory, albeit in a non-Championship race, the Imola 500 Km, in which Ickx led from start to finish on a streaming wet track.

The potential of the Mirage was undoubtedly limited and the team would have had a very thin time with this model in 1970. However, in late 1969 a deal was worked out between Porsche, Gulf Oil and Wyer whereby Wyer operated the works Porsche 917s throughout 1970–71. In the 1970s a new breed of Mirage appeared, powered by Ford and Renault engines, and enjoyed a reasonable measure of success.

Nash-Healey

In early post-war days the Donald Healey Motor Company of Warwick was one of the most successful of small manufacturers, building genuine 100 mph Riley-powered saloons and roadsters, competing with success in the Mille Miglia and the Targa Florio. From these was developed the 'Silverstone' sports 2-seater that was raced and rallied with success from its introduction in 1949 right through the 1950s. Donald Healey was anxious to break into the American market and a chance meeting on the Queen Elizabeth with George Mason of Nash Motors resulted in the Nash-Healey that was built in comparatively small numbers until 1954.

The Nash-Healey was based on a modified 'Silverstone' chassis with similar independent front suspension by trailing links and coil springs and rigid rear axle suspended on coil springs. In place of the usual Riley engine and gearbox there was a 6-cylinder ohv Nash engine and 3-speed gearbox with overdrive. The production cars had fairly luxurious roadster bodies, but the first Nash-Healey built for competition purposes featured a modified Silverstone body extended to greater width, with an air intake on the bonnet to clear the rocker cover of the rather deep Nash engine and left-hand drive (as on the production cars). Twin SU $1\frac{3}{4}$ in. carburettors replaced the single downdraft carburettor of the standard Nash engine. In this form power output was probably around 110 bhp and the maximum speed was only around 100 mph. The car ran in the Mille Miglia driven by Donald Healey, but with such an inadequate performance it was well out of the results.

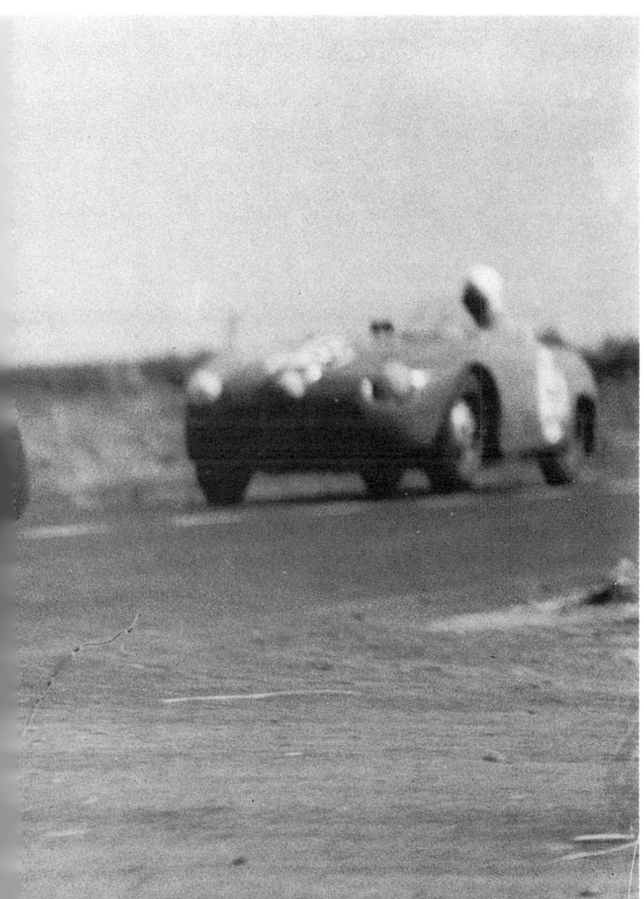

By June and the Le Mans race careful tuning and development work had boosted the power to 126 bhp at 4600 rpm, to comply with the Le Mans regulations the bodywork had been extended to envelop the wheels, there was a large headrest and streamlined scuttle panel topped by a perspex aero-screen. The result was a thoroughly ugly motor car, but, as results were to show, with a very effective performance. The Nash-Healey was driven by Tony Rolt and Duncan Hamilton (to become stalwarts of the works Jaguar team) and they drove a fine, consistent race, rising to third place until the Healey was rammed up the back by a Delage that had run out of brakes. The rear axle was damaged and the exhaust broken, but after the exhaust had been tied back on to the car by telephone cable it resumed the race to finish fourth.

For 1951 Healey prepared a modified production car with standard full-width bodywork (but non-standard radiator grille), tuned engine, Girling twin-trailing shoe brakes (instead of the Bendix servo brakes fitted to the production cars) and individual seats from a roadster (in place of the usual bench seat). Donald Healey drove the car in the Mille Miglia, finishing thirtieth overall (and fourth in his class), with Tony Rolt at the wheel it finished sixth in the Production Sports Car race at Silverstone in May and was driven by Reg Parnell in the British Empire Trophy in the Isle of Man, but retired because of a broken gear-lever. The car's final appearance was in the Tour de France, where it retired after a collision with a van. Earlier in 1951, Healey had built a new version of the Nash-Healey, a fixed head coupé, still retaining the familiar basic shape but with generally smoother lines, a high roof line and deep divided rear window. Wire wheels with knock-on hubs were fitted. This car was entered at Le Mans for Rolt and Hamilton and they enjoyed a trouble-free race to finish sixth overall.

Healey's 1952 competition season started again

Tony Rolt and Duncan Hamilton drove this Nash-Healey into fifth place in the 1950 Le Mans race (Quadrant Library)

G. JEUDY
la SOUPAPE des records
11

LEFT *A modified production car was raced in 1951. Here it is seen driven by Reg Parnell in the British Empire Trophy on the Isle of Man. Following is the 'Barchetta'-bodied Cooper-MG then owned by Lionel Leonard (Guy Griffiths)*

BELOW LEFT *The Nash-Healey of Johnson/Hadley at Le Mans 1953. It was classified 11th (LAT)*

with the Mille Miglia, in which Donald Healey, partnered by his son Geoffrey, drove the coupé raced at Le Mans and Leslie Johnson, partnered by Bill McKenzie of the *Daily Telegraph*, handled the 1950 car. Both Nash-Healeys were fitted with the lastest 4.1-litre Nash engines. Healey aquaplaned off the road and into a bridge, but Johnson drove a fine race to finish seventh overall (fourth in the Unlimited Sports Car class).

For the Le Mans race Healey prepared both the original 1950 car, with modified engine having a new cylinder head and power output of 157 bhp at 4000 rpm, and a new car based on the production chassis and with a body of generally similar proportions to the 1950 car, but much lighter. The 1950 car, driven by the French pair Pierre Veyron and Yves Giraud-Cabantous, retired because of a broken rocker shaft, while Leslie Johnson and Tom Wisdom finished third overall (winning their class) behind the two leading Mercedes-Benz 300 SL coupés. It was a fine performance, especially so because Nash-Healey were not serious contenders for outright victory, but 'waving the flag' with modified production cars.

In 1953 the Warwick firm built a further improved competition version of the Nash-Healey with very distinctive and rather more stylish full-width bodywork featuring a very large air intake and pronounced 'cutaways' beneath the headlamps to permit a good flow of air to the brakes. Laycock de Normanville overdrive replaced the standard Borg-Warner units. One of these cars was entered in the Mille Miglia for John Fitch, but retired early in the race because of final drive failure. At Le Mans two cars were entered for Leslie Johnson/Bert Hadley and Pierre Veyron/Yves Giraud-Cababtous, but the 24 Hours saw perhaps the strongest and most competitive entry in its history. The results were dominated by the works Jaguars, which finished first, second and fourth, while the sole Nash-Healey finisher of Johnson/Hadley was way down the field in eleventh place. The second car was eliminated by oil pump failure.

The racing days of the Nash-Healey were over, the production cars were phased out in 1954 and already at Le Mans in 1953 the team had started racing the new and very promising Austin-Healey 100.

Nomad

Back in the 1950s small teams could take on the works entries and through design expertise and hard work give them a sound thrashing. When Lotus Elite and Elan driver Mark Konig tried to do the same thing in the late 1960s, it was doomed to failure. The Nomad was well designed, well built and well driven, but Konig's small team simply lacked enough hard cash for the cost of development of a sophisticated prototype and to fund a full racing programme.

The mid-engined Nomad was designed by Konig's mechanic Bob Curl for Group 6 Prototype racing and was based on a multi-tubular space-frame chassis built of mainly 1 and 1.5 in. 16- and 18-gauge round tubing with reinforced areas formed by the sills and sections for mounting the front and rear suspension. Front suspension was by wide-based double wishbones with adjustable Armstrong coil spring/damper units. At the rear there was the equally familiar layout of single top links, wide-based lower wishbones, twin radius arms and Armstrong coil spring/damper units. Girling 10.5 in. disc brakes were mounted outboard front and rear. Under Group 6 rules, fuel capacity was limited to 90 litres and this was carried in two fibreglass clad aluminium side tanks. The tank on the right-hand side was shorter because the oil tank was mounted immediately behind it. Power was supplied by a Ford 1600 cc twin-cam engine developed and modified by Chris Steele and driving through a Hewland combined 5-speed gearbox and final drive unit. The radiator was mounted in the nose of the car and the twin intakes either side ahead of the rear wheels fed air to the engine compartment. Bob Curl designed the body, which was built in aluminium panels by Williams & Pritchard. It was a smooth, elegant coupé with cut-off tail, but it was rather on the large side for a 1600 cc car.

After 'shake-down' tests at Goodwood, Konig was at the wheel of the new car on its debut at the Crystal Palace on 29 May, 1967, and drove a cautious race to finish well down the field. Konig then made his first serious entry with the car on 18 June in the Auvergne 300 km race, finishing seventh and winning the 1600 cc class. At the Reims 12 Hours race Rollo Fielding was brought in as co-driver and the Nomad was holding second place in its class with 45 minutes to go to the finish when the clutch failed. In the Mugello 4 Hours road race Konig finished twelfth overall, but took third place in the 1600 cc Prototype class. He was holding sixth place in the Nürburgring 500 Km race when the fan belt broke and dropped well down the field. Finally Konig, partnered by Tony Lanfranchi, won his class in the Paris 1000 Km race at Montlhéry.

During 1967 the Nomad covered 2000 racing miles, during which it had needed no chassis modifications or repairs. Konig was well satisfied with the car and took it along to Brands Hatch for John Blunsden to track-test for *Motor Racing*. Blunsden wrote:

'It was quite a change to climb into a cockpit with all the room in the world. The pedals are well spaced, and there is a really good foot rest to the left of the clutch, which I was to find I needed for support through right-handers, the seat being if anything a bit too wide for me. A cowled instrument panel behind the steering wheel contains tachometer and oil pressure and water temperature gauges, the less important gauges being lined up to the left on the main dashboard surface. The master switch was conveniently placed low down on the right side of the dash panel just ahead of the right-hand gear shift.

'The latter had an open gate, which I sometimes find disconcerting with a five- or six-speed gearbox, but has the advantage on a long-distance car that it enables gears still to be "found" even if the linkage gets slightly distorted due to a chassis misalignment or even breakage (some chassis end up far from true after six hours on the Targa!) Also, in this case, the shaft itself was just about perfect, so that there was never any problem about finding the right gear.

'Chris Steele never reveals the output of his racing engines, but merely says that the 1967 version of his twin-cam delivers a minimum of 175 bhp at 7800 rpm. This particular example, which had been dropped in a few days earlier for a couple of British races, was a bit of a "super-tweaked" one, so presumably it was knocking out something in the region of 180 honest bhps. It certainly felt a real flier. It pulled pretty well from 5500 rpm, but really took off around 6800 rpm, leaving a useful 2000 rpm rev band up to the red line at 8800 rpm.

'. . . The handling can only be described as entirely predictable in the dry, with initial understeer fading out quite quickly to provide almost neutral steering with immediate response at the road wheels to steering corrections. You really get the message through to the steering column and the seat of your pants with this one, and although the tail can be broken away fairly easily the slide is not difficult to contain.

'. . . For a first-time effort it is an outstanding achievement, and the turn-out of the car in continental events has been a credit to the British specialist car-building industry. No trace of "back-yard-special-itis" here, but a thoroughly professional job all through . . . The prototype Nomad represents a capital outlay of roughly £3500, but of course the first car is always by far the most expensive, and anyone contemplating the hills and hairpins of the Targa, Mugello, Nürburgring and Clermont-Ferrand next year could do a lot worse than chat up Messrs. Curl and Konig.'

Over the winter the Nomad was fitted with fibreglass nose, tail and doors in place of the previous much heavier components and wider rear wheels with 10 in. rims were fitted (previously they were 8.5 in.)

At the start of the year the car was shipped to Daytona to compete in the 24 Hours race and the co-driver was again Lanfranchi. The Nomad rose to fifteenth place before dropping right back with gearbox problems and was eventually classified twenty-fourth. By the BOAC 500 Miles race at Brands Hatch in April the Nomad had been fitted with the lighter Hewland FT gearbox and an 1800 cc engine. In the 2-litre Group 6 class the Nomad led the Alfa Romeo 33s until the crankshaft broke after an hour's racing. Bravely Konig tackled the Targa Florio road race in May, but again there

In the 1968 BOAC 500 race the Nomad of Konig/Lanfranchi leads a 2-litre Alfa Romeo Tipo 33/2 (LAT)

was gearbox trouble and the Nomad finished right down the field in thirty-second place. Retirements followed at Montlhéry and Anderstorp, on both occasions because of engine trouble. At this point a BRM V-8 1498 cc engine and 6-speed gearbox were fitted and the results began to improve. Konig finished sixth overall and second in his class at the Jyllandsring in Denmark in August. Before the Nürburgring 500 Km race the Nomad was fitted with a larger radiator and oil cooler to counteract overheating problems and in this race he finished a sound fifth. Shortly afterwards he was seventh (third in class) in the Imola 500 Km race and with Lanfranchi as co-driver took fourteenth place in the Paris 1000 Km race and would have won the class for 1600 cc cars had there been one! During the year it was reckoned that the car had covered 12,000 racing miles.

For 1970 the small team built a new Mk 2 version of the Nomad and sold the existing car. The aim was to take advantage of the relaxation in Prototype rules so far as weight and windscreen height were concerned. The Mk 2 followed the basic chassis design of the Mk 1 car, but was an open *Spyder* with a body of ultra light fibreglass. To save time in construction a number of BRM components were incorporated in the design, including suspension uprights and wheels. The engine was the 2-litre BRM V-8 developing 250 bhp at 9500 rpm and used in conjunction with a Hewland FT 400 gearbox and DG final drive. The new car looked neat and purposeful with long sweeping tail and Konig was optimistic of some good results.

The Nomad's first outing in 1969 was in the Targa Florio, where Mark Konig was partnered by his wife, Gabrielle. They were out of luck, for a tyre punctured and the flailing rubber damaged the suspension. Next on the programme was the Martini International race at Silverstone where

Whoops! The Nomad in the ditch at the 1968 BOAC race (LAT)

Konig had a thoroughly miserable race on a wet track and trailed round to finish at the tail of the field. In the Le Mans 24 Hours race the Nomad retired after less than two hours because of the failure of a gearbox oil seal. At this stage in the season the Nomad was fitted with a new rear body section cut-off immediately behind the rear wheels, much shorter and lighter. The car was modified at the same time to take wider rims, 10 in. at the front and 13 in. at the rear.

During the remainder of the season not much success came the Nomad's way; the car ran at Brands Hatch on August Bank Holiday Monday, in Denmark once again, in the Nürburgring 500 Km race (in which Konig finished tenth and took a second in class), the Crystal Palace (Lanfranchi finished third), Zandvoort and the Paris 1000 Km race. At Montlhéry Lanfranchi crashed, damaging the car badly, and there was a frantic rush to get it ready in time for the Madrid Six Hours race. This was probably the team's best performance for the season, for Konig and Lanfranchi finished fifth overall and the Nomad was the first 2000 cc car to finish. To round off the year, Lanfranchi drove the Nomad in a minor race at Brands Hatch and won.

Konig pressed on with the Nomad project for 1970, offering the Mk 2 at £3188 as a rolling chassis or £5900 complete with BRM 2-litre—but Chevron was in the ascendant and their B19 looked a much more attractive proposition. For Konig himself a new car was built and the Mk 2 was retained as a back-up. David Piper drove the Mk 2 at Snetterton in March without success, Konig/Lanfranchi were leading their class in the BOAC 500 Km race at Brands Hatch when Lanfranchi crashed during the final hour and in the Nüburgring 1000 Km race they finished thirteenth.

By the Martini International meeting at Silverstone the new Mk 3 Nomad was ready. Basic design remained unchanged, but the chassis tubes were slightly smaller to save weight, the fibreglass body weighed a mere 60 lb, the suspension incorporated the team's own uprights, the Hewland FG400 Formula 1 gearbox was fitted and the car was running on Brabham wheels. Lanfranchi was up with the leading Astra of Roger Nathan in the opening laps, but he spun off and rejoined the race only to retire because of an engine misfire. At the

Vila Real 500 Km race in Portugal Konig drove the Mk 2 car and finished fourth—beaten by a couple of Chevron-BMWs. At Mugello, Konig was out of luck with the Mk 2 and finished well down the field in fifteenth place. Barrie Smith drove the Mk 3 in Denmark, but was eliminated in a multi-car crash just at the start of the first heat, retired in the second heat because of low fuel pressure and the car was withdrawn from the third heat. The Mk 3 reappeared at Brands Hatch at the end of August with Lanfranchi at the wheel, but was plagued by a misfire. Later in the year Konig, with Paul Vestey as co-driver, competed the Mk 3 in the Springbok series of races in South Africa, but failed to achieve any success in the face of strong Chevron opposition.

By 1971 Konig had given up the unequal struggle of financing this promising but unsuccessful project. It had provided variety on the Group 6 grids, achieved a small degree of success (especially in its first year), but was no real match for the Chevron opposition.

Revis-Borgward

Reg Bicknell, a motor trader in Southampton, was a keen Formula 3 competitor, running an Erskine-Staride and his own Revis 'Special'. The special was named after his business, Revis Car Sales, and featured tubular chassis, double wishbone and coil spring front suspension (similar to that of the Staride), swing-axle rear suspension suspended on rubber in tension and a Norton engine. In 1954 the Revis was distinguished by a full-width nose cowling, a primitive, but nevertheless effective, means of improving the aerodynamics. Bicknell also competed in 1953 in 1500 cc sports car racing, albeit without much success, at the wheel of a Tojeiro-MG with 'Barchetta' body and registered LOW 77.

For 1955 Bicknell constructed his own sports/racing car, the Revis-Borgward, the design of which closely followed that of the Formula 3 design, with the big difference that the engine was front-mounted. The tubular chassis had a wheel-base of only 7 ft, which was to cause handling problems; front suspension was again by double wishbones and coil springs and at the rear there were swing-axles, tubular radius arms and rubber strands, just as on the Formula 3 car. Well back in the chassis Bicknell installed a German Borgward 1493 cc push-rod engine (which Bicknell reckoned to be capable of being tuned to develop 100 bhp) and Borgward 4-speed gearbox. The exhaust

BELOW AND OVERLEAF ABOVE *Two views of the distinctive Revis-Borgward—a less than successful 'Special' seen here still unpainted. The rear view shows clearly the very short wheelbase of the Revis, the rather primitive exhaust system and the rear view mirror mounted at the back of the bulge in the bonnet*

emerged from the right-hand side of the bonnet and terminated in a motorcycle-type silencer just ahead of the rear wheel. Cooper wheels were fitted and drum brakes with a single rear brake mounted inboard. The body was a very compact design in aluminium panelling with a large hump on the bonnet to clear the carburettors (the rear view mirror was mounted on the back of this), a single door on the driver's side, full metal tonneau and very sloping tail.

The Revis-Borgward made its debut in the British Empire Trophy at Oulton Park. In practice for the 1500 cc heat Bicknell was third fastest in 2 min. 9 sec. to the Connaughts of Leston and McAlpine; he held second place until he spun on lap 2, dropping to third, spun again restarting in sixth place and crashed heavily at Druid's. The Revis had very real handling problems. Bicknell was still very much involved in Formula 3 (he crashed the Formula 3 car at Ibsley at the end of April when the suspension broke) and the Revis-Borgward was not seriously raced.

For 1956 Bicknell bought a place in Team Lotus and drove a 1500 Eleven with some success throughout the year. The Revis-Borgward was later sold to John Fisher, who registered it as NOW 1 and in 1958 it passed to C. J. Dade.

Tojeiro

Tojeiro-Bristol

It is inevitable with motor racing, as with so many other activities that successive designs were inspired by and based on their immediate contemporaries. Cooper pioneered the specialist British sports/racing car with independent suspension front and rear; John Tojeiro, who worked from tiny premises at Arrington, a village near Little Gransden in Cambridgeshire, took the theme one stage further by using a twin-tubular chassis—common enough of course on single-seater racing cars of the period and on post-war Frazer-Nash cars. Tojeiro used two 3 in. 16-gauge steel tubular members linked by a central 3 in. tubular cross-member and with sheet steel boxes at each end to carry the suspension. Following Cooper practice, Tojeiro used front and rear transverse leaf springs, lower wishbones and Girling dampers. Steering was Morris Minor rack-and-pinion, Tojeiro-modified Morris hubs were used and cast alloy wheels manufactured by Turner of Wolverhampton.

This first car was bought by Chris Threlfall before Tojeiro had completed it and was then finished off with a hybrid Wolseley/MG engine and neat sports body to which separate wings were attached. Threlfall raced the car with some success in Club events before selling it to Jim Fiander. The second Tojeiro was bought by Brian Lister and fitted with a Robin Jackson-tuned JAP twin-cylinder air-cooled 1100 cc engine mounted transversely in the chassis, and driving through a Jowett Jupiter gearbox, and a stark two-seater body. Lister, and later Archie Scott-Brown, competed with this car with some success (despite its appalling, inherent vibration problems) before it was sold to Peter Hughes, who enlarged the engine to 1200 cc. Chris Sears used a Tojeiro powered by a Lea-Francis engine and a chassis was ordered by

Cliff Davis with the famous Tojeiro-Bristol LOY 500 leads Alan Brown's Cooper-Bristol in the 1953 Goodwood Nine Hours race (Quadrant Library)

Lionel Leonard—but the story of Leonard cars is recounted elsewhere.

The first Tojeiro to make its mark on the British National scene was the car built early in 1953 for Cliff Davis. Davis, a well-known car dealer in the Shepherd's Bush area of West London, characterized by his check shirts, handlebar moustache and exuberant nature, had been racing JOY 500, a Cooper-MG, with considerable success, and the new Tojeiro, registered LOY 500, was to be its stablemate and bigger brother.

Chassis design followed that of the Tojeiros already built, but what characterized Davis's Tojeiro were its Bristol engine and gearbox and very elegant polished aluminium bodywork closely styled by Panelcraft Ltd. on that of the Superleggera Touring 'Barchetta' design used on a number of Ferrari sports/racing cars. The same design was of course used on Davis's Leonard-built Cooper-MG and on Leonard's own 1953–54 cars.

With the Tojeiro, Davis enjoyed a fantastic run of success in 1953, despite stiff opposition from Alan Brown's very fast Cooper-Bristol and a host of well-driven Frazer-Nash Le Mans Replicas. Davis raced both the Cooper-MG and the Tojeiro-Bristol almost every weekend during the season and it would be tedious to repeat every one of his many minor successes; among his successes, however, was a win in the *Motor Sport* Brooklands Memorial Trophy based on points gained with both Cooper and Tojeiro at BARC Members' meetings at Goodwood. He entered the Tojeiro in the Goodwood Nine Hours race with Les Leston as co-driver, but lost a lot of time when a fire started in the boot of the car. They eventually finished ninth.

During 1953 a small number of other Tojeiro chassis were sold and Formula 3 Revis driver Reg Bicknell raced a Tojeiro-MG with 'Barchetta' bodywork registered LOW 77. It seems that this car passed to Ormsby Issard-Davies in 1954 and was driven for him by Allan Moore. By the end of 1953 Davis's Tojeiro-Bristol had been adopted by AC as their production Ace and was to sire a long and successful line of sports cars that persisted into the 1960s. Cliff Davis continued to race the Tojeiro-Bristol in 1954, albeit with less success now that the opposition included Tony Crook's quasi single-seater Cooper-Bristol, Scott-Brown's Lister-Bristol and Salvadori's Maserati A6GCS. For 1955 the Tojeiro was acquired by the Rolls brothers, who ran it painted dark blue in the last of the Goodwood Nine Hours races, finishing fourteenth overall and fourth in the 2000 cc class. This Tojeiro still survives, having passed through many hands. The writer remembers it turning up at the 1965 Brighton Speed Trials, long after the runs had been completed, painted red and with crumpled front wing after a coming-together with a wandering Vauxhall.

In 1954 Tojeiro set up his company formally as Tojeiro Automotive Developments Ltd. and moved to new premises at Barkway near Royston to continue production of sports cars and to undertake development work for other companies. The following year there appeared the first of a new line of Tojeiros. This was a much more advanced design with a multi-tubular space-frame chassis with 7 ft 3 in. wheelbase constructed from 20-gauge 1.25 in. tube; front suspension was unequal-length wishbones and coil spring/damper units and at the rear there was a de Dion axle and coil spring/damper units. The de Dion tube running behind the drive shafts was located laterally by a bronze central sliding block and longitudinally by twin parallel radius arms. Disc brakes were fitted, mounted inboard at the rear. The body, again executed by Panelcraft Ltd., was inspired by the D-type Jaguar with smooth, low nose with large air scoop tapering inwards to the scuttle, metal tonneau and streamlined windscreen and headrest.

It is not clear just how many of these new-style Tojeiros were built. The first car, registered 8 APH, with Bristol engine and gearbox and Jaguar D-type magnesium-alloy wheels, was supplied to Percy Crabbe (there was talk of a Gordini engine being fitted later in 1955, but this came to nothing). Crabbe, who in his own words was an 'old (but enthusiastic) mug driver' raced this Tojeiro and its 1956 successor with Maurice Gomm body for three seasons in British Club and National events, enjoying himself immensely, but gaining little in the way of awards, before offering the car for sale in August 1957 for £1250. The later Tojeiro was bought by the Chequered Flag sports car dealership and continued to be raced by them with Crabbe at the wheel. Crabbe crashed when the steering broke at Goodwood on Whit Monday and the Tojeiro was sold shortly afterwards. Two cars were built with Turner 1496 cc engines for Chris Threlfall and Jim Fiander, and these were consistently raced and sprinted in British events without much success. There was a mystery Tojeiro-Jaguar entered by Prince Bira for M. Prasom at the Crystal Palace in July 1955—long before the Tojeiro works had started building Jaguar-powered cars—but it was driven by Morrice and crashed at South Tower. In addition, A. M. Park had a Tojeiro with Bristol engine and 'Mistral' fibreglass body; another Tojeiro-Bristol was delivered as a road car; Peter Bailey competed with a Tojeiro-MG and the 'Sun

TOJEIRO BRISTOL

Probably the most developed 2-litre car in the country. Space frame. De Dion axle. Disc brakes. Dunlop Centre lock alloy wheels. Six port head with twin choke carbs., etc., etc.

This car has lapped most circuits at very creditable speeds (Goodwood 1.40, Brands 63 sec., etc.) with an old (but enthusiastic) mug driver at the wheel. Heaven knows what its real capabilities are in expert hands. Could be modified to accept Jaguar engine, if someone really wants to pass Archie.

Bona fide enquiries only, please

Offers around £1,250

P. R. CRABB,

9, Winchester Park, Bromley, Kent

Tel: RAVensbourne 1282 **Mornings: BIShopsgate 2902**

Percy Crabb's advertisement in August 1957 for his second, 1956 Tojeiro-Bristol

Pat Special' in which Bert Rogers crashed and was killed on the first lap of the Sports Car race at Goodwood on Easter Monday 1956 was a Tojeiro-Bristol—this may have formed the basis of the Park car.

Using the same basic chassis design, Tojeiro built a Tojeiro-Jaguar in 1956 for John Ogier, a second car with longer wheelbase was built for Ogier in 1957 and two cars were supplied to Ecurie Ecosse. Despite handling problems with the first of the Ogier cars (attributable to its short wheelbase and narrow track), the Tojeiro-Jaguars proved the most successful of the breed, although never a match for the rival Listers.

Tojeiro-Climax

In 1956 Tojeiro built a Climax-powered sports/racing car for Chris Threlfall. So far as can be ascertained this was a one-off and was followed

Two views of the 1958 Tojeiro-Climax 1100, a design that achieved a good measure of success at Club level only

in 1958 by a Mk 2 version, of which several were built. It was the year in which Tojeiro built the AC prototype for Le Mans (at which a Tojeiro was also entered) and the two designs had much in common. The arrangement now was that at Barkway the Tojeiro organization carried out design and development, race preparation and the manufacture of some components. In new premises at Byfleet construction of the 1100 cc cars was to be undertaken.

The 1100 used a multi-tubular space-frame constructed from 1¼ in. 18-gauge and 1 in. 20-gauge mild steel tubing and the weight of the frame (complete with brackets) was 74 lb. At the front, suspension was by the familiar layout of unequal-length wishbones and coil spring/damper units and at the rear there was a de Dion axle; the tube was located longitudinally by parallel radius and laterally by a Watts linkage and suspended on coil spring/damper units. Steering was once again Morris Minor rack-and-pinion. The braking system was unusual in that while there were conventional 9.5 in. Girling disc brakes on the front wheels, there was a single 10 in. disc at the back mounted on the left-hand side of the differential housing. The Coventry-Climax FWA engine was used in conjunction with a very special VW gearbox mounted upside down. The body, built by Maurice Gomm in the Byfleet works, was particularly elegant, with low, curved nose-section that was fully detachable, detachable rear decking giving access to the final drive, fuel tank and spare wheel and neat and shapely tail fins.

Cars were built for Chris Threlfall, Alan Eccles and Richard Utley. Utley's car was ready by the Easter Monday meeting at Goodwood and Eccles' car appeared at the British Empire Trophy at Oulton Park shortly afterwards. Tommy Bridger drove a works car at the *Daily Express* Silverstone meeting in May. The cars were raced throughout the year in Club and National events, but the opposition was stiff—numerous Lotus Elevens and competitive Elvas—and not much in the way of success was gained. At Le Mans the works car was entered for Tommy Bridger/Peter Blond, but retired in the seventh hour because of rear axle failure. For 1959 Utley sold his car to Tony Hegbourne and both he and Threlfall advertised their cars for sale in August 1959. Threlfall was able to claim, 'Possibly this season's most successful club racing 1100. Has completed 16 out of 18 races, four firsts, two seconds, three thirds, never lower than sixth . . .' That said it all; the 1100 Tojeiro was a fine car for Club racing, but not a serious contender in major events.

Tojeiro EE type

Throughout the 1950s David Murray's Ecurie Ecosse team had been closely associated with Jaguar, running XK120s and C-types in 1952–53, ex-works C-types in 1954, D-types in 1955–56 and thereafter the ex-works D-types. Jaguars had withdrawn from racing at the end of 1956, but supported Ecurie Ecosse until 1960, and the Scottish team from 1958 onwards raced Lister and Tojeiro chassis with Jaguar engines. By 1961 Murray was thinking in terms of a successor to the long line of Jaguar-powered cars and agreed with John Tojeiro that he should design and build for the team a Prototype coupé to comply with the new regulations coming into force in 1962.

Tojeiro evolved a multi-tubular space-frame with mid-mounted engine constructed from 1 in. and ¾ in. round and square-section steel tubing. At the front, suspension was by wide-based unequal-length wishbones, coil spring/damper units and anti-roll bar. The rear suspension was also initially by double wishbones and coil spring damper units. The steering was rack-and-pinion, Dunlop disc brakes were fitted and the wheels were 15 in. magnesium alloy. In its first form the Tojeiro was powered by a 2495 cc Coventry-Climax engine used in conjunction with a Cooper-Knight 5-speed gearbox. The body was a very handsome 2-door light alloy coupé, designed by Williams & Pritchard Ltd., painted Ecurie Ecosse's traditional Scots blue and white, with three separate fuel tanks, with one on each side and one forward of the facia panel. Much of the construction work was carried out by Tojeiro at his Barkway works, but the cars were finished off—and subsequently rebuilt—by Ecurie Ecosse at their premises in Merchiston Mews, Edinburgh.

It is a sad truism that it is much cheaper and easier to design and build a competition car than it is to carry out a full and exhaustive development programme. Although Ecurie Ecosse tested the cars regularly, progressively modified them so that they passed through three different 'Marks', they were always underdeveloped, unreliable and largely unsuccessful.

Ecurie Ecosse had secured two entries at Le Mans in 1962, but only one car could be ready in time for the race. In the early hours of the race, the Tojeiro, driven by Dickson/Fairman, ran steadily in mid-field, but it developed gearbox problems and these caused its eventual retirement. It was, perhaps, unrealistic to expect an engine and gearbox designed for a two-hour Grand Prix to last a 24 hours race.

For 1963 Ecurie Ecosse concentrated their efforts on the development of the Mk II version of the Tojeiro to be powered by a Buick 3.5-litre engine and used with a 4-speed Chevrolet Corvair gearbox. The plan was to shorten the stroke of the Buick engine to reduce capacity to 3 litres. Under the Prototype regulations, if capacity was not reduced, the Tojeiro was too light to comply with the minimum weight limit and would have to be ballasted. An ambitious racing programme was drawn up, but none of these events was actually entered. In April it became known that the Le Mans organizers had declined to accept the Ecurie Ecosse entries, partly because Ecurie Ecosse could not warrant that the cars would be ready in time for the race, partly because the team was not sure what capacity engines they would be running and partly because they were not entrants in the Prototype Championship. The Tojeiro-Buicks eventually

---

OVERLEAF *Jackie Stewart on his way to sixth place with the Buick-powered Tojeiro EE coupé in the Sports Car race at Silverstone in May 1964 (T. C. March)*

DUNLOP
56

NLOP
DUNLOP
50

Stewart again drove for Ecurie Ecosse in the Guards Trophy at the Grand Prix meeting at Brands Hatch in July and finished eighth (Nigel Snowdon)

appeared at Charterhall at the end of June in the hands of Tom Dickson and young Jackie Stewart. Stewart and Dickson took the first two places in the GT race and then ran in the Sports event. Neither car ran well in this race—Dickson's was suffering from handling problems and Stewart's trailed a cloud of steam. Stewart spun, recovering to finish third and was followed across the line by Dickson. Long gone were the days of greatness of Ecurie Ecosse.

Three weeks later Doug Graham drove one of the cars in the Sports and GT race at the British Grand Prix meeting at Silverstone, but finished out of the results. At the end of August Ecurie Ecosse ran in a BARC Members' meeting at Oulton Park; the team had been testing at the circuit all week and were invited to run in the race meeting on the Saturday. Jackiet Stewart won four races with the team's Cooper Monaco and set a new class record in the GT race with the Tojeiro before retiring because of a broken rear wheel.

For 1964 David Murray continued to race the Mk II Tojeiro-Buicks with Jackie Stewart as the team number one driver. The decision was made not to enter Le Mans because of the very high costs involved and it was evident that the team's finances were becoming increasingly precarious. The first outing of the year was at Oulton Park in March, where Stewart led the GT race until a timing chain broke, but had the small consolation of setting fastest lap. One of the problems facing Ecurie Ecosse was finding suitable events in which to run the Tojeiros. They were not fast enough for British 'Sprint' events and not reliable enough for endurance racing. A further blow to the team came

when Jackie Stewart wrote off the Cooper Monaco in a practice shunt at Oulton Park in April.

At the May Silverstone meeting Stewart finished sixth in the Sports Car race (the opposition was very strong). Stewart reappeared with a Tojeiro at the European Grand Prix meeting at Brands Hatch, but finished well down the field in eighth place. A week later the team was in action again with John Coundley at the wheel in the Archie Scott-Brown Memorial Trophy at Snetterton, but although Coundley led initially, he fell back because of brake trouble and retired when the gearbox broke. The Corvair gearbox was the Achilles' heel of the Tojeiro-Buick, for the main shaft was not strong enough to transmit the power and it was not possible for technical reasons to increase its strength by enlarging the diameter. As a result much of Ecurie Ecosse's efforts in 1965 were devoted to a Formule Libre single-seater based on the remains of the Cooper Monaco crashed by Stewart.

During 1965 Ecurie Ecosse planned a Mk III version of the Tojeiro with Shelby-developed 4.7-litre engine and Hewland gearbox. The first car, EE1, was rebuilt as a Group 7 open sports/racing car, in which form it was known as the Ecosse-Ford. When the writer visited Merchiston Mews in the autumn of 1965, David Murray was still his old ebullient self, full of jokes at the expense of the English, still giving an impression of optimism. It was, however, evident that the team was near the end of the road. The Tojeiro design was now three years old and there were now no real prospects of turning it into a race-winner at a time when Prototype racing was being fought out between the hosts of Ferrari and Ford—and there was certainly not the money to even attempt serious International racing. Murray confided that it was the intention to sell the remaining Buick-powered Tojeiro and this was duly advertised in *Autosport* for 18 March, 1966: 'The Ecosse-Buick coupé is offered for sale. Rear-engine, Buick 3.4-litre V-8, considerably modified. Oulton 1.51, Silverstone 1.46, Brands 1.55. Suitable for sports car etc.

LEFT *The Buick-powered coupé photographed at Merchiston Mews late in 1965. In the background is the Ecosse single-seater (the author)*

BELOW LEFT *A view of the installation of the Buick engine in the Tojeiro chassis (the author)*

racing.' In the same issue Ecurie Ecosse advertised the open Ecosse-Ford. The Ecosse-Ford was not sold and crashed badly with Bill Stein at the wheel at the Grand Prix meeting at Brands Hatch in July. Eventually a receiving order in bankruptcy was made against Murray, and, very uncharacteristically for this straight and forthright man, he fled to Majorca to avoid his creditors.

Warrior-Bristol

The construction of the Warrior-Bristol is the repeat of a familiar tale. At the October Snetterton meeting in 1953 successful driver Rodney Nuckey crashed and overturned his Mk II Formula 2 Cooper-Bristol, which was to all intents and purposes a write-off. Bernie Rodger was commissioned to build the wreck up into a sports/racing car with a multi-tubular chassis frame (inspired by Cooper Mk II practice), but with the main frame tubes acting as the body superstructure. At the front, suspension was by a transverse leaf spring and double wishbones. Subsequently coil spring front suspension was substituted. At the rear Rodger incorporated a de Dion axle located by twin tubular radius rods and suspended on torsion bars. Cooper wheels and brakes were retained. The Bristol engine of course came straight from Nuckey's Formula 2 car and used with a Bristol gearbox from the same source. The body was a simple aluminium structure with very curved front wings, large scoop on the bonnet and small aero screen and the car was painted pale green. Construction was virtually completed by the end of 1953 and at the time it was said that a second car was being built for 500 cc driver Roger Biss.

In fact the Warrior was acquired by Roger Biss and, registered SAR 338, it was raced regularly, but

Rodney Nuckey at the wheel of the Warrior-Bristol leads Mike Sparken with the Gilby Engineering Maserati A6GCS at Silverstone in July 1954

J. DAVY *offer the*
LIMITED

BRISTOL-WARRIOR

an outstanding 2-litre Sports-Racing car

This is a car built regardless of cost to achieve one purpose—to win Sports car races. Race winning roadability is assured by a Bernard Roger chassis design that includes 45 ton steel tube space frame, De Dion rear end with outboard brake drums suspended by torsion bars, front suspension by double wishbones and coil, and Lockheed brakes with twin-master cylinders. The power unit is a Barwell developed Bristol B.S.4. A Borg and Beck racing clutch and Bristol close-ratio gearbox transfer the 142 b.h.p. that is reliably available.

For full details write, call or 'phone:

180, KENSINGTON HIGH STREET, LONDON, W.8.
WEStern 7181

This advertisement for the Warrior-Bristol in December 1955 shows off the tail fin which was a later addition

without conspicuous success throughout 1964. In one race report *Autosport* coyly described its exhaust note as 'outspoken'. For 1955 the Warrior acquired a single Jaguar D-type style tail-fin and a wrapround windscreen. In July 1955 the Warrior-Bristol was offered for sale by Kensington dealers J. Davy and it was acquired by J. D. Lomas, who won a 7-lap scratch race at Aintree in August from the Hon. Edward Greenall's Cooper-Bristol.

By the end of 1955 the Warrior-Bristol was back on the market again and was sold to Bernard Arnold, who exported it to Malaysia. Arnold finished tenth in the 1956 Macau Grand Prix after mechanical problems. The Warrior was still being raced by Arnold in 1961, by when it had been fitted with a Jaguar engine. Retirement came in the Johore Coronation Grand Prix, when Arnold ran out of petrol and the pit staff poured in two gallons of water before realizing their mistake. Later in the year Arnold finished fourth in the Singapore Grand Prix.

Index

Index

Index